Social Security Law in Greece

Social Security Law in Greece

Fourth Edition

Konstantinos Kremalis
Patrina Paparrigopoulou

This book was originally published as a monograph in the International Encyclopaedia of Laws/Social Security Law.

Founding Editor: Roger Blanpain
General Editor: Frank Hendrickx
Volume Editor: Willy van Eeckhoutte

Wolters Kluwer

Published by:
Kluwer Law International B.V.
PO Box 316
2400 AH Alphen aan den Rijn
The Netherlands
E-mail: lrs-sales@wolterskluwer.com
Website: www.wolterskluwer.com/en/solutions/kluwerlawinternational

Sold and distributed by:
Wolters Kluwer Legal & Regulatory U.S.
920 Links Avenue
Landisville, PA 17538
United States of America
E-mail: customer.service@wolterskluwer.com

Printed on acid-free paper

ISBN 978-94-035-1696-7

e-Book: ISBN 978-94-035-1396-6
web-PDF: ISBN 978-94-035-1406-2

Printed in the Netherlands.

The Authors

Professor Dr Konstantinos Kremalis (born in 1947) studied at the Universities of Athens, Munich and Vienna.

He holds the title of Supreme Court Attorney at Law. He practices in the areas of employment, social, insurance and health law issues. He is the Managing Partner at KREMALIS Law Firm, which is a member of *Ius Laboris Global Human Resources Lawyers.* Since 2002, Professor Kremalis has been the Director of the Research Laboratory of Social Insurance, Health and Assistance at Athens. In 2004, he became President of the Greek Health Law Association. Since 1990, he has been a member of the Greek Board of Mediators and Arbitrators and the National Representative of the International Scientific Society, European Institute of Social Security. He was awarded a PhD with Magna cum Laude in 1976 in the area of Labour Law, presenting the thesis *The Contractual Part of the Collective Labour Agreements*. After writing his monograph *The Social Insurance of Dependent Workers: Impacts from Labour Law Rules* (Habil.) (1982), he became an associate professor in 1983, substitute professor in 1987 and, since 1991, he has filled the position of Full-Time Professor at the Law School of University of Athens, Greece. For the academic year 1994, Professor Kremalis was a Visiting Professor a Fulbright Research scholar at Portland and Illinois Universities in the United States of America. Currently, Professor Kremalis teaches National, European and International Law of Social Security, Health and Welfare at the Law Department of Athens University for pre- and post-graduate students. During his career, he has also taught at the Catholic University of Leuven, the University of Paris II (Panthéon-Assas), the University of Rome, the University of Munich, the University of Tilburg, the University of Edinburgh, and the Kansai University of Osaka, among others. He is the author of the class books *Social Insurance Law* (1985), *The Right to Health Protection* (1987), *International and European Social Security Law* (1996), *Consultations of Social Law* (2000), as well as the author of many integral monographs and of over thirty special scientific works, many of which have been translated and published abroad. Professor Kremalis has participated in several experts and law drafting committees, playing a key role in the major employment, private insurance and social security law reforms. He contributes regularly as a university expert and offers legal advice to several ministries and organizations. He has participated as a university expert in the Communal Programme Equal 2006. He was also assigned as an independent expert for the national reports in the framework of the European project TRESS regarding 'training and networking on the European Coordination of social security systems'.

He is now participating in the frESCO project. frESCO is a European Commission (DG EMPL) funded network of independent experts in the fields of free movement of workers (FMW) and social security coordination (SSC). The overall aim of frESCO is twofold. On the one hand, frESCO is to provide the European Community (EC) with high-quality legal expertise in the areas of FMW and SSC, both by means of *reports* – informing the EC's analysis when considering developments in the European Union (EU) legal framework – and by means of ad hoc *analytical support* – assisting them with the investigation of complaints, petitions, parliamentary questions, etc. On the other hand, frESCO will also have a role in disseminating this expertise and increasing experts' and practitioners' knowledge of the relevant fields of EU Law, in particular by *organizing (training and other) seminars, sharing information* and *building networks* between stakeholders. He speaks French, German, English and Italian. *Distinctions – Awards: International Law Office Client Choice Award, K. Kremalis – Exclusive winner of the Employment & Labour category for Greece 2010* and *Global Law Experts – Labour & Employment Law – KREMALIS-Law Firm, Firm of the Year – Greece 2010.*

Patrina Paparrigopoulou is a professor of Law School at the University of Athens, Greece. She has been a member of the Bar of the Athens Lawyers and a lawyer in the Supreme Court since 1997. She specializes in administrative law and in social security law (social insurance law, health law and welfare law). She is married and has two children.

She has published several books, including *Public Health Law* 3d ed. Legal Library (Nomiki Vivliothiki), 2019, *Social Insurance Law*, 4th ed. Legal Library (Nomiki Vivliothiki), 2021, *The supplementary social insurance in the European competition law*, ed. Ant. Sakkoulas 2002. She has also published the *Insurance Reform for the New Generation, Law 4826/ 2021*, published by Legal Library (Nomiki Vivliothiki), 2022. She also has published many articles, including: *The Distinction between Basic Pension and Contributory Pension: The Paradoxes of the Recent Reform to the Greek Pension Scheme* (Laws 3863 and 3865/2010), Pensions, 2011 (16), pp. 51–62, *Constitution, Social Rights and Economic Crisis. The case of Greece*, Volume in honour of Professor Asbjørn Kjønstad, Velferd of rettferd, Festskrift til Asbjørn Kjønstad, 70ar, éd.Ketscher K., K. Lilleholt, E. Smith, A. Syse, ed. Gyldendal, Oslo, 2012, pp. 449–461, *Reflections on 3410/2014 and 3663/2014 decisions of the Council of State on pension reductions* (in Greek) EDKA 12/2014, pp. 823–834, *Social Security for Posted and Border workers, according to the rules 883/2004/EC* (in Greek), on the website Academia.edu, etc.

She was Deputy Ombudsman responsible for social protection during the period 2003–2008, member of the Commission for the preparation of the draft Law 3029/ 2002 and member of the Committee of Experts on pension reform (Law 3863/ 2010). She was a deputy member of the Council for Social Insurance (2012–2015) and the National Authority for Medically Assisted Procreation (2014–2016) and member of the Central Legislative Preparatory Committee of the Parliament (2016–2019). She has been scientifically responsible for the codification of the legislation of Welfare (for the Ministry of Labour, Social Assistance and Social Solidarity) and Organization for the Employment of Labour Force (DYPA). She is a member of the Ministry of Labour and Social Affairs' Committee for the acceleration of the award of pensions, a regular member of the Disciplinary Council overseeing the members of the National Telecommunications and Postal Services Authority and a member of the Special Court for disputes concerning remunerations and pensions of magistrates (paragraph 12 of Article 88 of the Constitution).

She has extensive experience as a counsel and advocate of social insurance agencies, occupational funds and private companies.

The Authors

Table of Contents

Table of Contents

List of Abbreviations

AP	Areios Pagos (Greek Supreme Court of Civil Law)
AYE	Decision of the Minister of Labour
KEPA	Centres for Certifying Incapacity
AYEO	Common Decision of Ministers of Labour and Economics
ASUYE	Supreme Army Medical Committee
KEN	Closed Consolidated Hospital Fees
D.El.Σuyn.	State Audit Council's Bulletin
D.IKA	IKA Bulletin
DEN	Labour Legislation Bulletin
DLOEM	Distributive Account of Family Allowances
EC	European Community
ECJ	European Court of Justice
ECHR	European Convention on Human Rights
EDKA	Review of Social Security Law
E-EFKA	Single Social Security Organisation
EED	Review of Labour Law
EHIC	European Health Insurance Card
EKKE	National Centre of Social Research
EOPYY	Single Organization for Health Services
ELSTAT	Hellenic Statistical Authority
EP.IKA	Review of IKA
EPIKAYP	Athens University Research Institute for Social Insurance, Health and Assistance
ETEAEP	Single Fund for Supplementary Insurance and Lump-Sum Benefits
ESM	European Stability Mechanism
ESY	National Health System
EU	European Union
FMW	Free Movement of Workers
GDP	Gross Domestic Product

List of Abbreviations

GNP	Gross National Product
Hell.Dik.	Greek Justice Journal
IKA	Social Insurance Institute
IKA-ETAM	Social Insurance Institute-Employees' Inclusive Insurance Fund
IKA-TEAM	Social Insurance Institute-Fund for the Auxiliary Insurance of Dependent Workers
ILO	International Labour Organization
KEA	Social Solidarity Income
IMF	International Monetary Fund
KEED	Code of Labour Law Review
KEP	Citizen Service Centre
KEPE	Centre of Planning and Economic Research
KNoB	Legal Tribune Code (Law Review)
MS	Member State
NAT	Maritime Pension Fund
NBG	National Bank of Greece
NHS	National Health Service
NoB	Legal Tribune (Law Review)
DYPA	Public Employment Service
OAEE	Institution of Freelance Workers
OGA	Organization for Agricultural Insurance
OKA	Organisation of Social Insurance
OPEKA	Organization for Welfare and Social Solidarity
OSE	Greek Railway Organization
OTE	Greek Telecommunications Organization
PIKPA	Patriotic Institution of Social Welfare & Assistance
SE	Council of the State (High Administrative Court)
SKLE	Greek Social Workers Association
SSC	social security coordination
TEKA	Supplementary Capitalisation Fund
TAE	Traders' Insurance Institution
TEA	Occupational Pension Schemes
TEVE	Craftsmen & Other Professionals Insurance Institution
TFEU	Treaty on the Functioning of European Union
TSA	Motorists Pension Fund
TSMEDE	Insurance Fund for Engineers
VAT	value-added tax
YYPKA	Ministry of Health, Assistance and Social Insurance

General Introduction

§1. Social and Economic Background

1. Greece is one of the medium-sized member countries of the European Union (EU) and is characterized by its extended coastline (15,000 km in relation to the 38,000 km of the European coastline) and its dominating position in international commercial shipping.

In a total population, according to the 2011 census, of 10.816.286 inhabitants (s. ELSTAT, Living Conditions in Greece, 6.5.2022, p. 1), the urban population is continuously increasing whereas the rural population is diminishing. The number of the semi-rural population remains almost the same. It is remarkable that the population of Athens in 1978 was more than 3.5 million inhabitants, and within seven years, it has increased to about 1 million inhabitants.

The average life expectancy of the Greeks has doubled in the last 100 years and is constantly increasing. From 36 years in 1879 to 69 years in 1961, it reached 81.04 in 2016. In 2009, 4.56 million people were employed in Greece. The number of employed people has decreased to 3.51 in 2013. In 2017 it was around 3.75 million. Just like the rest of Greece's economy, the job market has been adversely affected by the economic crisis of 2008; it has been struggling to recover ever since. The majority of the Greek population lives in urbanized areas, but lay-offs and job cuts affect the whole country; the unemployment rate in Greece has been increasing dramatically all over the country and has almost tripled since 2009. From 9.62% in 2009, it increased to 21.49% in 2017. In 2018 the unemployment rate was 18.6%.

Greece's economy relies heavily on services; most of Greece's gross domestic product (GDP) is produced in that sector. The gross domestic/GDP growth rate in Greece, however, has not improved since 2009 – on the contrary, after falling to an all-time low in 2011, GDP is now even lower than in the year recession hit the country.

Some of the most important industries for Greece are the maritime and shipping industries, as well as tourism. The export of goods has been on the rise, while imports have been decreasing, causing the trade deficit to improve slowly but steadily. Still, Greece is not out of the red and probably would not be for some time. National debt in relation to GDP is growing, and Greece is still ranked 2nd on a ranking of countries with the highest public debt worldwide. Austerity measures and rescue packages from the EU are now put in place to ensure Greece's recovery from the crisis. The immigration (internal and external) and the very low birth rate are two important demographic problems in Greece. However, it is not clear from the statistics how many employers work part-time and with a minimum salary.

2. A large percentage of Greeks are merchants, as they have had a tradition in commerce for many millennia (more than 10% of the financially active population). Yet, the value of the exports was always smaller than the value of the imports. This gap is particularly increasing of late because of the inclination towards consuming foreign products since the standard of living has improved continuously. The deficit of the trade balance is mainly covered by the shipping, tourist and immigration exchange.

Fundamental characteristics of the Greek industry are the medium extent of the enterprises, the preference for the light industry and the internal oriented market production.

3. According to Article 1§1 of the Greek Constitution (1975), the regime of a presidential parliamentary democracy is in force. The country is primarily divided into Districts, where the appointed representatives (General District Secretaries) from the government implement the governmental policy; at the secondary local government level, the country is divided into prefectures and at the third local government level into municipalities and some remaining small communities, where problems are confronted by the municipal or the communal authorities, which are directly elected by the people.

4. The substance of the actual Greek financial problem consists of the fact that the economy was not developed in quality and quantity, according to the consuming and investing needs. Thus, the financial development and relative prosperity have increased the technological and consuming dependence of Greece from the so-called rich countries. The balance of payments deficit, the high inflation rates (around 5%) and the unemployment rates (around 10%) are derivative phenomena of the aforementioned asymmetry between the supply and demand of products. For example, in the Five Years Programme of Economic and Social Development (1983–1987), it was presumed that there would be a gradual decrease in the unemployment percentage, if the average growth rate of the real Gross National Product (GNP) were higher than 3.5%–3.7%. These figures, however, were never reached and the real unemployment showed increasing tensions. The country shows the same weakness in meeting the European Union's targets for reducing unemployment, regardless of the period of the crisis. Moreover, a rather low productivity of the Greek industry, due to infrastructure problems, endangers the competition of the products directly. During the past years, important changes in the organizational structure and productivity methods of the various enterprises are attempted to confront this problem.

The deficit budgets in the public sector do not usually reflect a special improvement of the public services, but on the contrary, a structural inefficiency of the fiscal administration. The attempt to restructure the whole fiscal deficit, which is mainly due to the deficit of the public investments' budget and not due to loan needs of the public sector, is not yet in progress under decisive steps. The gradual replacement of an 'unavoidable' lending by a regular State subsidy to the IKA (Institute for Social Insurance) was, lately, considered as a measure towards the establishment of a rational tripartite financing mechanism (employers, State, insured people). Specifically, with the recent enactment and implementation of Law 3029/2002,

'Restructuring the social security system', IKA and other special insurance funds of employees have been incorporated into IKA-ETAM (The Inclusive Insurance Fund of Employees which was established by Law 3029/2002).

Greece has a mixed capitalistic economy with a large public sector that accounts for about half of GDP. Besides, Greece is a major beneficiary of EU aid, which equals about 3.3% of annual GDP. In addition, Greece is an agricultural country and one of the poorest countries in the EU with the second- to lowest-average income after Portugal. In January 2002, Greece adopted the euro as its currency.

The Greek economy averaged a growth of about 4% per year between 2003 and 2007, followed by a recession in 2009 as a result of the world financial crisis, which tightened credit conditions and marked Athens' failure to address a growing budgetary deficit. Greece met the EU's Growth and Stability Pact budget deficit criterion (of no more than 3% of GDP) in 2007–2008, but violated it in 2009, with the deficit reaching 15% of GDP. Austerity measures reduced the deficit to about 4% in 2013, including government debt payments. Deteriorating public finances, inaccurate and misreported statistics, and consistent underperformance on reforms prompted major credit rating agencies to downgrade Greece's international debt rating, which led the country into a financial crisis in late 2009. Under intense pressure from the EU and international market participants, the government adopted a medium-term austerity programme that includes cutting public spending, decreasing tax evasion, overhauling the health care and pension systems, and reforming the labour and product markets. Athens, however, faces long-term challenges while continuing to push through the unpopular reforms in the face of widespread unrest from the country's powerful labour unions and the general public.

In 2010, a leading credit agency assigned Greece the lowest possible credit rating as regards debt status. The International Monetary Fund (IMF) and eurozone governments provided Greece with emergency short- and medium-term loans worth USD 147 billion so that the country could make debt repayments to its creditors. In exchange for the largest bailout ever assembled, the Greek government announced combined spending cuts and tax increases totalling USD 40 billion over three years, on top of the tough austerity measures already implemented. Greece, however, struggled to meet the targets for 2010 set by the EU and the IMF, especially after Eurostat – the EU's statistical office – revised upward Greece's deficit and debt numbers for 2009 and 2010. European leaders and the IMF agreed in October 2011 to provide Athens with a second bailout package of USD 169 billion. In exchange for the second loan, Greece promised to invest an additional USD 7.8 billion in austerity measures during 2013–2015. However, the massive austerity cuts have prolonged Greece's economic recession and have depressed tax revenues. Throughout 2013, Greece's lenders called on Athens to step up efforts to increase tax collection, dismiss civil servants, privatize public enterprises, and reduce health spending. In June 2013, the Greek prime minister's efforts (Antonis Samaras) to meet bailout conditions were mostly successful and small measures worth about EUR 3 billion were demanded by the Troika in order to successfully complete the second Memorandum. The economy showed signs of recovery and the government was able to borrow money from the markets with low interest and the stock market prices showed great increase. However these efforts were halted by the dissolution of the

Parliament because the opposition refused to agree to support any proposition for a President of the Republic, whose term had expired, and demanded elections.

Parliamentary elections were held on September 2015. At stake were all 300 seats in the Hellenic Parliament. This was an early election, fourth since 2009, as new elections were not due until February 2019. The election resulted in an unexpected victory of 35.5% for the Coalition of the Radical Left (Syriza) party, which fell six seats short of an absolute majority, and was able to reform its coalition government with the right-wing Independent Greeks (ANEL). The key points for which the government has committed to the 'Institutions' are included in Law 4334/2015 (third Memorandum).

On 26 June 2015, Greece's new Prime Minister, Alexis Tsipras, announced a plan to put Europe's latest bailout offer to a public vote in a referendum that was held on 5 July. The people said no to the new bailout programme and voted for the 'Grexit'. However, the Prime Minister realizing the difficulties of the economic situation changed the meaning of the referendum and interpreted it as a 'consultative' referendum and proceeded to negotiate the terms of a New Memorandum, which were very harsh and costed Greece an extra EUR 85 to EUR 100 billion, according to the EU assessments.

As a partner in the negotiations, the EU has paid particular attention to the new programme's social fairness, to ensure that the adjustment is spread equitably, and to protect the most vulnerable in society, thus improving social cohesion. The European Community (EC) has published its assessment of the programme's social impact, which concludes that, if implemented fully and timely, the measures foreseen in the programme will help Greece return to stability and growth in a financially and socially sustainable way (Economic and Financial Affairs – Policy and Surveillance 6 January 2016). However, either the programme was not properly implemented or the measures were not the correct ones because even today (December 2018) still there is depression and only signs of weak economic recovery.

The European Stability Mechanism (ESM) support programme for Greece (Memorandum of Understanding 2015) included:

- phasing in a guaranteed minimum income scheme and providing universal health care;
- ensuring that the effort required from everyone is proportionate to their income;
- targeting savings in areas which do not directly affect the wallets of ordinary citizens, such as reduced defence expenditure, or addressing inefficiencies in many areas of public spending;
- challenging vested interests, such as phasing out favourable tax incentives for ship-owners and farmers, or a myriad of exemptions, e.g., ending unjustified subsidies or special value-added tax (VAT) rates for some islands;
- supporting the role of the social partners and the modernization of the collective bargaining system;
- fighting corruption, tax evasion, and undeclared work;
- supporting a more transparent and efficient public administration through moving towards a more independent tax administration, the reorganization of ministries, and the introduction of a better link between salaries and job responsibilities.

Since 2019, Greece has been out of the Memoranda, but has undertaken the obligation to continue the reforms of the Memorandum period.

In 2020–2021, the COVID-19 pandemic occurred. The state, with national and European resources, took increased measures to support jobs and income. Despite the pandemic, an effort was made to comply with the case law of the Council of State and the Court of Audit, regarding in particular the provisions of Law 4387/2016. Efforts were also made to improve the level of contributory pensions, rationalize contributions of non-employees and improve the quality and scope of social protection services as well as the process of awarding benefits, mainly through the use of digital technology.

In 2015, by decisions of the Council of State (Plenary Session), the pension cuts of Law 4093/2012 were judged unconstitutional. The court decided that the decision would apply retroactively only to applicants and to all other pensioners from July 2015. The government, according to the res judicata, was obliged to discontinue from July 2015 the unconstitutional pension cuts. But the government did not apply the court's decision and continued unconstitutional reductions.

In 2016, the government (Syriza, elected under the slogan of the 'abolition of Memoranda') chose to legislate on social insurance, in order to overcome the problems of implementing the jurisprudence of the Council of State, which declared invalid, as unconstitutional, the pension cuts of Law 4093/2012. The aim was to reduce the financial cost of the insurance system, but not to contradict the jurisprudence of the Council of State. In 2016 the Parliament adopted Law 4387/2016 on social insurance, which remains in force. This law introduced many major changes that are presented in this monograph. However, pension cuts still remain one of the major problems for the Greek government, the Greek political parties, the society and the sustainability of the social-insurance system.

A major challenge for the insurance system is now the implementation of the consolidation of the insurance legislation of the former main and supplementary insurance and lump-sum benefit organizations that have been integrated into e-EFKA. The single agency is nothing more than an umbrella under which the pre-existing insurance schemes are housed. The consolidation of schemes is far from straightforward. The first problem is that, according to a strongly held view, the insurance of civil servants is an aliud. It does not fall under Article 22 paragraph 5 of the Constitution, but is a continuation of the special civil service relationship and is regulated by special rules. Another issue is the different nature of paid employment and self-employment–in itself, the transition towards the adoption of uniform insurance rules is not an easy task because unification is bounded by the principle of equal treatment. In addition to this, however, there is another factor: digital governance. The digital operation of the Electronic National Social Security Institution (e-EFKA) and the digital pension provided for in Law 4670/2020 express the importance that the legislator attaches to digital governance. Important problems that are expected to be addressed in the coming years are the following:

- The records of the funds included in the e-EFKA have not been digitized for the period before 2002 with few exceptions. Therefore, the measurement of the insurance period and the control of the payment of contributions are based on physical records.
- The digital system is based on the assumption of clear and simple (in the form of a mathematical formulation) regulation. Insurance legislation is not formulated in this way and needs to be rewritten.
- Within and outside the e-EFKA, we are still thinking in terms of separate funds.
- Finally, the staff of the e-EFKA need support to cope with their new increased obligations.

The positive facts that facilitate the transition of the e-EFKA to the new digital and post-memoranda and COVID-19 era are that we are aware of the limits set by the Constitution, that the demand for consolidation and simplification of legislation has matured and that there is the will to proceed with digital governance and to take the necessary interim measures to ensure a smoother transition. Also, from 2022 the age limits are uniform with the exception of already established or vested rights which will continue to be a source of complexity for a few more years. Finally, the fact that the amount of the pension is easily calculated because it takes into account pensionable earnings from 2002 which have already been digitized.

Another important challenge is the implementation and extension of the minimum guaranteed income introduced for the first time during the Memorandum period. The minimum guaranteed income is now the main measure to fight poverty, but today only 273,000 households receive it (see the relevant announcement on the OPEKA website).

Of course, the fight against unemployment remains a top priority, especially in the post-crisis and post-pandemic era. The recent Law 4921/2022 with the ambitious title 'Work for all' reorganizes the services of the employment agency (OAED), renames it the public employment service (DYPA) and focuses on active employment policies (training, adaptation to market needs, etc.).

§2. Historical Evolution of the System

5. The prehistory of the several measures of social protection is quite extended in Greece.

Before the sixth century BC, some quite organized health services were offered by the Asklipieia, the sanctuaries of Asklipios, where therapy was combined with pleasure. The votive offerings to the temple were given in return for the services and they were rather obligatory than voluntary. From the sixth century BC, traces of social security against sickness can be found. Then, the institution of 'iatriko' must have been established. The cities, namely took measures for a general, equal and responsible health care of the citizens by engaging public doctors (dimosievontes iatrous) after a competition and for a certain term. These doctors were paid by the cities from the citizens' contributions that were called iatrika teli. They had public places at their disposal for the offer of open health care. The medical attendance took place at the patient's homes. The citizens could claim reimbursement or even penal punishment, if detriment of health occurred due to inappropriate medical care. Besides, the cash benefits from a special fund that were given to those who were unable to work in Athens by the Citizens' Assembly (eklisia tou dimou) can be paralleled with the today-disability-pensions. Aristotle mentions that there was a law in Athens, according to which the disabled people were entitled to receive a certain amount of money and public food. The beneficiaries had to be examined every year by the Parliament of the Five Hundred Citizens (Vouli ton Pentakosion) in order to confirm whether they still fulfilled the necessary prerequisites for this protection; one can see the relative account in Lysia's speech 'On behalf of the weak'.

In ancient Greece, it can be detected from isolated indications that every person was considered a possible receiver of social services. It is particularly mentioned that the city-state established a system of social protection for the entire population using the 'need' as a criterion. Besides, in order to eliminate the consequences of stigmatizing due to the social benefits, it was indicated in the 'Epitaph' speech of Pericles, that it was not a shame for somebody to confess that he is poor. Moreover, the welfare for the war victims and particularly for the orphans was actually a State concern with quite objective prerequisites, and therefore, it is possible that a genuine right to specific social services existed. From such indications, it can be suggested that also the poor had a right to social services, since they also had the opportunity of claiming the social services judicially. This interpretation could certainly be supported, as far as the cash benefits are concerned. For the benefits in kind, however, and the personal social services specifically, it seems that the citizen was faced still more as a 'mean' and less as a 'subject' of social protection. Despite the research, sources with a detailed description of social services have not been found. Therefore, it is rather difficult to conclude that there was a limited right of the person to claim social services. The possibility of every orphan to claim free food from the 'Prytaneio' is still doubtful, though this social policy measure has been mentioned several times.

6. During the Byzantine period, around the fourth century AD, State and ecclesiastical initiative established the first hospitals. These hospitals offered not only medical but also social and accommodation services to those who needed them, irrespective of their income condition. Social medical care, as we would determine it today, was financed by public or ecclesiastical funds and by extraordinary means, for example, by collections. Those who were responsible for medical errors were obliged to compensate for the damages (from loss of income) or even to abandon the specific region.

The welfare measures have a more anthropocentric character after the spreading of the Christianity. It was suggested that the children and the spouse of the dead were entitled to an adequate social protection. In this case, there are some terms for the acknowledgement of a claim to welfare protection, but the kind and the extension of the care were still under the discretionary power of the authorities. These authorities specified freely the 'adequate' social aid for each person in need. The welfare provisions were mainly provided in kind, as the so-called annones. This opinion is assisted by the fact that the social protection during this period, also due to the size and the variety of the Byzantine Empire, was based more on private or social charity principles rather than on the principle of social justice. The prerequisites for the welfare protection aimed mainly at the inadequate coordination of the assistance task that was enacted by the State, the Church, the emperors personally and the private initiative. The users of the charity services were not significantly 'humiliated' during that period because intense feelings of love and altruism prevailed due to the Christian teaching. We can mention the 'agapes', that is, the known meetings of the Christians, where it was not necessary, of course, to prove a real right to participate, and the 'ptochia', that is, the poor houses administered by clerics, where also idolaters were well accepted.

7. After the fifteenth century AD, during the Ottoman domination, some groups of workers were interested in organizing special social protection schemes under a corporative structure. There were funds composed by contributions for several risks, which threatened the members of the specific community, according to the insurance technique. For example, the maritime cooperatives in the islands of Hydra, Spetses and Psara safeguarded the medical care of the widows and the orphans from contributions calculated on part of the net profits of every voyage. An incomplete form of social insurance is also referred to in the statute of the shoemakers' and tanners' cooperative of the island of Zakynthos. All members were obliged to pay contributions every week, so that they could help the miserable ones in case of specific social risks.

8. The years from 1860 to 1930 can be characterized as the classic period of the Greek social security system because the developments of that period marked the nature of social protection measures until today. The absolute free market economy and the industrialization of the production caused so many social discriminations and risks, that the Greek legislator was forced to intervene without delay. Then the first insurance organizations started to function aiming at the protection of those, who worked in the private or public sector.

The history of the Greek social security system seems to start from 1852, when Law SE' of 19/25 August 1952 'about the military pensions' was published. Yet, the legislative activity was intensified right after 1860, which is also considered as a starting point of the industrial transformation of Greek economy. In Article 31 of Law XZ' (1861) a fund for the protection of the miners from accidents was mentioned and by virtue of the Royal Decree of 31 May 1882, a special fund was established for the realization of this protection. The first social-insurance organization is the Seamen's Retirement Fund (NAT). It was founded in 1836 and was established under a Law (1861), that is, twenty years before the well-known Bismarck's legislation in the imperial Germany. In 1861, the pension scheme for civil servants was established, followed by several social-insurance funds in the big private enterprises according to Law 2868/22. This legislation included obligatory rules for the establishment, structure and function of the social-insurance organizations of dependent workers in the industrial, handicraft and merchant enterprises. The first social-insurance organization for self-employed people was the Jurist's Fund (1928).

The substantial characteristics of the first social-insurance organizations correspond very much to the today's social security system. From that time, the following were established: (1) covering social risks in the framework of self-administered communities, (2) income redistribution based upon social-insurance contributions and (3) social protection irrespective of the insured persons' financial condition.

9. The modern period of the Greek social security system started in 1929, when the idea for a national social-insurance system covering the entire population was officially expressed. This idea has neither yet been accomplished nor abandoned. A rather crucial, but not efficient, step for its realization was the establishment of a general social-insurance Institute (IKA). This would cover, in some regions of the country all, the employed people who were not affiliated with another organization. Until recently, the relative legislation did not establish a unified social-insurance system for the working population. Not only did it maintain the former social-insurance organizations but also it could not prevent the appearance of new ones. After some hesitations, Law 6298/34 was voted and was put into force on 1 December 1937. This legislation was replaced by Emergency Law 1846/51, which is still in force after many amendments. The expansion of the social security system to the biggest part of the population was realized with two other important pieces of legislation: Law 6234/34 for the insurance of the artisans and craftsmen and Law 4169/61 for the insurance of the farmers. Nevertheless, Law 2676/1999 establishes the framework for the creation of the Institution of Freelance Workers (OAEE) which will consist of the social-insurance institutions TEBE, Motorists Pension Fund (TSA) and Traders' Insurance Institution (TAE), whereas Law 3029/2002 provides for the gradual merger of various social-insurance institutions with IKA (undisputedly, a fact that leads the way to an era of a unified social-insurance system).

Characteristic tendencies of the last period are: (1) the social-insurance coverage at a bearable protection level. Indications of this aim are the post-war establishment of numerous supplementary pension schemes, the obligation of all social-insurance institutions to provide at least the minimum benefits of the IKA and others; (2) the personal and territorial expansion of the basic social-insurance scheme for dependent workers. This generalization was realized by Article 3 of Law 1305/82; (3) the more centralized organization of the system in general social-insurance institutions. The incorporation of different social-insurance organizations or branches in the IKA is remarkable (*see* Law 997/79, Presidential Decree 633/82 and Law 1358/83, Law 3029/2002 and the establishment of OAEE, Law 2676/1999, etc.).

10. After the liberation from the Turkish occupation (1821) and for more than a century, the Greek State tried to organize social health services without a general planning, according to the needs of each period. It must be mentioned that a Section of the Ministry of the Interior, 'the Medical', was in charge of the public health (*see* the Royal Decree from 3 April 1833 and Law from 3 June 1846). This Section was also in charge of facing infectious diseases (with sanitary measures or in special therapeutic clinics) and for the free medical care for the poor people. The medical treatment was mainly based on private initiative because the State had other priorities and it was confined to a supervisory role or to preventive services. During the same period, those groups of workers who managed to be affiliated in a social-insurance scheme with a special health protection branch were the only groups who had a quite systematic medical care guaranteed by the State.

In the middle of the last century, the question of the coordination of the health services that are controlled by the State was raised, so that the whole population's basic needs for hospitalization or open medical care could be covered. For the first time, by virtue of Law 965/37, the public hospitals became part of a larger network and were organized into entities of public law. They were financed by State subsidies and they aimed at the medical care of the poor. Following then, the very important Legislative Decree 2592/53 was voted, which is still in force, to a certain extent, even after the establishment of the National Health System (*ESY- ethniko systima ygeias*) (1983). The State's concern has started to shift from the protection of the 'public health' to the 'medical care', and this notion had almost the same meaning as the one today. Unfortunately, this Legislative Decree has not succeeded in establishing a decentralized system of considerable health services to the citizens who really needed them, namely to the people who were uncovered by any kind of health insurance. During the same period, the medical care is mainly based upon the out-patients' departments of the public hospitals, the State health centres.

In conclusion, after the national reconstruction of the Greek State until 1983, a unified system of health services was not established but only isolated measures for the coverage of urgent needs or of pressure groups were taken. The citizen's legal position had to be protected defensively from excessive State interventions against the free development of his personality. Despite the fact that medical protection of the whole population had been recognized in the past as a social demand, only in the 1980s, the State undertook formally the responsibility of providing health services to all citizens.

11. During this first period of the national reconstruction, the 'welfare state' was addressed to the protection of the war victims, abandoned children, disabled people and rehabilitation of the refugees (Laws of 1867 and 1906) and of the earthquake-stricken (Law of 1886). Several measures of social welfare were still taken by the Church and the national benefactors, yet the main social welfare organizations were limited to public assistance services, with the present meaning of the notion. These social services, which covered unexpected and extremely urgent needs, were not possible to be combined with any kind of beneficiaries' claims. Even after the establishment of the first social assistance organizations, that is the Patriotic Institution of Social Welfare & Assistance (PIKPA) (Law of 1914), the social aid and the social action aimed at the protection from emergencies. Besides, the very limited means did not allow a timely social planning, as well as a specification of services that would prepare the recognition of respective rights.

In the last decades, social services are provided more systematically by several welfare institutions, such as the social welfare offices at the Prefectures, the Church funds for the relief of the poor and other public or private welfare organizations. Though at first, piecemeal beneficial regulations were in force for the fight against poverty, without any objective criteria and entitlement procedures (*see* the relevant Royal Decree from 1883), gradually, one can notice the intention of the legislator for a more specific description of this welfare protection. An important piece of legislation is Law 2646/98, which provided for the establishment and organization of the national system of social care (establishment of the national institution and national council of social care). Within the framework of several welfare programmes, the social services are usually predetermined in a way that the persons can imagine to which kind and extent of welfare protection they are entitled to specific needs, as long as the anticipated prerequisites occur. In the Royal Decree of 11 May 1946, a real obligation of the State to cover the basic needs of life of every person is provided. However, the citizen's position was not totally safeguarded because among the protection prerequisites, there were intentionally some undefined legal notions. Thus, if the demanded welfare benefit was characterized by the administration as unavailable or ineffective, then the refusal of assistance to a needy person was considered absolutely justified by the courts.

§3. General Structure of the System

12. The Greek social security system is promoted through the application of three different techniques: social insurance for persons within the labour market, social assistance for needy uninsured persons and national health service for all persons living in the Greek territory.

13. As far as its administrative structure is concerned, the social-insurance system and welfare policies are regulated and supervised by the Ministry of Labour, Social Insurance and Social Solidarity, while health care policies are monitored by the Ministry of Health.

I. The Social-Insurance System (*systima koinonikis asphaliseos*)

14. The social-insurance system is the basic cornerstone of the domestic social security model. Its function, as has been developed since the 1950s, aims at covering social risks of workers and employees through the provision of cash benefits and services, which address problems related to the reduction or loss of income gained through employment. The social protection system is based on three pillars:

- The First Pillar corresponds to the public schemes of compulsory main and supplementary insurance, which function through public organizations supervised by the Ministry of Labour, Social Insurance and Social Solidarity, except for EOPYY, which is supervised by the Ministry of Health.
- The Electronic National Social Security Institution (e-EFKA) is the general insurance institution for all employees, civil servants and self-employed in the private and public sector for main insurance, supplementary – distributive insurance, cash sickness benefits and lump-sum benefits.
- The Supplementary Capitalisation Fund (TEKA) is the general organization for supplementary capitalization insurance, compulsory for those entering employment from 1 January 2022 and optional for those born after 1987.

- At the same time, five compulsory insurance funds for specific professional categories operate under a capitalization system. Four of them apply occupational insurance rules and provide supplementary pensions. The EDOEP is the insurance institution for sickness, supplementary insurance and lump-sum benefits for its insured persons (owners, editors and journalists of daily newspapers in Athens and Thessaloniki, employees in the media, etc.). AN 248/1967, as in force.
- The National Organization for Health Services (EOPYY) covers the risk of illness by supplying health care to all insured persons in E-EFKA but does not provide health services in kind.
- The Public Employment Service (DYPA) is competent for the unemployment insurance for all employed and the unemployment allowances for self-employed.
- The second pillar has not been yet developed equally with the First Pillar. In 2002 the government adopted legislative measures to introduce occupational pension funds with the aim to extend the protection of insured persons and to strengthen the adequacy of insurance benefits. The second pillar also includes mutual funds.

II. The Healthcare System

15. Health services are provided by the National Health System and the private health care sector. The health services provided in kind by the insurance organizations during the Memorandum period were integrated into the NHS. The ESY was established by law in 1983, designed to guarantee free health care for all residents of Greece. Although, from a legal point of view, the ESY constitutes the cornerstone of healthcare protection, this harmonizing concept suffered serious drawbacks due to the parallel functioning of the healthcare branches of the various social-insurance schemes.

16. The government's GDP allocation to health care is quite low. The availability of public hospitals is limited to certain areas, which tend to cluster in big cities. These may be some of the reasons why Greeks have a perception of low-quality health care, despite the fact that hospitals in the metropolitan areas are of excellent standards. Currently, there are moves from the government to upgrade the health care system, having obtained funding assistance from the EU. Such improvements include the building of new facilities, developing mobile medical units, improving accident and emergency facilities and the installation of high-tech medical equipment. The public health system in Greece provides free, or low-cost, health care services to residents (and their families) contributing to the social security system. Other benefits include free laboratory services, maternity care, medical-related appliances or devices and transportation. Other EU nationals can also avail free healthcare benefits. Specialists can be consulted directly, but public hospital residents usually have long waiting lists. In urgent situations (but not in emergency cases), the patient may opt to see a private specialist and later reimburse. Because of the limited facilities of some hospitals, patients can be referred to other hospitals. In the case of non-urgent operations, waiting times can be lengthy. Emergency care is provided free of charge in public hospitals to anyone, regardless of nationality. There are also smaller outpatient clinics in rural areas which are attached to bigger public hospitals. These facilities provide faster emergency treatment than the bigger public hospitals. Dental and eye treatments are also free but non-essential medicines and health-related accessories such as dentures, dental crowns, and spectacles are charged at a substantial rate. Medications are of good quality and the pharmacists are highly trained. Medicines are also highly subsidized with only 25% of the cost of the prescription being charged.

17. A policy universal to all EU member countries is the E106 form or the European Health Card. The E106 can be accessed by the expatriate from his/her own country if he/she has paid two full years of social security contribution. The E106 card entitles the bearer to public health cover for a limited period of time.

Retirees from EU countries who are receiving their pension from their home country, and who intend to settle in Greece, are also entitled to state health benefits.

III. The Social Assistance System

18. The social assistance system forms the final safety net for needy persons without sufficient means. It is based on categorical minimum income schemes, which cover specific welfare target groups, such as the elderly, the disabled, the single-parent families and the children in need. These schemes were introduced in the 1960s and developed during the 1980s.

19. The categorical social assistance schemes normally require the Greek nationality and permanent residence in Greece in order to qualify for cash benefits and social services. However, EU citizens are equally covered as welfare benefits fall into the definition of social advantages, to which the principle of equal treatment is applied according to the provisions of EC Regulation 1612/68.

20. Greece was the first of the countries in the EU periphery engulfed in the so-called sovereign debt crisis that followed the crisis in the financial and banking sectors. The sovereign debt crisis exposed the serious weaknesses of the politico-economic regime that shaped Greece's development after the end of the military dictatorship in 1974. It also revealed the unprecedented power of unaccountable international financial institutions, banks and agencies to shape the dynamics of government bond markets across the globe and, therefore, the trajectories of national and regional political economies. More fundamentally, the Greek crisis exposed the limits of EU solidarity and accelerated changes in the future politico-economic governance of the EU: the institutional innovations pursued as a means for managing the sovereign debt crisis, especially within the eurozone, undermine national economic sovereignty to an unprecedented degree and, thus, place under serious question the role of national democratic politics in the process of EU integration. Our chapter begins with a brief discussion of the background to the crisis and explores how multiple and mutually re-enforcing causes created the 'perfect storm' conditions for its eruption. This is followed by a critical presentation of the key austerity and deregulatory measures adopted by the Greek government until the end of December 2011. Most of these measures were preconditions for the tranches of the 'bail out' loan agreed with the so-called troika of lenders, the ad hoc body comprising representatives of the European Central Bank, the European Commission and the International Monetary Fund (ECB/EC/IMF). A discussion of the impact of austerity measures on the economy, welfare and society more generally, as well as our final reflections, concludes the chapter. It is argued that the austerity measures and the deregulatory, pro-market, policy reforms prescribed by the ECB/EU/IMF and pursued by consecutive Greek governments have culminated into an anti-social policy that has done nothing to alleviate the crisis. Instead, it has severely reduced socio-economic security, traumatized social cohesion and democratic governance and sunk the Greek economy into the deepest and more prolonged recession in recent memory with detrimental effects on the state's finances and Greek society more generally.

21. Furthermore, the limited resources made available for social expenditure until 2014, when the minimum guaranteed income was introduced, do not reach those that should benefit from them. According to ELSTAT (Press release, 23 November 2021, Risque of Poverty, Household Income and Living Conditions Survey: Year 2020, Income reference period: Year 2019), the poverty threshold for 2019 was set at EUR 5,269 per year per single-person household and EUR 11,064 for households with two adults and two dependent children under the age of 14, and is set at 60% of the median total equivalent disposable household income, which was estimated at EUR 8,781, while the average annual disposable income of households in the country was estimated at EUR 17,263. In 2020 (income reference period 2019), 17.7% of the country's total population was at risk of poverty. This indicator, which stood at 19.6% in 2005 (income reference period 2004), increased until 2012. It started to decrease from 2014 onwards. Additionally, strengthening and improving the targeting of social expenditure towards families in relatively greater economic need is a matter of social justice that should contribute to a reduction of economic inequalities and poverty. The main inhibitory forces of relative poverty are the per capita GDP and social transfers as a percentage of GDP. It can be also argued that social democrat or corporatist social security systems are, in this respect, more efficient with the result that in such countries, an increase in per capita GDP reduces poverty more compared to Mediterranean or liberal countries. Exploiting these findings, the authors anticipate that in Greece relative poverty and standards of living will not improve in the years to follow.

22. Social benefits in Greece include social assistance (allowances for children under 16 years old who live in poor households, allowances to repatriates, refugees, persons released from prison, drug addicts, alcoholics, allowances to long-standing unemployed aged 45–65, benefits to households that faced an earthquake, flood, etc.) and allowances such as family, unemployment, sickness, disability/invalidity benefits/allowances as well as the education allowances. Pensions include old-age pensions and survivor's pensions and benefits. The population groups that genuinely deserve social support should be launched, as it would contribute considerably to the improvement of the effectiveness of social expenditure in Greece.

23. Based on the ELSTAT (Press release, 23 November 2021, Risque of Poverty, Household Income and Living Conditions Survey: Year 2020, Income reference period: Year 2019), the population at risk of poverty or social exclusion is 28.9% (3,043,869 persons) of the country's population, decreasing compared to the previous year (3,161,936 persons representing 30% of the population).

24. The risk of poverty or social exclusion is higher in the case of people aged 18–64 years (31.9%) (Table 1). Of the population aged 18–64 years at risk of poverty or social exclusion, it is estimated that 30.0% are Greeks and 52.2% are foreigners residing in Greece (Table 2). Of the population aged 18 years and over at risk of poverty or social exclusion, it is estimated that 27.0% are Greek and 55.7% are non-EU nationals of the twenty-eight countries residing in Greece (Graph 3, Table 2)

25. The at-risk-of-poverty rate before all social transfers (i.e., not including social benefits and pensions in the total disposable income of the household income) amounts to 48.3%, while when only pensions are included and not social benefits, it falls to 23.5% (Graph 7, Tables 14 and 15). With regard to social benefits, it should be noted that these include social assistance benefits (such as minimum guaranteed income, housing benefit, heating allowance, etc.), family allowances, social assistance (such as the minimum guaranteed income, housing benefit, heating allowance, etc.), family allowances and social security benefits, family allowances (such as child allowances), as well as unemployment, sickness and sickness benefits or allowances, disability or incapacity, or educational benefits. The at-risk-of-poverty rate after social transfers is 17.7%; therefore, it can be seen that social benefits contribute to reducing the at-risk-of-poverty rate by 5.8 percentage points, while, at the same time then, pensions by 24.8 percentage points. Total social transfers reduces the at-risk-of-poverty rate by 30.6 percentage points (Figure 7, Tables 7, 14 and 15).

26. The at-risk-of-poverty rate before all social transfers (i.e., not including social benefits and pensions in the total disposable income) for people aged 65 and over is estimated at 85.3%, while when excluding social benefits but including pensions, it is estimated at 14.8% (Tables 14, 15).

27. The poverty risk before all social transfers (i.e., not including social benefits and pensions in total disposable income) for persons aged 18–64 years old is estimated at 38.3%, while when social benefits are not included but pensions are included, it is estimated at 24.4% (Tables 14, 15).

28. § Social transfers (including pensions) account for 33.5% of the total equivalent disposable income of households in the country, of which pensions account for 86.7%, while social benefits account for 13.3%.

29. The most important developments in this area in the last three years are:

(a) the creation of the Organization for Welfare and Social Solidarity (OPEKA) with Law 4520/2018. It is responsible:

- for providing welfare benefits and social services for economic and social support and integration to vulnerable groups of the population (disabled, child benefits, uninsured elderly people, Social Solidarity Allowance, etc.); and
- for implementing and managing the actions and programmes related to the welfare policy of the Ministry of Labour, Social Insurance and Social Solidarity (i.e., actions for Roma, school meals, etc.).

(b) the introduction of the Social solidarity income (KEA) that aims to the income support, the provision of supplementary social services, which has already been renamed 'minimum guaranteed income' benefits and goods and activation services to people with low income and therefore promotes social inclusion and coherence; and

(c) the introduction of the Child Allowance replacing previous allowances and simplifying the legislation and the procedures. These very important benefits will be presented below in Part X.

§4. Sources of Social Security Law

30. Social Security Law derives from the Constitution, the International Agreements, EU Law, the specific laws, the regulatory acts, the general principles, jurisprudence, customs and the collective labour agreements.

I. The Constitution

31. Social insurance was introduced fragmentarily in Greece in the middle of the nineteenth century, following the Bismarck model and gradually expanded to all workers. The right to social insurance is a social right, the content of which consists of the obligation of the State to ensure the existence and continuous operation of social insurance services in order to enable workers to exercise their rights. The State undertakes the responsibility to organize and guarantee the social-insurance organizations by regulating the basic prerequisites and principles of their function. The legislator can neither abrogate the right to social insurance, nor hinder seriously the cover of certain risks and persons. It is not a right of the insured to claim a specific benefit from an insurance organization. It is only a guarantee of the social-insurance institution and a constitutional order to the legislator to specify the content of the various social-insurance schemes. The absolute exclusion of some people from the social-insurance protection, for example, of those who are under a certain age or before they complete a certain period of work, is considered contrary to the Constitution (*see* the Decision 867/75 of the SE, in EDKA 1975, 648, which has accepted the violation of a relevant general principle). In this sense, the state guarantees social insurance. The scope of the right to social insurance covers Greek citizens and foreigners legally residing in the country if they work. The Constitution allows for any kind of social policy measures to be introduced, under the condition that the right to social security will not be extremely restricted, and that the basic social protection will be administered by public social-insurance organizations.

Constitutional social rights are not enforceable. The right to social security is usually combined with other fundamental rights and principles, such as the preservation of the dignity of the individual (Article 2§1), the free development of the personality (Article 5§2), the welfare state (Article 25(1)) and the participation of the Greeks in public burdens according to their economic ability (Article 4(5)).

32. The Constitution also establishes two other social protection rights, health protection (Article 21(3)) and social welfare (the rest of Article 21). In 1983 the ESY was established on the model of the UK National Health Service. The National Health Service (NHS) follows the Beveridge model. Among the individual rights, which are relevant to the (open or closed) medical care from public organizations, lies the right to personal freedom. The provision of the free development of the citizens' 'personality', according to Article 5§2 of the Constitution, would have been without any sense, if the State had not undertaken the 'absolute cover of life' and, therefore, the elimination of health risks. Moreover, a patient could invoke §4 of the same Article, if he believes that during his hospitalization, his movements were unjustifiably restricted, Article 19, if the communication with his relatives was problematic and Article 9§1, if an entry into his home is forced by sudden controls of the health authorities. According to the classical defence function of the individual rights, a patient could only demand the omission of a specific and dangerous medical treatment, but not more freedom of movements, more extended visiting periods or health controls after previous notice. Despite the lack of a direct reference to the kind of health protection, the constitutional theory accepts the State's obligation for positive actions (health protection measures) with reference to individual rights and particularly, the right to personal freedom. One can note two really successful interpretative approaches: the first one analyses the general principle of the individual's dignity (Article 2§1 of the Constitution), while the second develops the legal notion of social interest (Article 25§2 of the Constitution).

33. Approaching the constitutional provisions, which safeguard particularly the social welfare beneficiaries, we end up again at Article 21 of the Constitution. The fact that between the draft and the final constitutional text the catalogue of the covered persons and of the social risks was expanded verifies the hypothesis that in Article 21 of the Constitution, a unified right to social assistance is established. The possible contrary interpretation, that in this Article, several social rights for various types of welfare services are established (e.g., for family protection and particularly, for families with many children, for disabled people and especially for the disabled during periods of peace, for the childhood protection and particularly, for the orphans, as war victims), would perhaps perpetuate the today's mosaic of several uncoordinated welfare programmes. Since, due to the character of the social welfare protection, the prediction of all the emergency situations, which can threaten a person is quite impossible, it should be considered that Article 21 of the Constitution anticipates a more general welfare right. However, in this Article, a social right is not recognized within the nature of a direct individual's demand against the State to take 'specific' social assistance measures. For example, the State's concern against the housing problem (Article 21§4 of the Constitution) is interpreted, either as a consequence of a special social right, or as an individual's claim for a specific home. It could, however, also include the demand for efficient State control of the housing programmes. Finally, the possible extent of the social welfare services derives also from constitutional regulations and particularly from Article 21, which includes special guidelines to the legislator for the establishment of specific assistance programmes.

34. Social assistance is based more on targeted programmes, but they have not managed to reduce the poverty rate, although they are often funded by EU funds as well. By Law 2646/1998, the 'National System of Social Care' has been established. Article 1(1) of that law states that 'Social care is the protection afforded to individuals or groups with prevention and rehabilitation programs and aims to create conditions for the equal participation of individuals in economic and social life and to guarantee them a decent standard of living. Family support is a key goal of these programs.' This provision highlights the modern aspects of social welfare, which is to ensure a decent standard of living and participation in social and economic life. Moreover, two basic principles govern the field of social assistance: namely, the principle of subsidiarity and the principle of individuality of welfare benefits. Social-insurance system, the NHS and the National Social Care System are distinct systems and they follow distinct techniques. However, there is no coordination between these three distinct systems that would allow optimal distribution of GNP resources and the achievement of their social objectives.

35. The minimum guaranteed income has been the main welfare programme for the fight against poverty since 2016. It was implemented on a pilot basis by Article 235 of Law 4389/2016 and then by Article 22 of Law 4445/2016, it was extended to all municipalities of the country. It supports households living in extreme poverty. It includes (a) income support, (b) access and linkage to complementary social benefits and services, as appropriate and depending on the needs of the beneficiaries, and (c) activation and promotion services for the beneficiaries of the Programme in actions such as covering a proposed job, participation in vocational training and experience programmes and returns to the education system. OPEKA grants and administers the Minimum Guaranteed Solidarity Income in accordance with Article 4 of Law 4520/2018.

Based on the whole of the constitutional stipulations, which concern the assistance protection (*see* Articles 9, 19, 25 of the Constitution), one could note that the hard core of the 'social assistance' institution derives. There is not an explicit institutional guarantee, as there is for 'social insurance' in Article 22§5 of the Constitution. Nevertheless, the existing constitutional provisions are considered equally effective, so that every unjustifiable violation of a minimum assistance level could be eliminated.

II. International and European Social Security Law

36. Among the sources of Social Security Law, the ratified international agreements are of great importance. Besides, according to Article 28§1 of the Greek Constitution, they form an inseparable part of our internal legal system and 'they prevail over any contrary national legislation'. There are bilateral, multilateral international agreements and the supranational EC Law.

37. Between Greece and those of the countries with which a continual and mutual flow of workforce is in progress, bilateral international agreements are contracted for the coordination of the different social-insurance systems. For example, there is a bilateral social security agreement between the Greek Republic and the Swedish Kingdom, which was contracted in 1978 and revised in 1984 (*see* the ratifying Law 1557/85). A bilateral agreement can be very useful because it imposes the adding together of several insurance periods in both countries. In that way, the completion of the entitlement conditions for the granting of benefits becomes easier (*see* Decision of the SE 965/76, in Social Security Law Review, 1976, 698). It usually provides equal treatment for the nationals of the Contracting Parties, the exportability of benefits into the territory of both countries, etc. Every social-insurance organization (under the condition that the insurance to which the migrant worker is affiliated) is burdened proportionally with one part of the benefit (*see* the Decision 3996/77 of the SE, in Social Security Law Review, 1978, 81). The bilateral international agreements, despite their characterization as 'social security' agreements in the ratifying laws, are in fact 'social insurance' agreements and they usually refer only to dependent workers. Their expansion to the entire population and the covering of more general social needs should perhaps concern the international social policymakers in the future.

38. Among the multilateral agreements established by the International Labour Organization (ILO), the most important is the Social Security (Minimum Standards) Convention No. 102 (1952), ratified by Greece in 1956. In addition, significant are the international legal texts, adopted by the Council of Europe members, such as the European Code of Social Security (1964), ratified by the Greek Law 1136/81 and the European Social Charter (1961), ratified by Law 1426/84. The International Convention about Economic, Social and Cultural Rights of the United Nations (1966) is also important as far as the improvement of health services is concerned, which was ratified by Law 1532/85. Furthermore, among the multilateral agreements for the coordination of national legislation on social assistance, of great significance is the European Convention on Social and Medical Assistance (1953), which was adopted by the Council of Europe and was ratified by the Greek Legislative Decree 401/59. The multilateral international agreements usually include abstract legal notions and flexible procedures. They comprise mostly guidelines to the contracted parties because their intention is the ratification from as many countries as possible. Any binding provisions, which are not in compliance with the socio-economic circumstances of a specific society, could delay or prevent their extension.

39. One of the founding principles of the EU is laid down in Article 45 of the TFEU (Treaty on the Functioning of European Union). It is a fundamental right of individuals, and an essential element of European citizenship. Free movement of workers (FMW) entitles EU citizens to search for a job in another Member State, to work there without needing a work permit, live there for that purpose, stay there even after the employment has finished and enjoy equal treatment with nationals in access to employment, working conditions and all other social and tax advantages that may help them integrate with the host country. It is estimated that there are 10.5 million migrant workers in the EU, 1 million people crossing EU borders for work every day and about 250,000 people who have worked in more than one Member State and need to export a part of their pension rights every year.

Ensuring the right of social security when the right of freedom of movement is exercised has been one of the major concerns for the EU Member States. To achieve this, it was necessary to adopt social security measures which prevent EU citizens working and residing in a Member State other than their own from losing some or all of their social security rights. This contributes to improving the standard of living of the migrant persons. Recognizing the importance of this issue, the Council adopted two regulations on social security for migrant workers in 1958, Regulations 3/1958 and 4/1958, which were replaced by Regulation (EEC) No. 1408/71, supplemented by Implementing Regulation (EEC) No. 574/72. Nationals from Iceland, Liechtenstein and Norway are also covered by way of the European Economic Area (EEA) Agreement, and from Switzerland by the EU-Swiss Agreement.

In 2004, Regulation (EC) No. 883/2004 of the European Parliament and of the Council on the coordination of social security systems was adopted to replace Regulation (EEC) No. 1408/71. On 16 September 2009, Regulation (EC) No. 987/2009 of the European Parliament and of the Council laying down the procedure for Implementing Regulation (EC) No. 883/2004 on the coordination of social security systems was adopted to replace Regulation (EEC) No. 574/72. The EU provisions on social security coordination (SSC) do not replace national social security systems with a single European one. Such harmonization would not be possible as the social security systems of the Member States are the result of long-standing traditions deeply rooted in national culture and preferences. Hence, rather than harmonizing the national social security systems, the EU provisions provide for their coordination. Every Member State is free to decide who is to be insured under its legislation, which benefits are granted and under what conditions, how these benefits are calculated and what contributions should be paid. The coordination provisions establish common rules and principles which have to be observed by all national authorities, social security institutions, courts and tribunals when applying national laws. By doing so, they ensure that the application of different national legislations does not adversely affect persons exercising their right to move and to stay within the EU Member States. In other words, a person who has exercised the right to move within Europe may not be placed in a worse position than a person who has always resided and worked in one single Member State. A migrant worker could face problems due to the fact that in some Member States, access to social security coverage is based on residence, while in others, only persons exercising an occupational activity (and the members of their families) are insured. In order to avoid a situation where migrant workers are insured either in more than one Member State or not at all, the coordination provisions determine which national legislation applies to a migrant worker in each particular case. Under national legislation, entitlement to benefits is sometimes conditional upon the completion of certain periods of insurance, employment or residence (depending on the Member State and the type of benefit, from six months up to fifteen years). The coordination provisions provide for the 'aggregation of periods'. This means that periods of insurance, employment or residence completed under the legislation of one Member State are taken into account, when necessary, for the entitlement to a benefit under the legislation of another Member State.

40. The principles of coordination of social security systems which were first established by the EU rules in 1957 remain the same today, though the text of the regulations has been changed several times.

These principles are:

- only one legislation applicable;
- equality of treatment;
- aggregation of the insurance, residence or work periods; and
- export of benefits.

In the new Regulation, a new principle has been added – namely, the principle of good administration. This refers to the obligation of the institutions of Member States to cooperate with one another and provide mutual assistance for the benefit of citizens.

Since 1 May 2010, the legislation in force in the field of coordination of social security systems in the EU includes:

- Council Regulation (EC) No. 883/2004 of the European Parliament and of the Council on the coordination of social security systems, as amended by Regulation (EC) No. 988/2009, hereinafter called the new Regulation;
- Council Regulation (EC) No. 987/2009 of the European Parliament and of the Council of 16 September 2009 laying down the procedure for implementing Regulation (EC) No. 883/2004 on the coordination of social security systems, hereinafter called the Implementing Regulation;
- Council Regulation (EC) No. 859/2003 of 14 May 2003 extending the provisions of Regulation (EEC) No. 1408/71 and Regulation (EEC) No. 574/72 to nationals of third countries who are not already covered by those provisions solely on the ground of their nationality; and
- Council Regulation (EC) No. 1231/2010 of 24 November 2010 extending Regulation (EC) No. 883/2004 and Regulation (EC) No. 987/2009 to nationals of third countries who were not already covered by these regulations, solely on the ground of their nationality.

An agreement has also been made to extend the personal scope of the new Regulation to nationals of third countries who are not yet covered by those provisions solely on the grounds of their nationality.

41. A number of significant changes have been incorporated into the new Regulation and implementing Regulation. A short summary of these changes is as follows:

- Extension of the personal scope of application to all nationals, active or non-active persons.
- Extension of the material scope, including the pre-retirement benefits and the paternity benefits.
- Extension of the principle of export of all cash benefits.
- Inclusion of only one general article concerning the aggregation of periods of insurance.
- Employment or residence (except for unemployment benefits, where for technical reasons, the original principle was maintained).
- Introduction of the new principle of the assimilation of benefits, income, facts and events.
- Replacement of all social security conventions applicable between the Member States.
- Extension of the initial period from twelve to twenty-four months in the case of posting.
- The provisional application of legislation and provisional granting of benefits.
- Inclusion of a provision for health care for the family members of a frontier worker, which constitutes a real improvement.
- Introduction of new dispositions regarding cross-border health care.
- Special reference to long-term care benefits.
- Introduction of the concept of a contact institution for pensions and the introduction of a summary note, which could be the basis for a review request.
- Introduction of special rules for taking into account the child raising periods in the pension calculation.
- Introduction of the possibility of coordination of unemployment benefits for self-employed persons, and extension of the possibility for an unemployed person to find jobs both in their State of residence and in the State of their last employment or in any other Member States, especially in the case of frontier workers.
- Introduction of clearer rules for the coordination of family benefits.
- Explicit introduction of the principle of good administration and establishing clear rules.
- Special attention is paid to providing information to citizens and employers.
- Introduction of clear rules regarding the responsibility of persons to provide information.
- Exchange of electronic data between the social security institutions through a database which will be maintained by the European Commission.

42. Article 76 of the new Regulation provides obligations for the competent authorities to communicate all information regarding measures taken and changes in their legislation which may affect the implementation of the Regulation to one another. The authorities and institutions of the Member States must lend their offices to one another, and act as though they are implementing their own legislation. The administrative assistance given by the said authorities and institutions is, as a rule, free of charge. In special cases, as established by the Administrative Commission, it is possible to set the reimbursable expenses above the amount of reimbursement that is due. The authorities and institutions of the Member States communicate directly with one another and with the persons involved, or with their representatives. The institutions and persons have a duty of mutual information and cooperation to ensure the correct implementation of the Regulation. The institution responsible for asking and responding to requests for information and assistance is the liaison body. The institutions, in accordance with the principle of good administration, shall respond to all queries within a reasonable period of time and shall provide the persons concerned with any information required for exercising the rights conferred on them by the Regulation. If difficulties arise in the interpretation or application of the Regulation which could jeopardize the rights of a person covered by it, the institution of the competent Member State or of the person's Member State of residence shall contact the institution(s) of the Member State(s) concerned. If a solution cannot be found within a reasonable period, the authorities concerned may call on the Administrative Commission to intervene. The authorities, institutions and tribunals of one Member State may not reject applications or other documents submitted to them on the grounds that they are written in an official language of another Member State, if that language is recognized as an official language of the Community institutions in accordance with Article 290 of the Treaty.

43. The Implementing Regulation establishes in Article 2 that exchanges between Member States' authorities, institutions and persons are based on the principles of public service, efficiency, active assistance, rapid delivery and accessibility, including e-accessibility, in particular for the disabled and the elderly. The institutions shall without delay provide or exchange all data necessary for establishing and determining the rights and obligations of persons to whom the basic Regulation applies. Such data shall be transferred between the Member States directly by the institutions themselves or indirectly through the liaison bodies. When a person mistakenly submits information, documents or claims to an institution in the territory of a Member State other than that in which the institution designated in accordance with the implementing Regulation is situated, the information, documents or claims shall be resubmitted without delay by the former institution to the institution designated in accordance with the implementing Regulation, indicating the date on which they were initially submitted. That date shall be binding on the latter institution. Member State institutions shall not, however, be held liable or be deemed to have taken a decision by virtue of their failure to act as a result of the late transmission of information, documents or claims by other Member States' institutions. Where data are transferred indirectly via the liaison body of the Member State of destination, time limits for responding to claims shall start from the date when that liaison body received the claim, as if it had been received on that date by the institution in that Member State.

44. In accordance with the principle of good administration, the institutions must respond to all queries within a reasonable period of time and shall also provide the persons concerned with any information necessary for them to exercise their rights. Member States must ensure that the necessary information is made available to the persons concerned, to inform them of the changes introduced by the new Regulation and the implementing Regulation and to enable them to assert their rights. They shall also provide user-friendly services for the persons concerned (Article 3 of the

Implementing Regulation). When collecting, transmitting or processing personal data pursuant to their legislation for the purposes of implementing the new Regulation, Member States shall ensure that the persons concerned are able to fully exercise their rights regarding personal data protection, in accordance with Community provisions on the processing of personal data and the free movement of such data. To the extent necessary for the application of the new Regulation and the Implementing Regulation, the relevant institutions shall forward the information and issue the documents to the persons concerned without delay and within the time limits specified under the legislation of the Member State in question. The relevant institution shall notify the claimant residing or staying in another Member State of its decision either directly or through the liaison body of the Member State of residence or stay. When refusing to issue benefits, it shall indicate the reasons for its refusal, the remedies and the periods allowed for appeals. A copy of this decision shall be sent to the other institutions involved. The persons concerned must inform the institutions of the competent Member State and of their Member State of residence as soon as possible of any change in their personal or family situation that may affect their right to benefits. If these obligations are not respected, proportionate measures may be taken against them in accordance with national law. These measures shall be equivalent to those applicable to similar situations under domestic law and shall not make it impossible or excessively difficult for claimants to exercise the rights conferred on them by the new Regulation. Persons for whom the basic Regulation applies shall be required to forward the information, documents or supporting evidence necessary to establish their situation or the situation of their families to the relevant institution. This is necessary to establish or maintain their rights and obligations, as well as to determine the applicable legislation and their obligations under it (Article 3 of the Implementing Regulation).

Article 87 of the new Regulation lays down the obligation for the Member States to ensure that the appropriate information is provided regarding the changes in rights and obligations introduced by the new Regulation and its Implementing Regulation. In the preamble of the Implementing Regulation, informing the persons concerned of their rights and obligations is mentioned as a crucial component of establishing a relationship of trust between the persons concerned and the competent authorities and Member States' institutions. Information should include guidance on administrative procedures. Special rules are stipulated in the new Regulation and Implementing Regulation regarding the provision of information to persons and employers concerned on the formalities to be followed for different types of benefits, or regarding applicable legislation (Article 19 of the new Regulation, Article 22 of the Implementing Regulation).

45. Former paper 'E-forms' will disappear under the modernized coordination, but in some cases, the information required by a citizen will be issued in the form of a portable document. There are, in total, ten portable documents, including the European Health Insurance Card (EHIC). Apart from the card, the other documents are in paper form. The EHIC is a portable document which proves one's entitlement to necessary health care during a temporary stay abroad, i.e., in another country than the country of residence. All persons covered by a statutory health insurance scheme in one of the EU countries, Norway, Liechtenstein, Iceland or Switzerland has the right to obtain an EHIC. The portable document S1 allows a person to register for health care if the person lives in an EU country, Iceland, Liechtenstein, Norway or Switzerland but are insured in another one of these countries. This is typically the case for pensioners retiring abroad. It can also be used for family members of migrant workers who have stayed in their country of origin but are now covered by the social security insurance of the country where their family member currently works. This replaces the old E106, E109, E120 and E121 forms.

III. Formal Law and Regulatory Acts

46. Under the term 'formal law', one defines the common laws, the emergency laws, the legislative decrees and the legislative acts.

The Greek social-insurance system is composed of a large number of laws, which establish the social-insurance organizations and regulate their administration and function. The scientific approach of the Greek social-insurance laws is rather difficult, as they usually include rules of mixed nature and their titles do not correspond to their content. Apparently, the codification of the basic rules of our social legislation would also make easier the dogmatic work out of the social-insurance institution.

47. The national legislator is often obliged to delegate the Executive for the regulation of social affairs under regulatory acts. These acts have mainly the form of presidential decrees, ministerial decisions and social-insurance boards or committees' decisions. Specifically, the establishment of social-insurance regulations with presidential decrees may correspond to practical needs, but it confines considerably the self-autonomy of the social-insurance organizations, since their administrations are not usually asked to express their opinions. On the contrary, before a ministerial decision, the administration of the relevant insurance organization formulates usually a proposal, which very often binds the competent minister.

IV. General Principles, Jurisprudence and Customs

48. The general principles play an important role among the sources of Social Security Law. As 'general principle', a commonly accepted (unwritten) fundamental rule is considered, which is justified from a logical necessity and derives from an explicit aim of the existing legal system. The general principles acquire their basic characteristic (the binding effect) from a legal provision that reflects their content and they are distinguished in principles which have the value of a constitutional provision and principles which have the value of a legal provision. Thus, these principles could form a legal ground for social-insurance claims, only if they are not expressed in Constitution and legislation. Otherwise, legal sources are the similar rules of law, where the principles are somehow expressed. We have to use first of all the methods of interpreting the positive law regulations, and additionally, we can refer to the general principles for the recognition of specific social-insurance rights. There are also court decisions, which follow the second interpretation, such as the Decisions of the SE 1427/83 and 2258/81, published in EDKA 1983, page 531 and 1982, page 203.

The social-insurance legislation is characterized by fluidity and gaps due to its very dynamic and occasional character. Thus, the legal science and particularly the courts' jurisprudence attempt to cover the legislative defects by forming relevant general principles; the general principles, recognized by jurisprudence, have a major impact on the real meaning of the social-insurance provisions, as they are extracted from the given economic and social circumstances. General principles with a constitutional value, which are often referred to by the recent case law of the High Courts (Council of State and Court of Audit) are the principle of social solidarity which allows redistribution of income, the principle of the financial viability of the insurance system, the principle of actuarial studies when regulating social insurance, the principle of carrying out social and economic impact studies when the legislator takes measures restricting the property rights of pensioners. But the contributory principle is not a constitutional principle. Therefore, there is, namely, no guarantee that the amount of benefits will be proportional to the amount of contributions. On the contrary, according to the principle of solidarity, the benefits of low pensioners can be much higher compared to the amount of contributions that they have paid.

49. As it is commonly acknowledged, jurisprudence in Greece is not a source of law, and therefore, not of Social Security Law. The court decisions simply reveal the real and effective meaning of the law provisions, which are interpreted. However, if the jurisprudence of the SE is altered constantly, then the social-insurance organization must re-examine every other similar case for its adaptation to the last case law (*see* the Decision 1460/73 of the SE, in EDKA 1973, page 420 and the Decision 4444/84 of the First Instance Administrative Court, in EDKA 1985, page 350, and also Decisions 2709/82 and 3692/82 of the SE, in EDKA 1983, pages 82 and 153).

50. The customs are not considered sources of Social Security Law because the dynamic character of this law branch is not compatible with the prerequisites of a custom's creation (factual, steady and generally approved application of an unwritten rule, with a legal conscience). There is only a limited sector of referring to a custom in Social Security Law. The conviction of an 'existing procedure' (a long, continual and unified behaviour of the insured people and the social-insurance authorities) could be based on a custom or an administrative practice, as we usually say.

V. Collective Labour Agreements

51. For the promotion of a unified and state-coordinated social-insurance policy, the Greek legislator had forbidden (by Article 21§3 Law 3239/55) the establishment or the modification of social-insurance rules in collective agreements. The clauses that violated this prohibition were considered as null because of exceeding the collective autonomy limits. Yet, it was difficult to eliminate the relevant social pressures through such a legal prohibition. The professional organizations and trade unions refused to be deprived of such an important means for the protection of their social insured members. They went on contracting collective labour agreements, which obliged the employers to finance several social-insurance schemes (*see* the Collective Labour Agreement from 24 April 1985 for the technical personnel of the Urban Transport Enterprise, in the Code of Labour Law Review (KEED) 1985, page 489). According to Article 2§3 Law 1876/90, 'a collective labour agreement can regulate: … social insurance matters, except the ones related to pensions, if they are not contrary to the constitutional order and to the policy of the social insurance organizations'. This regulation was later specified by Article 43§3 Law 1902/90, where the meaning of the 'pension matters' is extremely enlarged. These two pieces of legislation have not proved very successful. They, on the one hand, include self-evident provisions, such as the need for compliance to the Constitution and on the other, criteria that cannot be judicially estimated, like the organizations' policy. Besides, the distinction between pension matters and others does not have any special meaning, since, finally, the contracting parties can never replace the *jus cogens* of the most social-insurance rules. In the future, the collective labour agreements might form another source of Social Security Law, under the guarantee, of course, that the State-coordinated social policy would not be substantially neglected.

Collective labour agreements are an integral part of the employment relationship mechanism in Greece. They can regulate social-insurance matters under two conditions: first, regulation should not be involved in pension matters, and second, it must abide by the Constitution and be compatible with the general policy framework of the insurance institutions. Thus, social partners are regulating insurance matters by expanding employee protection on particular insurance hazards. On the other hand, social partners were not able to establish special funds or accounts that provide occasional pension benefits or lump-sum payments by placing the burden on the employer, until now. The recent amendment of 2002, however, enables social partners to establish, under the initiative of the employees or the employers or under an agreement between both parties, occupational pension schemes (TEA) which fall within the second pillar of social insurance.

According to Article 37 of Law 4024/2011, throughout the application of the Mid-term Frame of Fiscal Strategy (which will remain in force until 2015), one should always apply the business collective bargaining agreement, as opposed to that of the sector or profession, as long as it is at least as favourable to the employee as the national general collective bargaining agreement (e.g., setting minimum wages and, in general, minimum working terms and conditions for all employees). Although this change is expected to help businesses avoid, or at least reduce, redundancies, it has been met with scepticism by union leaders and many politicians and lawyers, who unfortunately still seem unable to grasp the simple fact that employment law is effectively meaningless if there are no jobs. Collective bargaining agreements: previously, only unions could sign collective bargaining agreements (on behalf of employees). However, at least twenty employees are needed to form a union, placing small businesses at an unfair disadvantage. For example, small businesses with no unions were unable to sign business collective bargaining agreements which would have enabled them to employ personnel with wages lower than those provided for by the collective bargaining agreements of the sector or profession (as noted above). Paragraphs 1–4 of Law 4024/2011 address this problem, providing that if a business has no union, then a simple association may sign the collective bargaining agreement instead, as long as it comprises at least three-fifths of the business's personnel. This rule is expected to allow small businesses to take advantage of the new law so as to become more competitive. Since around 60% of employees in Greece work for such small businesses, this may well result in less unemployment than anticipated.

Part I. The Institutions

52. The need to drastically change the organization and functioning of the social security system is demonstrated in the actuarial studies in 2010. They result that if there were no drastic changes, in 2040, 24.1% of GDP would have to be allocated to pensions instead of 11.4% allocated in 2009. It is clear that if Greece spent 1/4 of GDP on pensions, the resources that would remain for other public purposes (such as health, welfare, unemployment, education, investment, defence, public order) would be limited. In this case, retirement would be a deterrent to growth but also to social cohesion. The main reasons that led to the problem are explained below in section 1 and the measures taken by the legislator in section 2. One of the most important measures was the creation of E-EFKAs by merging the existing ones and the unification of the legislation for the award of benefits and the collection of contributions.

§1. The Main Reasons That Led to the Problem

53. The main reasons that led to the problem concerning the viability of the social-insurance system are:

- Demographic ageing. In 2010, the dependence ratio, i.e., the ratio of the population over 65 to the population of productive ages 15–64, was 28.41%, in 2030, it is expected to be 37.74% and in 2060, the ratio is expected to reach 56.65%.
- The large number of social-insurance organizations and the particular large number of schemes that governed the insurance of different categories in each organization. Unfortunately, this problem has not been solved, as the number of insurance organizations has been reduced by the merger into a single organization called Unified Social Security Fund (E-EFKA), but the distinct schemes that existed in each merged organization have been maintained within E-EFKA.
- The high replacement rates, the early retirement opportunities (in particular for married women with underage children and civil servants) and the low insurance contributions compared with the amount of benefits awarded. In 2011, less than 40% of Greeks aged 55–64 were working. As Eurostat data shows, expenditure on pensions jumped from 13.5% of GDP in 2009 to 17.5% in 2012 (the highest level in the EU-28). The continuous decline of Greece's GDP during a recession stretching over five years (2008–2012) partially contributed to the above-mentioned increase. After the crisis broke out, some small-scale pension reforms involved lowering replacement levels, raising contributions, preventing early

retirement, and merging dozens of small social-insurance organizations into a few larger ones. However, a decline in social insurance contributions, which resulted from growing unemployment combined with lowered salaries and wages from 2010 to 2014, meant that any stabilization effected would be through a lower level of contributions and benefits.
- The unequal distribution of state funding, and of social resources (indirect taxation), mainly for insurance organizations that have a strong lobby, such as workers in the media.
- The pay-as-you-go financial system that applies to both main and supplementary insurance. This system is sensitive to recession and ageing.
- Extensive uninsured work and tax evasion.

From 1 January 2022, the funded system in supplementary insurance will be operated by the Supplementary Capitalization Fund.

§2. The Measures Taken by the Legislator after 2010

54. The most important measures taken on the reform of the social-insurance system are:

- The merging of social-insurance organizations, but not of their particularly large number of different schemes that governed the insurance of different categories in each one of the merged organizations.
- The development of e-government systems (KEAO, EDIKA, ERGANI, SILIOS, etc.). These systems have made tremendous progress in collecting contributions, but no progress has been made on the level of processing of the pension claims, mainly because there are no records in electronic form before 2002.
- The adoption of automatic spending limits on pensions so that they do not exceed a predetermined percentage of GDP. Automatic restrictions result in immediate pension cuts and/or increases in contributions. Most of the arrangements are made first in Law 3863/2010 and 3865/2010 and are restated in Law 4387/2016.
- The retirement age limits are based on demographic indicators for population survival in Greece.
- The age limits and insurance periods have risen.
- With regard to supplementary pensions, all supplementary insurance organizations were merged into one, which is called ETEAEP, by Law 4670/2020, ETEAEP was incorporated into e-EFKA, and a sustainability clause was introduced. This clause stipulates that pensions are adjusted in a way that ensures that ETEAEP's viability is not jeopardized.
- A maximum pension is foreseen (Article 13 of Law 4387/2016), according to which the main and supplementary pension may not exceed EUR 2,000 per month. If one has more than two pensions, the maximum amount is set to EUR 3,000 per month. It should be noted that the contributions are paid up to a maximum salary of, i.e., EUR 5,860 per month which is almost three times higher than the maximum pension.
- Successive pension cuts: initially for a main pension of over EUR 1,000 and for a supplementary pension of EUR 300 (a total of EUR 1,300).

- From 1 January 2017, the basis and method of calculating contributions for self-employed and liberal professionals changed. In particular, the contributions are calculated on the taxable income. This regulation did not apply for more than a short time to self-employed persons. In compliance with the jurisprudence of the Council of State, the legislator with Law 46702020 provides that self-employed persons pay contributions on the basis of insurance categories.
- The minimum pension for persons insured after 1 January 1993 amounted to EUR 497.74 and with the supplementary pension and EKAS reached a total of EUR 700. Law 4387/2016 replaces the minimum pension with the basic pension which amounts to a maximum of EUR 384.

§3. The Different Policies of the Parties: Lack of Consensus

55. However, the political parties did not share the same vision on the social insurance reform. The main differences in their policy are the following:

- By 2015, the government (New Democracy and Pasok) wanted to create three main pension organizations: one for the employees and civil servants, one for the self-employed and liberal professionals and one for the farmers. After the elections of 2015, the government (Syriza) opted for a single pension fund for main insurance and a single pension fund for supplementary insurance. The difference is not arithmetic. The nature of the employment is different and the degree of viability of each fund is different. In some funds, pensions were under-funded by contributions and over-funded by social resources. The consolidation of dissimilar categories and situations raises legal problems (violation of the principle of equality, infringement of property rights, infringement of legal certainty) and administrative problems.
- Until 2015, there was no question of changing the basis and method of calculating the contributions of self-employed and liberal professionals. Law 4387/2016 imposes contributions for all categories on the taxable income. Contributions are calculated at the same rate. For example, for the main pension, the rate is 20%. Of course, the legislator has a wide discretion to choose the basis and method of levying contributions. But when choosing taxable income by invoking equal treatment, the income has to be similar to all categories. In fact, the income of EUR 10,000 of the employees after deduction of insurance contributions and taxes resulted in a net income of about EUR 9,000, but for the self-employed, the same income after deduction of taxes and contributions resulted in a net income of only EUR 5,000. Obviously, this is a problem concerning the implementation of the principle of equal treatment because the self-employed and liberal professionals contributed more to the public debt than the employed and the civil servants. The income of the self-employed and the liberal professionals dramatically decreased especially for those with low income.
- A problem also appears to exist with regard to sustainability. Concerning contributions, the Ministry of Labour, Social Insurance and Social Solidarity claimed that while 20% of the self-employed paid the minimum contributions, with Law 4387/2016, 80% are paying the minimum contributions. Concerning pensions

(which represent the overwhelming expense for E-EFKA), the government announced that there will be no cut for pensioners that received their pension before 2016. All this without any actuarial study with the argument that no study is needed because Greece achieved surpluses for 2018 and there will be surpluses in 2019. This argument underestimates macroeconomic data.

§4. Law 4387/2016, Its Goal and Principles

56. The principle of social solidarity in the jurisprudence of the Council of State is of constitutional level, while the contributory principle has the force of the level of a simple law. This is a paradox because the Greek system is mainly funded by contributions. As a consequence, the legislator in period 2010–2015 reduced higher pensions based on the principle of social solidarity. However, the Council of State decided that the cuts were unconstitutional (for the period after 2012) due to the lack of sufficient actuarial and economic studies. The new government (Syriza) was urged to find a solution in response to the annulment of all previous measures.

57. In this context, the new government adopts Law 4387/2016, known as 'Katrougalos law', which aims at removing social injustices, unnecessary expenses, and administrative problems of the prior system under consideration of two major restrictions – the persisting financial crisis and the limitations set by Law 4336/2015 (known as the 3rd Memorandum between the Greek Republic and its creditors). This reform introduces unified rules for all past and future pensioners, for all people employed in the private and public sector, and for all dependant workers and the self-employed. Moreover, the establishment of a basic part of the pension without means test requirements promotes income redistribution, the elimination of inequalities, and the provision of minimum living standards for all insured people.

§5. The Basic Arrangements of Law 4387/2016

58. The basic provisions of the new legislation are summarized as follows:

- A single main pension organization (E-EFKA) is established, which includes all pre-existing main pension funds (IKA for employees and civil servants, OAEE for self-employed, ETEA for liberals, Organization for Agricultural Insurance (OGA) for farmers and ETAP-MME for employed and self-employed in media). At the same time, all lump-sum benefits organizations and all supplementary pension organizations merged into a single organization (ETEAEP) and, since 2020, merged into e-EFKA.
- The supervision of social-insurance organizations is exercised by the Ministry of Labour, Social Insurance, and Social Solidarity. Moreover, a high-level advisory board, the National Council of Social Security, has been created for working out

and following up on the various social policy measures, for information on public opinion, for the planning of the relevant research, and for efficient communication with international organizations, etc. However, the National Council of Social Security is still on papers.

- It is foreseen that all insured persons in the E-EFKA will pay a single insurance contribution rate (20% for the main pension and 6.95% for the sickness insurance attributed to the National Health Insurance Organization (EOPYY) on their taxable income from work. Also, all insured persons for supplementary pension and lump-sum benefits in ETEAEP will pay uniform contributions, i.e., 7% for the supplementary pension and 4% for the lump-sum benefit. Total contributions amount to 38% of taxable income from work.
- Shortly afterwards, Law 4472/2017 provides that the contributions of self-employed and farmers are not deducted from the previous year's income as an expense. If one deducts contributions and taxes from taxable income, the 'net disposable income' for active insured persons is very small and there is a disproportionately low net income for self-employed and liberal professionals. In income categories of EUR 10,000, the insured person without a family has income at the poverty level while the insured with a spouse and two children has income less than the poverty threshold.
- The law reiterates, with slight variations, the distinction of the previous Law 3863/2010 (known as Loverdos law) into a basic pension (funded by the state budget) and a contributory pension (funded by contributions). The final pension received is the sum of the two parts (basic and contributory). The logic is that the 'state guarantee' is limited to the financing of the basic pension (*see* below for the calculation of the pension).
- The National Actuarial Authority produces actuarial studies as of 1 January 2017 and every three years. These studies are ratified by the EU's Economic Policy Committee to monitor the evolution of basic pension expenditure.
- By special law, pensions are readjusted to ensure the long-term viability of the insurance system. In particular, the pensions are adjusted as of 1 January 2016 and thereafter by a joint Ministerial Decision of the Ministers of Finance and Labour, Social Security and Welfare, based on a 50% rate of change in GDP and 50% by the change in the Consumer Price Index of the previous year and the adjustment does not exceed the annual change in the Consumer Price Index.
- Retirement age limits are determined on the basis of demographic indicators for population survival in Greece.
- The level of pension expenditure projected up to 2060 should not exceed the margin of 2.5 percentage points of GDP growth with a reference year in 2009.
- For supplementary pensions, ETEAEP's sustainability clause is foreseen.
- There is a ceiling on pensions.
- In addition, Law 4387/2016 provides that the pensions already paid will be recalculated by 2018 based on the method of calculating the pensions provided by this law. The resulting difference (between the 'old pension' and the new one after the recalculation) is paid as a 'personal difference' and offset annually until it is completely eliminated by the annual increases in pensions. It is clear that an increase in pensions is not expected until the Greek economy enters development and the GDP grows. However, by recalculating, very low pensions are expected to

increase slightly because the basic pension part is more important than the contributory part in low pensions; that is why the Minister (Katrougalos) had stressed that his policy is 'class-oriented' and favours low pensioners. This law overlooks that a system based on contributions presupposes a fair relationship between contributions and benefits. In addition, poverty in the Greek system is primarily addressed by social assistance rather than social insurance (*see* below for the parallel programme of the Government in Part X, §1), as the insured and the retired are not considered poor because they have income above the poverty line either as employees (minimum wage) or as pensioners (basic pension).

- Just one year afterwards, Law 4472/2017 amended Law 4387/2016 on recalculation and provided that from 1 January 2019, if the amount of such pensions is greater than that resulting from their recalculation, the excess amount is reduced. The amount deducted in this way may not exceed 18% of the amount payable at the time of entry into force of the beneficiary's main pension. If the amount of the pension paid is greater than that resulting from the above-described recalculation, the additional amount shall continue to be paid to the beneficiary as a personal difference, set off each year and up to its complete elimination by the adjustment of pensions. If the amount of pension paid is less than that resulting from their recalculation, then it shall be increased by one-fifth of the difference progressively and equally within five years from 1 January 2019.
- Already, Article 1 of Law 4578/2018 provides that the social security contribution of self-employed persons and liberal professionals is now 13.33% and not 20% of their net taxable income from their professional activity. In this way, the legislator replies to the claims made by the Trade Unions and the Associations of Liberal Professionals that the setting of a uniform rate of contributions overlooks that they do not have an employer who pays part of their contributions and that the sum of taxes results to a disproportionate reduction in their income (*see* above in Part I, §3).
- Law 4578/2018 is a major crack in the logic of Law 4387/2016 because it overturns the logic of assimilating the social security scheme of wage earners, civil servants, self-employed, professionals and farmers. This crack was expected, as they are categories with different insurance and employment characteristics. In fact, in the name of equal treatment, Law 4387/2016 had introduced unequal arrangements that selectively degraded self-employed and professionals. In compliance with decisions of the Council of State, Law 4670/2020 follows, which provides that self-employed persons pay contributions to predetermined insurance categories and choose the category in which they wish to be insured. Of course, a low insurance category implies a low pension. The logic of the unilateral nature of the contributions in Law 4387/2016 was found to be contrary to the Constitution and, in particular, to the principle of equal treatment. The new law has the acceptance of the self-employed.
- Law 4387/2016, in its Explanatory Memorandum, states that it aims to the sustainability of the pension system and the restoration of equality between the insured persons and between generations. It is clear that the legislator meant intergenerational equality as a reduction of unjustified differences between pensions, awarded at different times. Therefore, pensions already paid are recalculated, and the differences are reduced, as above-mentioned. However, for political

reasons, personal differences were largely retained in 2019. The Ministry of Labour, Social Insurance and Social Solidarity so far has no data on the recalculation of pensions and, when asked, states that with recalculation low pensions are rising. In fact, the average pension category of EUR 700–EUR 1,300 is expected to suffer significant reductions for the first time, while the high pensions category, i.e., over EUR 1,300 which have suffered very high reductions since 2010, is expected to keep the reductions. The logic is that those who have 'enough income' will be burdened. Only 'enough income' goes down and it should be laid down in law, or even by courts, what the limits are.

Part II. Contribution and Financing

§1. Introduction

59. In the beginning, the social-insurance schemes were based on the contributions of the insured people. Besides, social insurance was historically and functionally related to private insurance. This way of financing, which is in force until today, responds to the feeling of mutual help in the closed insurance societies. Personally interested in the payment of contributions were, apart from the employees, all those who took indirect advantages from the social insurance, for example, the employers, family members. As time passed, the cost of social-insurance protection increased reversibly to the income of the active population. During periods of unemployment, for example, as the expenses for the relevant benefits increased, the resources from contributions decreased because they presupposed payment of wages. Therefore, the burden of financing became a concern of the entire population. Special taxes (direct and indirect) were introduced for the regular financial support of the social-insurance organizations and the State guarantee for the covering of the various insurance risks was established approximately. The legal nature of contributions has given rise to scholarly debates. The view of a charge similar to tax is based on the provisions that disconnect the obligation of contributions from (a) the payment of remuneration (Presidential Degree 278/82, Article 29(a)) and (b) the immediate expectation of benefits (Law 1302/1982, Article 4 VII).

§2. First Pillar

60. First pillar scenes are funded by:

(a) Mixed insurance contributions (by employers and insured persons) to the social-insurance organizations for dependent workers.
(b) Contributions of insured people to the social-insurance organizations for self-employed.
(c) Social contributions.
(d) Regular or special State subsidies.
(e) Revenues from the exploitation of E-EFKA's property.

I. The Main Pension

61. E-EFKA legally constitutes the general successor to the merged social-insurance organizations and assumes all related rights and obligations. For specific issues which have not been regulated under the new legislation, the rules governing the merged organizations apply accordingly. Exempted from the E-EFKA, there are various public pension recipients, who are, in fact, being compensated by the State for specific reasons, e.g., if they have become victims of terrorist attacks, war veterans, invalids after a State service or mission. The Ministers of Finances and Labour will regulate their protection until their definite affiliation to the Unified Social Security Fund has been established.

62. The basic part of the pension is financed, through tax revenue, from the State budget. The contributory part is entirely financed through social insurance contributions. The total employer's and employee's contribution, which amounts to 20% (13.33% for the employer and 6.67% for the employee), is calculated on the basis of all kinds of monthly salaries. The upper limit of insurable earnings for the calculation of the monthly insurance contribution of employees and employers consists of ten times the amount corresponding to the respective minimum basic wage of an unmarried employee, which as of 1 February 2019 amounts to EUR 6,500. That is, 13.33% of their taxable income for the previous year as it appears in the tax declaration, and can be justified accordingly. Moreover, from 1 January 2017, the social security contributions for health protection (in cash and kind) amounts to 7.10%, and is shared by employers and employees, based on a range of salaries. Regarding the self-employed, the relevant percentage amounts to 6.95%.

63. As far as the property of the social-insurance system is concerned, a 'private' assets management company has been planned in the form of an anonymous society totally owned by the Unified Social Security Fund and supervised by the Ministers of Finances and Labour. This company will be responsible for the administration, management, and investment regarding the real estate of the pre-existent social security organizations. All income received from its activities will constitute additional capital at the disposal of the Unified Social Security Fund. A similar company has also been planned as far as other kinds of property are concerned. This second company will be operating through a mutual fund following the successful example of the two pre-existing (merged) companies. In addition, new capital shall be collected from the fight against contributions avoidance, from ongoing privatizations, etc.

64. The invalidity pension is fully paid (for invalidity over a degree of 80%), but it is reduced to 75% (for invalidity to a degree between 67% and 79.99%) and to 50% (for invalidity between 50% and 66.99%). The multiplicity of entitlement conditions among the invalidity pension schemes forced the legislator to avoid a unified regulation, and to establish a specific Committee of Experts for recommendations on all necessary amendments to the existing system. On the contrary, entitlement conditions for the survivors' pension have been fully harmonized. Family members will profit significantly from this simplification.

65. The survivors' pension for widows and widowers is granted after the 55th year of age because thereafter, accessing the labour market is extremely difficult. The required length of the marriage (or marital pact) has been reduced to three years from five years, so that abuses due to fictitious behaviours are limited. The national pension is shared among survivors according to the percentage of the inheritance legislation. In the case of pension accumulations (from various professional activities), only one full pension is provided.

II. The Supplementary Pension

66. Supplementary pensions are almost exclusively financed by the social insurance contributions of the persons involved. From 1 June 2016 to 31 May 2019, the social insurance contributions, based on the total salary, will amount to 3.5% for employees and 3.5% for employers.

Self-employed persons, with the exception of farmers who pay slightly lower contributions, choose one of the following insurance categories and pay the corresponding monthly contributions for the main pension and sickness.

Categories	*Main Pension (€)*	*Sickness (€)*	*Total (€)*
1η	155	55	210
2η	186	66	252
3η	236	66	302
4η	297	66	363
5η	369	66	435
6η	500	66	566

67. The Minister of Labour, Social Insurance and Social Solidarity is authorized to modify upwards or downwards the above percentages, according to the efficiency of the contribution collection. This constitutes a new incentive to reward the lawful payment of contributions on the part of the insured. Furthermore, protection by way of a supplementary pension in e-EFKA, which operates on the basis of the distribution system, is linked to the 'sustainability clause'. In other words, its payment at a certain level depends on the maintenance of sufficient (actuarially justified) reserves, on the actual demographic data (death rates), on the development of the main pension level, etc. In the TEKA which operates on the capitalization system, contributions are calculated in the same way as e-EFKA and are actually collected by it and paid to TEKA. The supplementary pension depends on the amount accumulated in the individual account based on the contributions and their returns.

III. The Lump-Sum Social Insurance Benefits

68. Lump-sum benefits are provided by e-EFKA that, since 2020, merged to e-EFKA, and have to be recalculated in relation to the credited insurance periods.

Only periods for which the appropriate social insurance contributions have been paid (exclusively by the insured) are taken into account. The relevant contributions amount to 4% of the real salary or income, and they are managed in conformity with the capitalization system. According to the new method of calculation, the lump-sum benefits level is submitted to a considerable decrease (of up to 35%) compared with the previous system. Although these benefits are the result of a compulsory individual savings procedure, they could not remain untouched by the current trend of using 'private property' to improve public finances and satisfy international creditors.

§3. Second Pillar

69. The funding of the second pillar which was established institutionally in 2002 by the introduction of professional insurance funds is covered by employers'–employees' premiums. Occupational pension funds provide pension benefits and operate on the basis of a capitalization system.

Funding sources of TEA are the insured's regular and extraordinary premiums, the employers' regular and extraordinary premiums and the return from the scheme's capital gain and reserves. The schemes are obliged in setting up reserves that will cover the obligations towards the insured and the beneficiaries. Reserve exploitation is allowed under the following conditions:

- Up to 10% of the technical reserve is to be invested in real estate.
- Up to 70% of the technical reserve is to be invested in shares and corporate bonds.
- Up to 20% of the technical reserve is to be invested in bank deposits and interest bills.

Investment of the technical reserves of the scheme in financial means that are issued by the scheme itself is also allowed, provided that it does not exceed 5% of these reserves.

An open discussion has been started as to the way in which the second pillar (mutual supplementary insurance or occupational pension funds) should be structured in general. What rather prevails is the preference for an actualization and improvement of the existing pension funds legislation. These funds have been regulated as legal entities of private law on the basis of a capitalization system according to Directive 2003/41/EC. After the economic crisis, the State could not guarantee to uphold the obligatory second pillar (supplementary pensions) anymore. Some trade union representatives admit that the private supplementary plans or accounts could constitute an alternative option to the declining supplementary insurance schemes. Consequently, a social consensus appears in favour of the maintenance of the pay-as-you-go public system for a mandatory First Pillar, and of the actualization of the capital-funded private system for a voluntary Second Pillar.

Only recently, a new trend for the reform of some quite old legislation regarding mutual funds, dated from 1920, has been gradually emerging. These mutual funds, which are closely connected to the trade unions, provide for the supplementary protection of their members.

Last but not least, private insurance companies are considering the drafting of new group life insurance plans with strong social characteristics (*see* initially Article 13§2 Legislative Decree 400/1970), which would profit from tax exemptions.

All these trends are facing the same difficulty. There is not enough money left for the payment of voluntary contributions, since the obligatory ones (together with the tax obligations) constitute a large part of the monthly salaries and yearly incomes. Two proposals have been set for consideration: either the introduction of an 'opting out' mechanism in favour of some certified supplementary pension schemes, or the establishment of a private-public mix cooperation between the Unified Social Security Fund and some generally acknowledged occupational insurance plans. Nevertheless, under the current political and economic circumstances, there are many reservations regarding the efficiency of similar strategies.

§4. Temporary Special Contributions

70. In the Greek legislation, there are no such special contributions. Perhaps the previously mentioned reduced contributions for enterprises in the border areas could be characterized as (five years) temporary contributions.

Relatively there are the so-called special contributions, to which one is obliged when a special event occurs, such as the receiving of the first increased salary, the marriage allowance and so on

§5. Contributions on Benefits (Participation of the Insured and Pensioners)

71. Health care beneficiaries receiving benefits in kind from the sickness insurance branch are burdened with a part of the relevant expenses.

According to Article 19 of Law 1902/1990, as amended after Article 38 of Law 4025/2011, the participation of insured persons in out-hospital care costs amounts to 25% of the value of the medicinal product. The participation is reduced by 10% for the beneficiaries of the EKAS benefit and the members of their family. Participation is excluded for drugs for women during pregnancy and childbirth, for occupational accidents, for antiretroviral drugs administered to HIV-positive patients and prescribed by recognized centres for the diagnosis of the acquired immunodeficiency syndrome (AIDS) and for hospital infections.

With Law 4368/2016 and KYA A3(c)/GP/oik.25132/4-4-2016, the right of free access to all public health care facilities for the provision of nursing and medical care to uninsured and vulnerable social groups is established for the first time. The most fundamental change introduced by the above institutional framework is the equalization of the right of the insured, the uninsured and former holders of the Individual Account for the Economically Disadvantaged or Uninsured to access the public health system. The health coverage guaranteed by the new framework is comprehensive and includes hospital, diagnostic and pharmaceutical coverage.

§6. Government Funding and Other Sources of Revenue

72. The State subsidy mentioned above must not be confused with the obligation of the State to cover the social-insurance organizations' expenses for general social policy purposes. For instance, if a law charges a social-insurance scheme with protection measures characterized as social assistance benefits, the State budget has to cover the cost.

73. The total assets of social-insurance organizations (cash, securities and real estate) after deducting their financial liabilities are their assets. In the past, the most neglected source of revenue was the exploitation of the social-insurance organizations' reserve funds. For many decades, the social-insurance organizations were obliged to invest their reserve funds only to values with a State guarantee, to a State-bank account with lower rates of interest, etc. For the purchase of real estate, long-term procedures were imposed, which used to disorientate the administrations of the organizations from their main duties.

This situation has changed significantly. Article 12 of Law 1902/90 provides that investments in mutual funds are allowed and Article 13 of the same Law anticipates that the above organizations can receive for their deposits the common rate of interest. Law 3586/2007 regulates the investment of the above-mentioned assets and its main provisions are:

- The excess capital, except for the amounts that are used in the cash management accounts, must be deposited in the Bank of Greece reserve account. Part of the funds may be invested.
- The principles of investment policy and asset management defined in Article 17 must be followed by the managers of their assets.
- The assets are invested and liquidated without any limitation on fixed or floating rate securities of the Greek government, other than compound bonds, and in Greek government securities in the form of the repos or in the form of reverse repos. Greek government in the form of repos or in the form of the sale repurchase agreement (reverse repos).
- The assets are invested with limits and under conditions in other products (shares etc.)
- Investments in mutual funds are carried out only through the Mutual Fund Management Company – Social Insurance Institutions (AEDAK-FKA) or through the Mutual Fund Management Company – Insurance Organizations (AEDAK-AO).
- A certified custodian must be appointed for safekeeping the transferable securities.

Part III. Health Care

Chapter 1. Who Is Entitled to Health Care?

§1. Directly Insured

74. From the several health insurance branches, all the persons who are obligatorily or voluntarily affiliated to a social-insurance scheme are directly covered, according to their work, if they have fulfilled the necessary insurance period. For example, those who provide a salaried dependent work as a main profession are considered as directly insured persons for the health care by the IKA if they have carried out at least hundred insurance days during the previous year or during the previous fifteen months (without the estimation of the last three months in that case). As working days apart from those days where the payment of contributions is obligatory are also considered the days of sickness, maternity, accident or unemployment subsidy. Relatively to the insured at Craftsmen and other Professionals Insurance Institution (TEVE), the practice of the work of craftsmen or professionals is demanded and also the acquirement of an insurance ability with the expiration of six months, for the first registered and with the payment of all the owed contributions.

75. Moreover, health care is offered by the ESY hospitals and units to all citizens according to Article 1§1 of Law 2071/92. The most recent law concerning the ESY is Law 2519/97.

According to a prevailing point of view, the State has to be concerned for the health care of all citizens. It seems, however, more fair that the health protection from the ESY should be provided to the total population, regardless of the specific citizenship or explicit international obligations. The right to the health protection corresponds not only to a social right (Article 21§3 of the Constitution) but also to the human dignity (Article 2§1 of the Constitution) and to the life protection (Article 5§2 of the Constitution) principles, which impose an absolute protection of all the people living on the Greek territory. Article 1§1 of Law 2071/92 referred to the 'citizens' without a real exclusion of some parts of the population. The refusal of admission or stay of a foreigner in a hospital, a health centre or a peripheral consulting room, until his citizenship was correlated to an international obligation would have also provoked the sense of justice.

§2. Dependent Persons (Indirectly Insured)

76. Contrary to other legislations, the covering of every (directly) insured or retired person's family members is a self-evident characteristic of the most social-insurance schemes in Greece. The international declarations and agreements, which suggest that among the dependent persons, only spouses and children have to be included, have not prevented the Greek legislator from extending the coverage to the whole family according to the traditional structure of the Greek society. Thus, in some cases, the circle of the protected persons includes, apart from the directly insured, the wife or widow, the under-aged children or the adult disabled children, the supported parents and also the brothers and sisters, the grandchildren and the stepchildren. This circle is enlarged or narrowed in the specific social-insurance schemes according to Article 36 of Law 2084/92.

77. For example, affiliated to EOPYY are the (directly insured) employed or retired person and his (indirectly insured) spouse, his unmarried children (natural, legally recognized, adopted), his parents and the orphan brothers, sisters and grandchildren (Article 33§1 of Law 1846/51). Particularly, the children are entitled to sickness benefits until the 18th year of age, unless they are: unemployed (until the 24th year), continuing their studies (until the 26th year), or unable to ever work. In the last case, their right corresponds to the whole period of their incapacity.

All the previously mentioned persons have to live together with the directly insured person so as to be considered 'family members' protected by the EOPYY. In other words, the maintenance of all these people, apart from the spouse, have to burden mainly the directly insured.

For the avoidance of unjustified insurance protection, there is a rule that the quality of the indirectly insured yields to the parallel quality of the directly insured, when benefits are going to be provided by the same organization. From the moment an insured's wife to EOPYY starts a dependent work, she cannot keep on demanding services from her husband's health insurance organization.

Chapter 2. How Does Health Insurance Operate?

§1. Insurance Sickness Benefits: EOPYY

78. Law 3918/2011 (Articles 17–31) establishes the Single Organization for Health Services (EOPYY) which is competent for sickness benefits in kind and is supervised by the Minister of Health. The Uniform Health Benefit Regulation has already been issued by the Decision of the Minister of Labour and Social Insurance Φ90380/25916/3294/2011 (Government Gazette B 2456) which establishes in a uniform way the sickness benefits in kind provided for all insured persons. The amended Uniform Health Benefit Regulation of EOPYY (Government Gazette B3054/2012) is today into force.

79. Under Law 4238/2014, the aim of the EOPYY changed. The primary care clinics and primary care units were transferred from EOPYY to the ESY and function in the context of the Regional Health Administrations (DYPE). After that, EOPYY aims to: (a) the purchase health services for the entities transferred to the PEDY according to EOPYY's Regulation; (b) the establishment of rules on the design, quality, development, evaluation, safety and efficiency of the health services, the management and the control of the funding and the rationalization of human resources; (c) the definition of the criteria and terms of procurement for the purchase of health services with public and private law bodies and contracting physicians, as well as the revision and modification of these terms; (d) the negotiations with all contractors regarding their fees, the terms of the contracts, the prices of medical devices and medicines.

This law completes the ESY which now includes primary care (outpatient care) and secondary (nursing).

80. The EOPYY provides and health insurance in kind, which consists of medical, hospital and pharmaceutical care.

Under the term *medical care* we mean the use of health services for the general prevention, diagnosis and treatment of an illness, and every necessary paraclinical examination or special treatment. The general and special doctors' or dentists' services are here included, as well as the duties of the helping medical personnel (nurses, physiotherapists, etc.). The provision of therapeutic means and orthopaedic devices, like pacemakers, artificial dentures, hearing aids, invalid chairs, belongs also to the medical care.

Given that the health restitution mainly depends on a successful diagnosis, medical care beneficiaries can demand not only an appropriate treatment but also services for additional diagnosis.

Under the term 'paraclinical examinations', we consider the radiological, microbiological and other examinations for the diagnosis or the observation of a disease, though special medical treatments like radiotherapy, physiotherapy, etc., are considered.

Hospital care means the stay, feeding and treatment (cure, education) in a health institution, until the consequences of a disease are seriously reduced or disappeared. This care is usually decided, when the insured suffers from a contagious disease or he/she needs intensive treatment (e.g., confined women in maternity clinics).

Some additional benefits are also justified together with the hospitalization, as the expenses restitution for the employment of an exclusive nurse, the cost reimbursement for the urgent transportation to the hospital and the financial support (income maintenance).

The hospital care abroad is particularly costly for the insurance organizations. In such case, an important part of the expenses for the hospitalization, transportation of the sick and of the necessary companion and even for their temporary stay at a hotel can be covered. Naturally, this payment presupposes a very serious illness and a difficulty to be cured in Greece. By virtue of the Greek administrative practice, a person is entitled to hospitalization at a public clinic or to a private clinic of a public hospital abroad: (a) when he suffers from an illness which cannot be treated in Greece, either because the appropriate scientific means of treatment or of diagnosis do not exist; (b) when he suffers from a serious illness that cannot be treated in time in Greece; (c) after his departure to another Member State, without having previously acquired an authorization due to the necessity for urgent medical treatment abroad; and (d) when there is a need for urgent medical treatment, while he is already abroad for any reason, professional or tourist.

With particular reference to the provision of emergency treatment during a stay in another Member State, significant problems arise in practice, as stated by numerous Greek SSIs, on the occasion of using the S documents. Though their use is very frequent, in cases of a posteriori authorization of medical treatment abroad, questions arise, on the one hand, due to the evaluation of the insured person's condition made by the institution (hospital) of the place of stay concerning the concept of 'urgent' medical treatment (Administrative Court of Athens 10630/94, StE 1983/94, StE 4370/95, Administrative Court of Appeal of Thessaloniki 724/96, Administrative Court of Appeal of Athens 4710/96) and, on the other, on the prolongation of the therapy (E HIC) (Administrative Court of Appeal of Thessaloniki 4710/96). Because of the nature of the competent institution, all cases requiring hospitalization will most probably be considered to be urgent. Therefore, insured persons obtaining an EHIC form enjoy benefits, the covering of which should depend on following the procedure for obtaining an S2 form. It should also be noted that according to the opinion of the administration of Greek SSIs, child delivery is not covered by the aforementioned procedure. However, in concrete cases, the Greek administration has accepted that for the strict application of Article 22(1)(a) of the Regulation 1408/71 (now Article 19(1) of the Regulation 883/2004), the institution competent to decide on the urgency of treatment is that of the state of stay. As far as the provision of authorization before moving to another Member State from the Greek competent institution is concerned, the above-mentioned problem is also of relevance.

The stay in institutions for chronic or incurable diseases can sometimes be considered as a marginal case of hospital care, but not the stay at old peoples' homes providing also health services. The insurance risk of sickness includes only cases of irregular function of the body or mind, but not the old age, which is an unpleasant, but natural development.

Following a series of European Court of Justice's (ECJ's) rulings since 1998 (in the case *Kohll* and *Decker*), which entitled patients to obtain healthcare in any other EU MS and to have these healthcare costs reimbursed by their own health systems (competent institution) in their home country (the competent MS), the European Commission submitted a proposal for a Directive (on 'patient mobility') of the European Parliament and the Council on 2 July 2008.

The Directive on cross-border healthcare entered into force on 24 April 2011 (JO L 88, 4 April 2011) and MSs have until 25 October 2013 (the date it becomes applicable) to implement it, that process being closely monitored by the Commission with the aim to ensure its full implementation across the EU by the deadline agreed.

Overall, the Directive 2011/24/EU is set to clarify the right of patients to seek healthcare in another MS while being reimbursed by the national (health/sickness insurance) system they are subject to in the MS of origin.

The stated aims of the said Directive are threefold, namely to:

(1) help patients exercise their rights to access cross-border health care;
(2) guarantee safety and quality of cross-border health care;
(3) contribute to the establishment of increased EU cooperation on healthcare.

The main outstanding issues of articulation between the Regulation and the Directive, coming out from the Greek competent authorities' contribution to the debate launched by DG EMPL and DG SANCO, which would need to be further elaborated for the purposes of better delineating the scope and mechanisms of both instruments, with a view to the application of insured persons'/patients' rights by all actors involved, could be summarized in the following points.

I. 'Residence Outside the Competent MS'

A. Rights in the Competent MS Other than the MS of Affiliation

81. The scope of Article 7(2)(a) and (b) of the Directive 2011/24/EU needs further clarification:

– *In respect of Article 7(2)(a)*, the question is raised regarding the type-range of healthcare provided to pensioners and members of their family as well as to members of the family of a worker. Given that the above-mentioned three categories have full coverage under the Regulation during their stay in the competent MS, it then becomes clear that the healthcare which is to be provided under this Directive concerns treatments received by non-contracted healthcare providers. However, as the said healthcare, as expressly stated, is provided in accordance with national legislation (the competent MSs), the question arising is about the precise impact of Article 1(4), second sentence, i.e., how these provisions have to be interpreted for such an application of the Directive. Otherwise, how Article

7(2)(a) should be implemented by the competent MS, where the latter 'does not reimburse costs of healthcare provided by providers established on its own territory if those providers are not part of the social security system or public health system of that MS'.

- *In respect of Article 7(2)(b)*, implying competent MSs which are not listed in Annex IV of the Regulation 883/2004, healthcare to pensioners and their family members under the Directive is provided either by contracted providers but under a private regime or by non-contracted ones. On the contrary, as the members of the family of a worker are fully covered by the respective provisions of the Regulation (Title II, Chapter 1), healthcare under the Directive would imply that the said treatment is exclusively provided by non-contracted healthcare providers. The question of the impact of Article 1(4) last sentence is once more arising regarding healthcare by non-contracted providers.

B. Different Applications and Entitlements under the Two Instruments

82. The aim is to clarify all pending issues, in a way to eliminate the complicated character or overlapping of provisions under two different instruments, which is already an obstacle per se. Yet, clarification of grey zones or complex approaches requires highlighting the different applications of the Directive in situations where the MS of residence is different from the competent MS:

- Where the MS of residence is not listed in Annex 3, then the competent MS is the MS of affiliation. Thus, a person may receive in the MS of residence healthcare under the Directive, while such healthcare (under the Directive) cannot be received in the competent MS, by virtue of Article 7(2)(a) and (b) provisions. This is a topic which needs to be expressly defined, notably following the court's most recent ruling of 15 June 2010, in case C-211/08, *Commission v. Spain*.
- Where the MS of residence is listed in Annex 3, then the said MS is also the MS of affiliation. Consequently, a person residing in that MS is not entitled to healthcare under the Directive, while the person concerned may receive such healthcare in the competent MS, in conformity with the provisions of Article 7(2)(a) and(b).

If, following what has already been analysed, the application of Article 7(2)(a) and (b) provisions seem clearer, however, this application leads to different entitlements which derive from the different way the general principle on equal treatment of TFEU is conceived and implemented under the Regulation, on the one hand, and the Directive, on the other.

Under the Regulation, equal treatment, as a fundamental horizontal principle, is implemented in the light of FMW/insured persons, one of TFEU's fundamental freedoms. This approach, based also on the general principle of a sharing of responsibilities between MSs involved, as sustained by ECJ's settled case law, means in practice that, it is the MS of residence that bears the responsibility to guarantee that persons subject to the legislation of another MS (competent) are equally treated on its territory, as the said insured are expressly assimilated with persons properly insured under the legislation of the MS of residence: the former are entitled to the same (rights to) sickness benefits in kind (healthcare). It goes without saying that the principle of equal treatment is likewise implemented also in the MS of stay.

The implementation of equal treatment as above is finally reflected in the Regulations financing mechanism, whereby the competent MS reimburses the MS of residence or stay for healthcare costs incurred in their territories. Thus, the reimbursement mechanism established by the Regulations guarantees the implementation of the principle of equal treatment in all MSs involved, as it is based on the general principle deriving from the court's jurisprudence on the equal/balanced distribution of healthcare costs. Under the said mechanism, the competent MS always remains responsible for the reimbursement of healthcare costs except where responsible for the reimbursement of costs abroad is the MS of residence listed in Annex 3, Regulation 987/2009.

Under the Directive, the general principle of equal treatment is, on the contrary, mainly implemented in the context of TFEU's fundamental freedom to provide services. This approach is based on the assimilation of the patient's healthcare received in another MS with the same or similar healthcare in the MS of affiliation. This, in practice, means that the implementation of the said principle concerns reimbursement of costs by the MS of affiliation and by the competent MS (under the Regulation) where the latter is not the MS of affiliation.

Of course, reimbursement of costs under the Directive is in no way comparable with the mechanism of a balanced distribution of costs at a European level between all MSs involved under the Regulation. Moreover, in the years to come, the question to be answered is whether and to what extent the reimbursement of costs established under the Directive undermines the balanced distribution of costs under the Regulation.

However, the diverging application of the principle of equal treatment between these two instruments (in the MS of residence, under the Regulation, and in the MS of affiliation, under the Directive) implies discriminatory treatment depending on whether the competent MS is also the MS of affiliation or not.

Focusing on healthcare in the MS of residence, insured persons are not equally treated depending on that MS being listed in or excluded from Annex 3 of Regulation 987/2009. Apart from that, for persons residing in an MS not listed in Annex 3, administrative complexities and the financial burden deriving from their communication with the competent MS, may result in creating essential obstacles to their free movement. That situation may be even worse in cases where the costs to be reimbursed are comparatively low, which means that the above-mentioned insured often chooses to give up such reimbursement (bearing finally themselves the total costs).

These obstacles could possibly be eliminated by means of best practices to be developed between the MSs concerned. Yet, the question remains whether MSs would choose (in which cases/with which MSs) to apply the reimbursement mechanisms of the Regulation or the actors involved would follow the free-of-charge mutual administrative cooperation principle, since these alternatives might be still deemed considerably expensive for the MS concerned.

Following all the above-stated, the overall question remains whether there is still a conflicted relationship between two fundamental freedoms of the Treaty: freedom to provide services versus free movement of (insured) persons – which in more concrete would be translated into Directive versus Regulation.

Anyway, whatsoever the overall/utmost response to such a theoretical in principle question may be, the crucial priority for the Directive is to guarantee, as soon as it becomes applicable/implemented, that the said secondary-law instrument fulfils EU legislature's aim, actually functioning as a supplementary tool to the comprehensive system of overall protection established by the Regulation.

It is true that strong concerns have been expressed so far, regarding a possible, negative evolution, whereby the Directive could progressively act as a challenging alternative, substituting in every-day-practice the Regulation, i.e., taking in reality priority over the latter and, in a way upsetting the horizontal rule, expressly or indirectly governing the Directive, the Regulation's implementation always preceding the Directive's. The impact of such a supposedly adverse effect would be the limitation (confinement) of the Regulations' material scope, the reduction (in terms of quantity and quality) of the benefits falling under EU coordination. In fact, a derogatory (fraudulent) 'use' of the Directive would underpin the EU legislator's political choice per se, to use a coordination mechanism as a means to establish (achieve and enhance) freedom of movement (Article 48 TFEU).

The above-mentioned concerns are also reinforced by the increasing number of derogations in EHIC's implementation, mostly but not exclusively by healthcare providers, without the appropriate, effective intervention of the institutions involved, mainly those of the place of stay (healthcare treatment), which would remedy such problematic situations. The outcome of contracted providers' unwillingness to accept/recognize a 'foreign' EHIC, on the one hand, and hospitals' attitude to demand an S2 in place of the already submitted EHIC, on the other, is quite burdensome for the patient who is finally called to bear the costs of healthcare provided in another MS.

It is worth noticing that such derogations are usually the case where the competent institution reimburses healthcare costs with a considerable delay. Obviously, as the Regulations' reimbursement mechanism leaves some space to (allows for) quite time-consuming procedures, it is rather self-evident that direct/upfront payments by the patient could be sought by providers, as the latter would give priority to their financial interests, and would be indirectly well-come by institutions concerned, as the latter would be released from perplex and time-consuming reimbursement procedures.

Keeping the above-mentioned observations in mind, we consider that a well-informed and fully aware patient would better protect him/herself in respect of both the kind/type and quality of healthcare sought 'abroad', matching also the latter with his/her economic capacity. In parallel, it should be stressed that MSs, in the context of their complex competencies regarding cross-border healthcare in general, are responsible and obliged to enhance and intensify their administrative supervision over all institutions and contracted providers involved.

However, we are afraid that comprehensive information and analysis would not be sufficient to overcome problems that may always arise from the parallel implementation of the inherently 'conflicting' secondary-law instruments. So, a new 'intervention' in the framework of the Regulation, either in the form of more visible provisions or in the form of amendments extending the scope of coordination, is deemed indispensable as it would serve the aim of ameliorating in real terms the protection of the patient's rights and would guarantee that EU coordination Regulation is the most effective means of legal security, a prerequisite for the smooth exercise of the right of free movement.

II. 'The Authorization System'

A. Scope

83. It would better be clarified what seems as obvious under the existing provisions, that the type of healthcare provided in the other MS is defined according to the legislation/system of the MS of treatment. This leaves intact differences in ESYs (scope, structure and organization). Yet, this discrepancy may result in discriminatory treatment between mobile and non-mobile patients – i.e., a patient may have to seek authorization under the Directive for healthcare which in the MS of origin is considered as 'outpatient' while in the host MS is falling under the categories/classification of Article 8(2)(a) and (b) of the Directive 2011/24/EU.

Another point/provision which is not so visible concerns the limits between treatment under Article 8(2)(a) points (i) and (ii): for example, where hospital accommodation for a specific treatment (e.g., a laser operation) does not coincide with an at least one-night accommodation but is accomplished within some hours daily stay in hospital (inpatient treatment from X hours in the morning till early afternoon). The question is whether, for the purposes of the Directive, the said healthcare should fall under (i) or (ii).

B. Procedure

84. The perplexity in the smooth application of both prior authorization's procedures lies exactly in the involvement of different legislations on the basis of different health care systems under the Directive, on the one hand, and the Regulation, on the other, for certain categories of persons residing outside their competent MS. That perplexity leads to different entitlements (*MS of affiliation v. MS of residence*) which, in their turn, result in situations of patient discrimination on the basis of their MS of residence.

The MS of residence not listed in Annex 3 of Regulation 987/2009 is indeed, under the Regulation responsible, at least initially, for processing the patient's applications for authorization for treatment in a third MS (Article 26, Regulation 987/2009) and in other words, responsible for the application of Article 20, Regulation 883/2004, as far as the conditions by virtue of the said Article are met in its territory according to the legislation it applies; this means that decisive criterion for authorization is the MSs of residence capacity to provide or not the requested health care.

However, under the Directive, it is the MSs of affiliation's exclusive responsibility to grant or refuse authorization based on its capacity to provide or not the requested health care on its territory. This means that the respective capacity and opportunities in the MS of residence are irrelevant, i.e., are not taken into consideration and exercise no influence whatsoever on the former MS's (of affiliation) decision, although it is the overall situation in the MS of residence which is decisive for the patient's initiative to seek health care in a third MS. Moreover, the authorization in the MS of affiliation is subject to limitations (Article 8(2), mainly points (b) and (c)) which are linked/connected with the latter's health system and/or population, yet completely irrelevant with the patient's individual situation/state of health. This also happens in cases where the MS of affiliation is listed in Annex 3 ('competent' MS), but the insured/patient resides in an MS not listed in Annex 3.

It is to be noticed that the whole interplay may become even irrational, since the patient has nothing to do with the MSs of affiliation with either system of health or its own population. Under such conditions, granting or refusing authorization is, in our opinion, based on criteria which could hardly be considered as related to/connected with the concrete patient's state of health/need for specific treatment.

A more perplexed situation may arise where the MS of affiliation may (be called to) grant authorization for receipt of health care under the Directive's terms in the territory of the very MS of residence, just because the patient requested 'otherwise' (*see* Article 8(3), last sentence). In other words, although the patient could receive the same (similar, equivalent) health care in the context of the system of the MS of residence under the Regulation, the criteria for granting or refusing prior authorization are once more connected exclusively with the MS of affiliation. Thus, the patient's 'interests' finally take precedence over the Regulation's in principle priority, i.e., the patient's right in the context of freedom to provide services takes precedence over his/her right in the light of the principle of equal treatment in the MS of residence (in the context of free movement of persons).

C. *Reasons for Refusal*

85. It is still though essential to go deeper in the analysis of the topics/areas where the two instruments may overlap, especially in cases where 'undue delay' is absent and taking into consideration the reasons for which the Directive allows considerable derogations from its general principles for reimbursement of costs (*see* Article 7(9) or even (7) the last sentence, regarding administrative formalities), which are in the light of ECJ case law criteria and, thus, coincide with Community criteria applying *mutatis mutandis* for cases falling also under the Regulation (another case of overlapping).

So, while at the beginning it may seem that the scope of authorization is quite different, even exceptional in principle under the Directive, the way the latter shall be integrated into each MS's internal legislation and administrative practice risks to blur seriously, at the end, the exact points where the two instruments may diverge or converge in every-day-practice. A 'remedy' provided under the Directive in the form of MSs' obligation to make publicly available which health care is subject to prior authorization and relevant information on their respective system (Article 8(7)) is not, in our opinion, sufficient to shed light on all above-mentioned grey zones. The question remains how an MS could prove that the ECJ's criteria expressly mentioned under Article 7(9) are met under the Directive's terms (in general, more balanced reimbursement of costs), where no MS has been able to prove so far that the same Community criteria governing EU coordination are met in cases falling under the Regulation (assumption of considerably higher costs). Consequently, similar issues should be revealed and closely examined in order to demonstrate in which cases the Directive may seriously affect – eventually undermine the implementation of the Regulation.

III. Status of Health Care Providers

86. The question is whether MSs will actually and progressively choose to implement the Regulation only/as a rule for the health care provided by contracted providers and the Directive for the health care provided by non-contracted ones. Yet, what should be pointed out, right from the start, is that the application of the Regulation (and/or the Directive) does not depend solely on the status of healthcare providers. On the contrary, the difference in the application of either of the two instruments in question lies on whether the health care is provided in the context of the health system/sickness insurance or under a purely private status (even by an in principle contracted provider).

In other terms, where (prior) authorization has been granted for non-contracted providers, and the MS concerned (the competent one) 'usually reimburses on his applicable rates and assumes the cost of treatment', we would like to comment that the said reimbursement may be governed:

- either by the rules of the Regulation, namely the provisions of Article 26(7), Regulation 987/2009, where the Vanbraekel complement is equal to the tariffs applicable by the latter MS (in case of same/similar treatment on its territory); or
- by the system of the Directive. Thus, the essential issue is to delineate in a clear-cut way the Regulation's scope of application, in other words, to demonstrate the cases where private status health care should be covered by the Regulation. In our opinion, it remains to be expressly clarified that '*Keller/quasi Keller* – cases' as well as cases of 'undue delay', i.e., where the provision of health care under a private status proves to be 'compulsory' – one way, should be considered as falling under the Regulation. In the above-mentioned cases, the patient is practically 'driven' to receive healthcare either under a semi-private (e.g., private clinic/ accommodation within a public hospital/contracted provider) or under a fully private status.

So, it is of decisive importance for the competent MS, before proceeding to a posteriori authorization and the assumption of the costs incurred, to know, via the institution of the MS of stay providing the most accurate information and reliable assessment on the patient's overall situation and/or national (regional/local) health system's capacity-availability, whether the ad hoc case actually consists of an *ex post* implementation of the Regulation. The issue under a posteriori implementation of the Regulation can be described, in general terms, as a problem of loyal (effective and efficient) cooperation between the competent and the institution and the MS of stay. It is precisely the moment where the question on the extent of and responsibility for cooperation between all stakeholders concerned arises.

In other words, what is mostly missing is cooperation in substance from the MSs of stay part, so that the competent MS is fully aware of the circumstances in every mixed-type concrete case, i.e., whether private health care was the patient's individual and informed choice or the latter was 'quasi referred' outside the national health/sickness insurance system as he/she had practically no other alternative but to be treated 'under a private status' (derogatory situations already observed where a valid EHIC is not respected by health care providers in the MS of stay).

The obligation for such cooperation is not self-evident, since it does not come out straightforwardly either by Article 25(5) provisions (Regulation 987/2009) or by the Regulations' horizontal rules on overall cooperation, mainly because private sector agents are also coming into play; so, covering that gap means that we point out the need to extend the Regulation's scope in that specific but crucial domain, precisely for the purposes of safeguarding the latter's priority/taking precedence over the Directive.

87. Under the term *pharmaceutical care,* we mean the provision or the cost restitution for some medicines (substances for the relief or the cure of a disease).

Within the broad sense of this care belong also substances for diagnostic purposes, i.e., for the X-ray examinations.

From a socio-political point of view, the overproduction and overconsumption of drugs in our country must be mentioned, besides the international problems.

For facing these phenomena, three organizations have been established by virtue of Law 1316/83: the National Medicine Organization, the National Pharmaceutical Industry and the State Pharmaceutical Store. In this way, a centralized-strictly controlled planning of the production, import and promotion of the pharmaceutical products in the Greek or in the foreign markets was intended. The function of these institutions has not proved very successful, and recently, there has been a new tendency towards the privatization of several activities concerning medicines. Moreover, the doctors who are affiliated with insurance organizations are obliged to recommend medicines according to specific lists.

§2. Prerequisites of Entitlement and Exceptions

88. E-EFKA grants a sickness allowance to employees directly insured. The conditions for the award of the allowance are: (a) incapacity to work, (b) abstention from work, (c) hundred working days in the previous year, (d) three days after the E-EFKA notification. The allowance is granted for a period of six months. If the insured person has three-hundred working days in the last two years before the notice to E-EFKA, the allowance is granted for a further six months. It is possible to qualify for the subsidy for more than 360 days. The amount of the allowance corresponds to 50% of the presumed wage of the insurance class in which the employee is classified according to the average salary he had the last thirty days before the illness and is increased by 10% for each member of the family of the insured. The sickness allowance is paid by the Department of the Local E-EFKA of the insured person's place of residence, where the following original supporting documents must be submitted:

(1) Social Security Booklets (Extract from the Personal Social Security Record or Social Security Identity & Contributions Card – DATE – or, if no Extract from the Personal Social Security Record has been issued, then a certification issued by the employer, validated by the EOPYY office of the employer's area). These are submitted and remain at the branch during the whole period of the payment of the allowance.
(2) Personal Health Booklet and family Health Booklet, if any, for the calculation of the increment due to family burdens.
(3) A certification issued by the employer, certifying that the insured has stopped working and is absent from work during the period of payment of the allowance.
(4) A medical opinion certifying that the insured is not fit for work (work disability report in triplicate signed by the treating physician and Director of the Local EOPYY Unit (or his/her substitute) in the case of unfitness for work of up to fifteen days. In the case of unfitness for work for a period of more than fifteen days, such a report is required by the Primary Health Committee of the Health Unit upon referral of the case by the treating physician.

Additional Supporting Documents for Special Cases:

(1) *Accident*: In the case of the allowance being paid because of an accident at the place of work or outside the place of work, in addition to the above-supporting documents, a decision of the Director of the competent EOPYY is required, characterizing the accident as such, following the notification of the accident within five working days from the date thereof or the date of discharge from the hospital, if hospitalization was involved.
(2) *Hospitalization at a State Hospital or EOPYY Affiliated Clinic*: In the case of hospitalization at a state hospital, the discharge notice and the admitting and treating physician's report are required.
(3) *Hospitalization at a Non-EOPYY Affiliated Clinic*: In order for the sickness allowance to be paid for the period of hospitalization at a non-EOPYY affiliated clinic, an opinion is required by the Primary Health Committee, which must be notified to the EOPYY instruments within thirty days from the date of admission into the Clinic.

Chapter 3. How High Is the Reimbursement for Expenses?

§1. Primary Care

89. The insured people demand medical care from salaried doctors or from hospitals belonging to or contracted with the EOPYY. In the case of indirect health protection, they apply to health services of independent professionals contracted or not with EOPYY.

Basic medical services are usually offered in the outpatients' departments of the ESY and in the contracted health care institutions.

In cases of urgent need, non-contracted doctors or other necessary health care assistants can be consulted, but only for one visit. The doctor's or the assistant's payment is initially covered by the insured. Afterwards, the social-insurance organization pays back to the insured a certain amount of money subjected to the State control. The reimbursed amount can be increased with the doctor's or assistant's travelling expenses.

With the same conditions, non-contracted doctors can also be called, when for a specific treatment there are no doctors affiliated with the social-insurance organization.

A special doctor, who has not a contract with EOPYY or is not a doctor of ESY, can be consulted and the relevant cost can be covered in cases of lack or temporal absence of employed doctors of the specific speciality. Also in such cases, the reimbursement refers only to fixed (State controlled) prices. When no rule indicates the specific price, the administrative board of EOPYY has to decide accordingly.

Every necessary health care with specific chemical or mechanical means and remedies, like the X-ray treatment, radiotherapy, electrotherapy, external lithotripsy, can be considered as a specialized therapy. These therapies are provided by contracted or non-contracted private clinics or by public hospitals. The health care expenses are also here partially covered. The social-insurance beneficiary can claim a prescribed price of the specific health service after the deduction of his contribution (e.g., 25% of the total cost).

§2. Hospital Care

90. The insured can even freely choose a non-contracted health care institution (private, public, municipal) in other cities, except Athens, Pireus and Thessaloniki. In this case, the sick can ask for reimbursement according to the class he is entitled to be hospitalized, in relation with his insurance periods and his contribution records (*see* Article 37 of Law 1846/51).

Exceptionally, if the insured suffers from a 'particularly serious disease', which needs operation by specialized doctors, he can be hospitalized in a non-contracted institution after the permission of EOPYY. Then, apart from the hospitalization costs, the EOPYY undertakes the special surgeon's fee (SE 4328/85, EDKA 1986, page 361).

91. EOPYY will reimburse the expenses incurred for the emergency hospitalization of its insured members and pensioners in non-EOPYY affiliated clinics (private clinics) on the basis of the State-set rates. The following prerequisites must be met in order for the expenses to be reimbursed:

- the beneficiary must notify his/her emergency hospitalization to the EOPYY unit in whose area the non-affiliated clinic is situated, within thirty days of the date of his/her admission; and
- the urgent nature of the case must be verified by the competent EOPYY auditor-physician.

Required supporting documents:

- Verification of the insurance link on the basis of the electronically kept Individual Social Security Register.
- An application was submitted to the EOPYY Health Unit, which supervises the clinic, with the original expense certificates attached. The expenses will be reimbursed by the Benefits Department of the Local EOPYY of the insured's place of residence, where the above original documents were submitted.

EOPYY reimburses the cost of medical tests and procedures to its insured members and pensioners, when these tests and procedures are made in non-EOPYY affiliated laboratories, on the basis of the State-set rates, provided the case is characterized as an emergency by the EOPYY auditor-physician.

In order for the costs to be reimbursed, the following prerequisites must be met:

- the beneficiary must notify the case to his/her Local EOPYY Unit, within thirty days of the date of provision of healthcare; and
- the urgent nature of the case must be verified by the competent EOPYY auditor-physician.

The costs are reimbursed by the Sickness Benefits Department of the Local EOPYY of the insured member's place of residence.

Required supporting documents:

(1) Verification of the insurance link on the basis of the electronically kept Individual Social Security Register.
(2) An application submitted to the Local EOPYY Unit, with the original receipts attached.
(3) In the case of tests performed at the outpatients' clinics of State Hospitals costing up to EUR 100, the application is submitted directly to the Benefits Department of the Local EOPYY Unit and the opinion of the EOPYY auditor-physician concerning the urgent nature of the case is not required.

§3. Pharmaceutical Care and Appliances

92. This covers expenses for all medicines prescribed by EOPYY doctors. The prescription has to be executed at the latest within five days, otherwise it is not valid.

Chapter 4. Amount of Fees and Prices

§1. Doctors and Dentists

93. The doctors and the dentists who practice their profession independently demand fees according to the law of supply and demand. Most of them, however, are also contracted with EOPYY. In these cases, the insured usually pay directly the same fees for the doctor's visits and services, claiming afterwards a partial cost restitution, which is specified with regulatory acts of the administration, such as Presidential Decrees and administrative board decisions.

For the specification of the doctors' and dentists' fees, very important are the following pieces of legislation: Law 1565/39 (Article 29§1) 'About the code for the doctors' practice', the Royal Decree from 22 April/4 May 1939 'About the expansion of Law 1565/39 to the dentists' and the Legislative Decree 3623/56 (Articles 1 and 9) 'About the doctors' minimum wages and working conditions. From time to time, new regulations appear for the readjustment of the estimated fees or for the addition of new medical actions to the State-controlled lists.

For the doctors of the ESY who are civil servants (Article 30 of Law 1397/83), a special scale of basic payments according to their position and their employment period is defined (Article 55§4 of Law 1759/88). There are also extra monthly allowances regulated for the family burdens (Articles 11 of Law 1505/84 and 27§3 of Law 1579/85), for the provision of services in problematic and infertile areas (Article of Presidential Decree 131/87), for studies and library expenses (Article 1 of Law 1471/84), as well as for dangerous and unhealthy working conditions (Articles 17 of Law 1193/81 and 1 of Law 1471/84).

§2. Paramedical Professions

94. The persons who exercise paramedical professions, work in the private sector, as independent professionals (i.e., as physiotherapists), or as dependent workers (i.e., as assistants of laboratories).

In the first case, they are paid directly by the customers without restrictions. In the second case, however, the following mechanism of minimum wages is established.

If there are no professional organizations covering all the employers, the minimum wages are regulated by a common decision of the Ministers of National Economy and Labour. (*see* Law 435/68). Otherwise, they are defined by a collective labour agreement, or settled by an arbitration concerning the specific paramedical profession (*see* the Decision 51/89 of the Athens Administrative Arbitrating Court of Appeal about the wages and working conditions of the personnel in private clinics, in the old people's home, etc.).

95. When persons with paramedical professions work in public hospitals, they are usually paid as the other civil servants, if they have permanent positions. Otherwise, their wages are usually provided by special collective labour agreements, or arbitrary decisions (*see* the Decision 73/82 of the Athens Administrative Arbitrating

Court of Appeal about the wages and working conditions of the personnel in public or communal institutions of hospitalization).

§3. HOSPITALS

96. It is important to define the various categories of hospital charges, which break down into three, basic types: (1) Open or Common Hospital Charges, (2) Inclusive Hospital Charges, and (3) Semi-inclusive Hospital Charges.

The 'Open' or Common Hospital Charges

The common hospital charges are composed of a price set for health care rendered by the private clinics which includes both the hospitalization cost per day as well as a profit percentage. This category of hospital charges includes accommodation-type expenses such as:

(1) Personnel salaries and insurance fund contributions.
(2) Food supply expenses.
(3) Rents.
(4) Depreciations.
(5) The clinic's overhead (general) expenses.

Naturally, a private clinic also provides other services that a patient may need. These services are charged separately and beyond what insurance funds grant for hospital charges. Such services are: (a) medications; (b) surgical and anaesthesia expenses; (c) medical exam fees (laboratory, diagnostic, etc.); and (d) a variety of implantable and non-implantable materials (such as pacemakers) used in surgical procedures.

The Closed Consolidated Hospital Fees

97. As of 1 January 2012, the way of billing for services in all nursing institutions has changed. Until then, insurance funds paid for the hospitalization of their insured persons based on invoices for materials and drugs and days of hospitalization. The Ministry of Health introduced Closed Consolidated Hospital Fees (KEN) by therapeutic category of conditions. Under the new way, billing is based on a code with the patient's condition category, to which a predetermined amount will be assigned for all hospitals.

What should the doctor do?

98. The attending physician completes the admission form, where he or she selects the patient's admission diagnosis code. The attending physician completes the patient's discharge form, where the discharge diagnosis (ICD – 10) and medical procedure are indicated (more than one diagnosis and medical procedure may be selected, but the principal diagnosis should be identified and an effort should be made to avoid listing the admission diagnosis code, which is usually a symptom or sign, as the discharge diagnosis). ICD code – 10 is mandatory and without it, the discharge cannot proceed. The IT Department exports in excel format the patient data from the discharge notes and forwards it to the Patient Accounting Department (in case there is no automatic link through the ICD) for billing the patient's hospitalization charges. This is done at the beginning of each month in aggregate for the previous month (in total for up to 28/2/2012). The Patients' Accounting Department, using the Ministry of Health – Coding Matching System (KEN) application, can enter the ICD – 10 and medical procedure code(s), and the application gives the KEN code(s) corresponding to the above diagnoses and medical procedures. The selected CCN code is entered into the information system (OPSY), in order to charge the patient. In cases where the Patient Accounting Department cannot find the appropriate CCN code, it asks the CCN Management Team, consisting of doctors and nurses, for help in selecting the correct CCN directly. The submission list of hospitalized patients is printed at the beginning of the month for the previous month and sent to the insurance funds. In cases where the Average Duration of Hospitalization (ADI) exceeds that of the KEN, the information system invoices the additional days of hospitalization based on the invoice of the CPS, as well as the additional drugs, materials and tests. For private patients, the same procedure is followed by the Movement Office in collaboration with the Patient Accounting Office for billing the inpatient stay and payment of the expense.

In practice, the closed consolidated hospital fees do not differ much from the maximum medical fee schedule of a private insurance plan. We are talking about a table that lists the majority of medical cases with a coding (not our concern here) and the maximum amount covered by the government but in a public hospital.

99. Based on the EOPYY contract with private hospitals, in cases of hospitalization in a private institution, the KEN table is still in force but with a 30% participation. Therefore, the public coverage in a private hospital is up to 70% of the relevant KEN.

100. For example: In an operation costing EUR 9,000 in a private hospital, the NHIF will cover an amount of EUR 9,000 x 70% = EUR 6,300 and the difference (EUR 9,000 – EUR 6,300 = EUR 2,700) will be borne by the patient or a private insurance policy.

§4. Pharmaceutical Care

101. The pharmaceutical care, like the other medical services, within the framework of the ESY units (hospitals and health centres) is provided free of charge.

For the different sickness and maternity insurance branches, special Regulations (Ministerial Decisions) are in force. They are issued after an opinion of the administrative boards of the competent social-insurance organizations.

Chapter 5. Health Services in Greece

102. Health services in Greece are provided mainly via two avenues:

(1) Primary care, which includes health services not requiring hospitalization. These services are provided primarily by primary health care services of ESY, outpatient units at public hospitals, as well as the private sector through:
   - private practices of all specialities;
   - small laboratories (microbiology, radiodiagnostic) at the neighbourhood level;
   - organized diagnostic centres of multiple capacity; and
   - private hospitals' clinics and laboratories.

(2) Hospital coverage for patients treated in hospitals, which includes:
   - public hospitals, which 42.4% are financed by the State, and public social security organizations;
   - independent, non-profit hospitals (few in number); and
   - private hospitals, which cover approximately 57.6% of hospital beds in all of Greece.

103. Companies in the private market of secondary treatment fall under two categories, depending on the type of services they provide, i.e., private clinics and maternity hospitals. Private clinics are, as a rule, small treatment units with a limited number of beds (the average number of beds per private clinic is seventy-seven) and which can be characterized as either big or small treatment units. Small treatment units cannot cope with the increasing demand for integrated health services. As a result, they face significant problems and cannot survive easily. The problems in their operation are mainly attributed to the fact that they depend on public social security organizations, where the price of services is lower than the cost. Due to low financial fluidity, they are not in a position to carry out investment programmes in order to upgrade their accommodation facilities and medical and mechanical equipment and it is particularly difficult for them to act in accordance with community regulations. Big clinics of multiple capacities are mainly located in Athens and Thessaloniki. These are well-organized units with modern equipment, offering a variety of services both in primary and secondary treatment. This category has far fewer clinics compared to the first. Private maternity hospitals operating in Greece today are, in essence, clinics offering obstetrics and gynaecological services. However, most have moved on to create modern examination centres for the provision of diagnostic services.

The market of private clinics has shrunk due to Law 1397/1983, which prohibited the issue of new licenses for clinics or the expansion of clinics already in operation. So the number of clinics declined from 391 in 1983 to 224 in 1993, while, at the same time, public hospitals increased from 122 to 140. The foundation and expansion of private clinics was again allowed in 1991. The very low costs for patients at public hospitals, urbanism and the great need for equipment and investment led to a further reduction in the number of private clinics, mainly in small towns.

Today the total of existing beds (in the private and public sector) is not enough to cover all needs and Greece in 2019 had 438.5 beds per 100.000 inhabitants. Also, a large number of beds, mainly in provincial hospitals, are not full, due to a lack of equipment and staff, in big public and university hospitals there are waiting lists, since they lack special units such as intensive care. An important development in recent years is the evolution of the private health sector, which is being carried out both independently and in alliance with the public sector. The private health market is progressing autonomously, as far as the strategic choice of quality and not the financial services provision is concerned, in response to the demand for such services by a significant part of the population who did not previously have access to such services. The private health market is also developing in parallel to the public sector because the private health sector took advantage of the public sector's weaknesses in general, operating in secondary markets such as diagnostic services or maternity hospitals. However, the imposition of claw back and rebates during the economic crisis and its prolongation until today has contributed to the reduction of activity, especially of small regional hospitals, and has had an impact on the quality of services provided.

104. Moreover, within the framework of ESY, it is considered that the public health services are provided by 'state units'. This characterization, nevertheless, emerges only from the unified planning in health care matters (*see* Articles 3§2 of Law 1397/83 and 8§1 of Law 2071/92). It does not estimate the legal nature of the hospitals (entities of public law), which actually offer health services. The State authorities contribute mainly to the supervision and the staffing of the public health care institutions, according to Articles 2, 3, 53, 63 and 64 of Law 2071/92. Thus, contrary to what happens in other countries (e.g., in Great Britain), the Greek ESY does not correspond to a 'unified health organization'. Primary care serves as a necessary pathway for an individual for the promotion of health, the prevention of debilitating disease and the reduction of disability has also been recognized in Greece. The ESY, established in 1983, provides primary and hospital health care and emergency pre-hospital care; it was the same year where primary health care was recognized as a formal part of the Greek ESY since 1983 (Health Act No. 1397) and it was put into action with the main aim of improving the quality of care throughout the implementation of regional health systems. Up-to-date, 200 national health care centres are operating in Greece, and all of them serve the rural and semi-urban areas, in addition, 250 SSI polyclinics are located in urban areas. The medical speciality of general practice was considered as a cornerstone for this system and a vocational system of three years was established in 1986 (today, the vocational training in general practice requires a four years residency with three years and two months in the hospital setting). The central government through State insurance funds and private insurance schemes finance health care, upon this there is universal coverage for pharmaceutical care and various social-insurance organizations are available for the citizens. Although all those are in favour, it has been reported that integrated primary health care needs extensive efforts.

A general impression is that the primary care system in Greece has failed in reaching its targets and especially continuity of care, integrated and coordinated care and patient-family focused care. Among these hardships in Greece, many attempts have been made to surpass these roadblocks to improve the efficiency of primary care, yet it is still an issue of debate and remains as a difficult discussion among the policymakers, providers and primary care practitioners. In addition, a national electronic patient record (EPR) system using is available for the prescriptions of pharmaceutical products. However, the future of primary care in Greece has been discussed extensively and certain proposals have been submitted and among them is to increase the quality and efficiency of primary care by introducing quality indicators, the distribution of practice guidelines and clinical protocol for the most common diseases and health problems, the development of an electronic file for recording data, establishing a specialist nurse in primary health care education and a separate budget to each health centre recorded in each regional administration. Such proposals are a great first attempt to help shape the current system. Today, the current government has decided to focus on primary care and develop a mechanism for controlling the high health care cost through the implementation of the family doctor, taking into account that the relevant arrangements to date have not been successful as insured persons do not choose a family doctor.

Part IV. Family Allowances

Chapter 1. Who Is Entitled to Family Allowances?

§1. General System

105. Family allowances, in general, aim at covering extra costs caused within a household by the existence of children or other dependent family members. Law provisions related to such benefits may refer to the professional relations, such as the family benefits laid down in collective agreements, or to civil servants (Article 6 paragraph 1 of Law 283/76). Other family benefits may be integrated into different social security branches, as in the case of the increment of old age and invalidity pensions and sickness, unemployment, etc., benefits (Article 33, paragraph 1 of Emergency Law 1846/51, Article 51, paragraph 1 of Law 1539/85, or into the social assistance programmes, such as the Child Allowance granted by OPEKA, according to Article 214 of Law 4512/2018 which is financed out of the State's budget. Finally, in the framework of the general social policy, several law provisions are related to the protection of the family and the maintenance of family income (special advantages for large families, as regards the access to employment in the public sector, housing, education, taxation, etc.).

106. (a) Family allowances granted by the Distributive Account for Employee Family Allowances (DLOEM):

In the DYPA, an account for the cover of the dependent workers' family burdens is established (Legislative Decree 3868/58). This account is called DLOEM and is basically financed by insurance contributions (*see also* Law 1346/83 and Law 1414/84). It covers employed persons who offer dependent work with labour contracts of private law. It is not important, if the dependent work is offered as a main profession or if the insured are affiliated with the main insurance of IKA or of other organization.

Family allowances are available until the child reaches the age of 18, or permanently if the child has disabilities certified before the age of 18. The amount paid depends on the family income, how many children there are in the family, and where and if the parents are employed. The employer takes care of this and the amount is paid together with the salary.

The Distributive Fund for Employee Family Allowances (DLOEM) is financed equally by employees and employers, and gives family allowances to employees who do not receive an allowance from their employer. This is paid annually in a lump sum. The amount is higher for parents with more children, disabled children and for single parents.

Conditions

Completion of fifty working days in the calendar year preceding the year of subsidization or two months of being in receipt of ordinary unemployment benefit or two continuous months of incapacity for work. The child for whom the allowance is claimed must be:

- under 18 years of age, or under 22 years of age if a student;
- incapable of work, in which case payment is for the duration of the incapacity;
- unmarried;
- resident in Greece or in a member country of the EU.

The application for the allowance is submitted to the DYPA or to a Citizen Service Centre (KEP).

107. (b) *E-EFKA subsidies* directly insured women for fifty-six days prior to the birth and for sixty-three days following the birth. The insured women must fulfil the following conditions: (a) 200 working days in the last two years before the expected date of birth (b) abstention from work. The amount of the allowance is equal to the sickness allowance plus the family allowances.

Insurance cover for maternity is provided both for women who are insured directly and for indirectly insured women (non-working spouses of employed men). Directly insured women are protected both during the pregnancy and for the birth and post-natal period. Indirectly insured women are protected only for the birth. Maternity assistance consists of the birth benefit and the maternity benefit. The birth benefit is given to all insured women (directly and indirectly insured), and the maternity benefit is given only to women who are directly insured:

- The birth benefit consists of a lump sum to cover the cost of treatment in a maternity home or hospital. The amount is thirty times the day wage of an unskilled worker.
- Maternity benefit is paid to insured women who have completed at least two-hundred days of insurance in the two years before the expected delivery date. The amount is thirty times the day wage of an unskilled worker, and is increased by 10% for each dependent family worker.

However, where the employer benefits and the E-EFKA benefits do not cover the earnings, which an indirectly insured woman would have received, if she had worked during that period, the woman is entitled to an additional lump-sum maternity allowance from the DYPA. This allowance lasts for as long as the E-EFKA maternity and covers the difference in amount between the E-EFKA benefit and the earnings which the insured woman would have received from her work.

E-EFKA is also responsible for the social security scheme for civil servants. Retired civil servants who had been employed by the Greek State are entitled to children benefits irrespective of any conditions related to years of previous insurance (Article 12 of Law 2470/1997 and Article 5, paragraph 6 of Law 2592/1998); the retired civil servants or assimilated persons are to be granted children benefits in the form of a lump-sum allowance (Article 12 Law 2470/1997 and Article 5 paragraph 6 of Law 2592/1998).

108. (c) Child Allowance granted by OPEKA:

According to Law 4520/2018, the OPEKA was established and, as of 22 January 2018, is the universal successor of the OGA, concerning welfare. OPEKA is competent to provide welfare benefits and social services for economic and social support and integration to vulnerable groups of the population and to implement the welfare actions and programmes of the Ministry of Labour, Social Insurance and Social Solidarity (i.e., actions for Roma, school meals, etc.).

OPEKA is responsible for the child allowance provided by Article 214 of Law 4512/2018 that is granted to Greek citizens and Greek expatriates living permanently in Greece, recognized refugees, persons who enjoy a humanitarian status and stateless persons residing legally and permanently in Greece and aliens who legally reside in Greece for at least five years prior to the submission of the application. Proof of permanent residence is made on the basis of their tax declaration, or the tax declaration of their spouses or their parents, provided that they were not liable to tax declaration and their dependent children reside in Greece.

The benefit is exempted from any tax, levy or charge in favour of the State or a third party and is not added to family income for tax or other purposes unless explicitly provided for by law.

§2. Special Systems

109. For the family burdens of the personnel of some big enterprises, special (employment-related) systems are established, with sometimes peculiar entitlement conditions. The courts then interpreted the ambiguous legal rules. For example, a sex discrimination in the system of DEI has been judged as contrary to the Greek Constitution and to the EC Law, which offered family allowances to the husband without prerequisites, but to his wife only if he was poor or totally invalid. (Decision 17326/89 of the Athens First Instance Administrative Court, in EDKA 1990, page 182). The augmentation of the wages with family allowances belongs also to such special systems, which are provided in collective labour agreements, and the legislative regulation of such allowances for the civil servants.

Consequently, some professional groups may receive more favourable family allowances than the ones offered by the social-insurance scheme of DLOEM/ DYPA. For example, according to the collective labour agreement from 15 June 1985, concerning the 'Olympic Airways', the employed persons of the regular personnel who have children are entitled to a lump-sum benefit for the childbirth's expenses and to a full pay leave for three working days.

110. Besides, the earnings-related and flat-rated pensions are usually increased with family allowances to the insured with children. For instance, after 1 January

1993, the old age and the invalidity pension of a civil servant will increase with a percentage of 8% for the first, 10% for the second and 12% for the third and the rest children (Article 13§2 of Law 2084/92).

As noted in a research by the Centre of Planning and Economic Research (KEPE) (1990), the classification of several population groups (employed persons of private and public law, retired people, etc.) regarding the family protection is socially unjustified. Ensuring of adequate living conditions for the family with children concerns the whole population, and it has to be unified for everyone.

111. There are, finally, some important social assistance benefits for the family protection. These include: (1) the financial support for women in pregnancy, who are deprived of an adequate life level, if they are not insured or they do not yet have a right to insurance benefits (Article 4§5 of Law 1302/82, which has ratified the ILO Convention 103/52), and (2) the monthly allowance for the unprotected children, when they 'stay' with their natural family or with a family of relatives (Article 2§1 case b' of Presidential Decree 147/89) and the Child Allowance (Article 214 of Law 4512/2018).

Chapter 2. For Which Children?

112. The Law provides for following cases of child protection:

(a) The entitlement prerequisites for the protection from DLOEM are that the parent is a dependent worker, that fifty days of insurance period have passed during the previous calendar year and that the family consists of children under aged and unmarried.

Underaged are the children who have not reached the 18th year of age. Nevertheless, the insurance risk of 'family burdens' exists as long as the children are studying and until their 24th year of age. When the children are disabled and unable to work, the protection continues accordingly. In the notion of 'children' belong to the natural, the legitimatized and the adopted children (Article 1 of Presidential Decree 527/84). Additional prerequisites are that the children have to live permanently in Greece or in another EC Member State (Articles 73 and 74 of the EC Regulation 1408/71).

(b) OPEKA awards benefits to children until they become 18 years old, or if they are students until the completion of the 24th year of age.

(c) In the special systems, the entitlement conditions for the cover of family burdens are slightly differentiated.

Chapter 3. Payment of Family Allowances

§1. The Normal Case: Child Staying Within the Family

113. The right to the family allowance from DLOEM begins the first day of the month, which follows the child's birth, and it ends on 31 December of the year, during which the age limit is completed or the other entitlement prerequisites are removed. In the case of the beneficiary parent's death, the above right is transferred to the living parent or to a third person, e.g., to a legal trustee, who is in charge of the children's upbringing (Article 6 of Presidential Decree 527/84).

The payment of the children's benefit from OPEKA begins on the 1st of January of the year, during which the relevant application is submitted.

§2. Child Placed in an Institution or a Foster Family

114. The social-insurance organizations usually cover the expenses of the employed person's children for educational establishments, boarding schools, asylums, or other institutions. More specifically, the sickness insurance branches undertake the main part of the financial burden for the corporally or mentally disabled and maladjusted children. The possible contribution of the insured cannot overcome one-fourth of the training or other expenses (Article 6 of Law 861/79). For example, the parents' contribution to children living in asylums is 10% of the amount paid by the IKA for the medical or board charges (Circular IKA 156/87, in EDKA 1987, page 755).

For the protection of preschool-aged children (0–5, 5 years), who cannot live in a family environment (e.g., orphans, illegitimate, abandoned), welfare institutions are functioning. Their services are offered gratis until the adoption or the placement of the children in foster families.

When the parents of the orphans and the unprotected children face financial problems, they receive a family allowance (until the 16th year of the child's age) according to Law 4051/60. Exceptionally, when such children are living in institutions, which provide free services all over the year (on a twenty-four hours basis), and which are subsidized by other welfare or social-insurance organizations, they do not receive the above financial support (Article 2 of the Presidential Decree 270/85 and Article 2 of the Presidential Decree 286/88).

Moreover, according to the former regulations, a means-tested allowance is provided to the parents' or relatives' family, in which the 'unprotected' children are living. This cash benefit is also offered for such children, who are guests in families of relatives for educational reasons.

Chapter 4. Calculation of the Allowances

§1. Basic Child Allowances

I. Granted by DLOEM

115. A salaries increase with marriage and child benefits is usually stipulated in various collective labour agreements. There are, however, legal provisions for the avoidance of accumulation of more than one family allowance. For example, in Law 1346/83 (Article 18§4), it is mentioned that DLOEM provides the family allowances for the dependent worker's children, only when such allowances are not to be granted in equal level by the employer according to the existing collective labour agreement. It has also been accepted by the jurisprudence (AP 1887/1988, B' section, NoB 1989, page 905) that if one spouse is a permanent civil servant and the other a lawyer employed in and paid by a legal entity of public law, the family benefit is allowed only to one of the spouses.

In the case of the insured's or pensioner's death, the survival pension amounts the 50% of his (possible or received) pension, increased to a percentage of 25% for each child (Articles 12§1 and 31§1 of Law 2084/92).

The old age and invalidity pensions increased from 1 January 1993 with a percentage of8% for the first, 10% for the second and 12% for the third and the rest unmarried, underaged and unemployed children (Article 13§2 of Law 2084/92) not only for the civil servants, as it is already mentioned (about special systems), but for the dependent workers and the self-employed as well (Article 30§1 of Law 2084/92).

It has to be underlined that the tax reductions for the children have significantly increased from 1975 until today. It is estimated that the elimination of public revenues from the relevant tax regulations exceeds the amounts which are spent for family allowances from DLOEM and OGA. Namely, the tax legislation seems to offer a more dynamic mechanism for facing the demographical problem in Greece.

II. Child Allowance Granted by OPEKA

116. The Child Allowance under Article 214 of Law 4512/2018 replaces the previous Special Child Allowance for Three Children and Child Allowance for more than three children, as well as the Uniform Child Support Benefit.

It is paid on the basis of the number of dependent children and the 'equivalent family income'. That is the total actual income in Greece or abroad before taxes and after the deduction of social security contributions. Taxes not counted towards taxation are not counted. This income is divided by the so-called scale of equivalence as follows:

(a) first parent weighs one;
(b) the second parent weighs one-half;
(c) for each dependent child weighing one-fourth;

(d) for single-parent families, the first dependent child weighs one-half and each next one-fourth.

In order to determine the beneficiaries and the amount of the monthly child allowance, three categories of equivalent income are defined as follows:

Category	*Income in Euro*	*Allowance for the 1st Child in Euros per Month*	*Allowance for the 2nd Child in Euros per Month*	*Allowance for the 3rd Child and for More Children in Euros per Month*
A	0–6,000	70	70	140
B	6,001–10,000	42	42	84
C	10,000–15,000	28	28	56

Source: Article 214 of Law 4512/2018.

In the event of the parent's death, parental breakdown, divorce and abandonment of children, the allowance is paid to the person who has custody of the children.

§2. Increments Due to Age, Disability and Orphanhood

117. There are some special legal provisions for disabled children, orphans and families in difficult situations.

The child's incapacity to work is usually a reason for the continuation of the family allowances. For example, the children receive the survival pension after the 18th year of age or after the 24th year of age, in cases of education, until they regain the working ability (Article 27§3 of Law 2084/92).

Moreover, the above 25% (survival pension's increase) for each child becomes 50% if the child is an orphan from both parents (Articles 12§1 and 31§1 of Law 2084/92).

Finally, Article 1§3 of Presidential Decree 412/85 provides (in the framework of DLOEM general system) a monthly augmentation of GRD 1,250 for every beneficiary child because of the difficult situation of the parents or the children in his family (*see* the Circular of DYPA 98655/13 September 1985, in DEN 1986, page 370).

§3. Birth Grants

118. The various social-insurance schemes normally include lump-sum benefits to cover childbirth expenses. Childbirth is considered as the main consequence of the maternity insurance risk. Therefore, the entitlement conditions are not different from the prerequisites of maternity care. These are also the same with the prerequisites for sickness protection, especially where a unified 'sickness and maternity insurance branch' is established.

119. Beneficiaries of this cash benefit are women, who are insured or pensioners, under the obvious condition that the childbirth has not taken place at a maternity home established or paid directly by the social-insurance organization.

The birth grant differs among the various professional groups. It is usually a remarkable amount, which is automatically readjusted. In the case of IKA, for instance, it is thirty times the daily wage of an unskilled worker (Article 31§7 section B' of Law 1846/51, as replaced by Article 5§10 of Law 825/78). In the case of Mutual Fund of the Railway Personnel, it is three-fourths of the managing clerk's basic salary (Article 19§1 of the Presidential Decree 278/82) and so on.

The students can claim from the University Fund a birth grant, equal to the one received by the civil servants (Article 12 of Presidential Decree 327/83). This allowance, however, is based on a special social security system, regardless of the specific working status of the beneficiaries.

§4. OTHER SPECIAL GRANTS

120. By virtue of a Decision of the Minister of Labour (from 1984), as amended on 7 and 20 December 1989, a *marriage benefit* in cash is established.

Its prerequisites are: (1) the valid marriage, (2) the status of the insured worker, pensioner or unemployed, (3) the insurance period of thousand days (from which hundred days at least in each year of the three years before the marriage), and (4) the limited income of the spouses. This benefit is allowed from the fund of the Workers' Home Organization, and amounts twenty-five times as much as the lowest daily wage of the unskilled worker.

121. Another benefit in cash, extended in specific professional groups, is the so-called *allowance for family or professional independence* (*see* Law 1329/83). The first marriage is considered as family independence, and the first employment of the insured's children as professional independence, according to the judgment of the competent social-insurance organization.

The prerequisites for this allowance are alternatively two, within the framework of the obligatory social insurance: (1) the legally contracted marriage or (2) the reach of a certain age of the child (e.g., 30 years old). A characteristic example is the family allowance for the children of the active participants or beneficiaries of the Share-Capital Maritime Fund (*see* the relevant Decision of the Ministers of National Defence and Financing in the year 1985). The specific insurance branch for this family allowance is financed by a contribution of up to 3% on the basic salary of the active participant or up to 5% on the benefit of the dividend receiver after the date of declaring the child. The amount of the allowance is fluctuating correspondingly to the insurance period following the above declaration and it is estimated up to an amount multiple of the earnings or the salary of the parent. In the case of the child's death, the contributions (increased with interests) are paid back from the fund to the direct insured parent.

122. In some social-insurance schemes, even loans are anticipated for those facing family burdens. By the occasion of marriage, of childbirth, etc., the Subsidiary

Insurance Fund for the Employees of the National Tobacco Organization can allow a loan (with interest) up to Drachmas 80,000 (Presidential Decree 19/87). This financial support can be asked by the persons who have been insured for more than two years, and it never exceeds the total amount of the already paid social-insurance contributions.

Chapter 5. Procedures

§1. Request for Family Allowances and Birth Grants

123. (a) The supporting documents required for the family allowance must be submitted to DYPA. Alternatively, they can be sent by post or through a KEP. More specifically, the following supporting documents are required:

- Employer's certificate, if the claimant receives a monthly salary (download the relevant model here).
- Personal and family health booklet for children-dependents (updated by IKA); updated health booklet of wife/husband if she/he is insured with a Social Security Fund other than IKA.
- Family status certificate for the third child allowance; National Bank of Greece (NBG) account, of which the claimant must be the first beneficiary.

The family protection benefits are usually recognized without any serious procedural problems.

They are directly paid to the beneficiary. If he cannot receive the allowances, the payment is permitted to another authorized person. Up to a certain sum, which is defined by the administrator of the social-insurance organization, a proxy is sufficient, with an ascertainment of the signature by the police or other public authority. For higher amounts, a notary authorization is needed.

124. (a) Regarding the family allowances from the general system of DLOEM, the payment is realized once a year (*see* the Presidential Decree 1178/80). Nevertheless, they are considered as benefits of periodic character. For practical reasons, this financial support starts from the beginning of the child's birth year, until the end of the calendar year when he comes of age or when he has completed the 22nd year, if he is still studying.

The application and the supporting documents for the birth grant have to be submitted in a short (predetermined) period, so that the control of the prerequisites is easier. According to the regulations of TAE, the submission of the supporting documents has to be made within six months from the day of the birth.

Exceptionally, the decision of a family allowance must be approved by the competent minister, as the already referred decision for a loan to the insured of the Subsidiary Insurance Fund for the Employees of the National Tobacco Organization.

(b) Family Allowance granted by OPEKA.

The allowance is granted:

- from 1 January of the year for children born until 31 December of the previous year of the application and up to the age of 18;
- from the 1st of the following month of the birth of the child for children born in the year of submission of the application;
- from 1 January of the following year to enrol in a school for students and students up to the age of 24.

For the discontinuation of the allowance, the birthday is considered to be 31 December of the year of birth, and in the case of students, the end of the academic year or the student year.

§2. Granting of Information

125. The officials of the social-insurance organizations and OPEKA grant the necessary information about family allowances to the beneficiaries or to their representatives. Important information can also be found on the websites of the insurance organizations and OPEKA. Guidelines to the clerks are given with circulars of the administrative board, though for matters of special difficulty or significance, written standpoints from the competent Ministry are usually asked by the organizations.

In case of false information, a juridical decision for the reimbursement of the resulted damage is quite possible, but the juridical nullification of such information is not conceivable.

Chapter 6. Institutions for Benefits to the Family

126. Summarizing, in a way, the former presentation, we point out that the main organizations which provide benefits for the facing of family burdens are: (1) the DYPA and especially its account DLOEM, (2) the OPEKA, as an agent of the Ministry of Labour, Social Insurance and Social Solidarity.

In addition, there are several specific schemes of maternity and family protection branches incorporated in E-EFKA. Also the employers play a very important role in the family protection of their personnel.

127. The State can also be classified in the family protection institutions, particularly the Ministry of Financing, which permits considerable tax reductions for family expenses. Moreover, family welfare programmes are organized by the Ministry of Labour, Social Insurance and Social Solidarity, the local authorities and some benevolent societies or public welfare organizations.

Part V. Incapacity to Work

Chapter 1. Temporary Incapacity

§1. Beneficiaries

128. Sickness cash benefit is paid only to insured employees who, because of physical or mental illness, are unable to work and absent from the workplace for more than three days. The eligible period of benefit increases with contribution history:

> Sickness benefits in kind are granted to insured persons and their family members by the EOPYY from 1 March of each year and for a period of 12 months if the insured person has made at least 50 working days which from 1 January 2009 are increased by ten days per year and gradually reach 100 working days. In the case of insured persons working in the construction sector only 80 working days are needed in either the previous calendar year or the last 15 months before the sickness was announced without taking into account working days made during the last calendar quarter of the 15-month period.
>
> To claim sickness benefit, the insured have to submit the following documents:

– the personal social security account statement;
– the health booklet (personal and family);
– a statement from the employer specifying the time the employee has been off work;
– a certificate from your an EOPYY doctor that the insured is unable to work.

129. Other prerequisites are the incapacity to work, which will be analysed in the following paragraphs, the absence from work, and a three-day waiting period before the relevant application.

The incapacity to work, which took place abroad, is also covered, provided that the insured can ascertain an active social-insurance relation, according to the unexpected and urgent circumstances of hospitalization (Council of State 4919/87, NoB 1988, page 1721).

§2. The Concept of Incapacity to Work (Sickness)

130. In the social insurance, sickness is considered every irregular body or mental condition, which causes a need for therapy, incapacity to work, or both.

Analysing these characteristics, we point out that there has to be an irregular disorder of functions of the body or the mind. The location of neoplasms' is considered a sickness that needs to be cured, even if they have not caused a functional disorder to the human organism. On the contrary, in the case of pregnancy or childbirth, the health treatment and the temporary incapacity are usually caused because of a normal function; and that is, therefore, the reason why 'maternity' is addressed as a separate social-insurance risk. Moreover, the predisposition of a person to become sick under certain circumstances (i.e., in case of allergy) cannot be considered as an 'irregular health condition'.

Whether the need for therapy exists, this has to be judged under objective criteria. The expectation for total health restitution is not necessary. An offer of services for health improvement is enough. The social aim of sickness insurance branches imposes a large interpretation of the legal rules. Thus, even cases without a direct need for therapy are classified into diseases (i.e., the hernia from birth).

131. The abnormal corporal or mental condition is also considered as sickness, if it cannot be cured and causes an inability to work. The provision of short-sighted glasses from a sickness insurance branch is not actually a remedial measure, but a necessary measure for the exercise of a profession.

132. 'Sickness', as a social-insurance risk, seems to be interpreted sometimes within a narrower and sometimes within a broader sense than the relevant medical notion. The first is in force, when an incurable mentally sick continues without any problem his professional duties. The second is in force in the case of a professional driver who is unable to work because of his dependence on alcohol. For the referred insurance risk, the point of the medical diagnosis is not as important as the moment of the necessary treatment or the day of the obligatory break from work. During the waiting period, for example, until the operation of a 'cataract' is permitted, the insured cannot claim inability to work demanding insurance benefits, despite his serious eye disease.

§3. Sickness Benefit for Employees

133. The sickness benefit is granted if there are cumulative: (a) incapacity for work, (b) abstention from work, (c) hundred working days in the previous year, (d) waiting period for three days after the notification of the sickness to E-EFKA. During the economic crisis as well as the COVID-19 pandemic, the required days were reduced to fifty. The benefit is granted for a period of six months. In the case that 300 working days preceded the previous two years, the allowance is granted for another six months, it is possible to qualify for the subsidy for more than 360 days.

134. Cash sickness benefits are calculated on the basis of the insurance category, which depends on the average pay for the last thirty days worked in the preceding calendar year. The base rate is 50% of the reference pay of the insured category. This is increased by 10% for each dependent in your family, but the total amount cannot exceed 70% of the reference rate, or the reference rate for insured persons in Category 8. For those who are in receipt of hospital care, the benefit is reduced by two-thirds if they have no dependents. For the first fifteen days, the total ceiling for sickness benefits plus supplements for dependents (maximum four) is EUR 15.99 per day. After fifteen days, the total ceiling for benefits plus supplements for dependents (maximum four) is EUR 29.39 per day.

§4. Funeral Expenses for Employees

135. A lump sum grant equal is paid for the death of an insured person with hundred insurance days in the year before the year of death, or in his or her last fifteen months (not counting the final three months), or for the death of an old-age pensioner or a person receiving an invalidity pension or a death benefit. This compensation is not paid for the death of a dependent. The compensation is paid in principle to the widow/widower or the person who paid for the funeral. The supporting documents required for payment of this grant are:

- the deceased's health booklet;
- the death certificate;
- the insurance booklet;
- the pension (for a pensioner);
- the original funeral bills.

The funeral expenses for employees correspond to EUR 759.52.

§5. Special Schemes for Other Groups

136. The description of the sickness benefits and the funeral expenses from the specific social-insurance schemes would be inadequate because of the variety and the rapid evolution of the special legislation.

The amount of money, which is paid for funeral expenses, is different among the various social-insurance organizations. It rarely corresponds to the real expenses of the beneficiary. For example, for self-employed to EUR 1,200 and for retired self-employed to EUR 762, for farmers, it corresponds to EUR 800 and for civil servants to EUR 800.

Worth mentioning, however, is the monthly allowance for paralytic persons. It is offered by all the social-insurance organizations like a 'pension', but it is actually a special form of sickness benefit (Article 42§1 of Law 1140/81, amended by Law 2042/96). The insurance risk of tetraplegia or paraplegia can exist irrespectively of the working status of the person concerned. That was the case of a tetraplegic manager of a company (StE 2241/88, in EDKA 1988, page 563). A special committee is competent for the ascertainment on whether the affiliated or the members of his family suffer from tetraplegia or paraplegia.

In addition, Law 1897/1990 provides allowances to victims of terrorist actions and to their families; for instance, lump sums due to death or full disability of the employee, monthly allowance to those who are partly disabled due to terrorist action and remain still in the service.

Chapter 2. Industrial Accidents and Occupational Diseases

§1. Beneficiaries

137. In Article 25§1 section a' of Law 2084/92, it is regulated that a permanently invalid insured person can claim an invalidity pension, if he/she has at least 300 working days without having completed the 21st year of his/her age. This number of days has to be increased by an average of 120 extra working days for every additional year of age until the completion of 1,500 working days for a pension after the 31st year of age.

In other words, for an invalid pension before 30 years of age, one needs an insurance period from 300 to 1,380 working days or one to four years of insurance. After this age, one must have completed at least a period of 1,500 working days or five years of insurance.

The reasons of incapacity must be located for the exclusion of any responsible behaviour of the insured. In addition, of great importance is whether the invalidity was caused by a common sickness or from a labour accident. In the second case, the insurance protection is provided, even if no insurance period was preceded. If more than one reason takes place, the invalidity is considered to be caused by the most serious one.

Among the substantial characteristics of invalidity belongs also a probable duration of incapacity to work. For the relevant insurance risk covered by the IKA, this incapacity has to last more than one year, according to medical diagnosis (Article 27§4 of Law 1902/90).

138. For acquiring a right to an invalidity pension under any Greek legislation, it is further necessary that the risk has occurred while the person concerned was still insured or, in other words, the prerequisite of the 'existing insurance bond' should be fulfilled. According to the same provision, an invalidity pension can be granted, even if the invalidity has occurred before the beginning of insurance under the Greek legislation, provided that the invalidity after insurance is equal to half of the invalidity in each concrete case. The Greek jurisprudence has repeatedly (latest decision: Three-Member Administrative Court of Appeal of Athens 7723/95) ruled that the 'insurance bond' is not broken unless insurance is definitely interrupted or the person concerned has started another occupation and has applied for an invalidity pension.

139. The disabled can enjoy benefits, only when he is forced to interrupt or eliminate his/her occupation. This is justified because he/she sometimes prefers to stay at the productive procedure, with an intensiveness of his/her strength, until his/her final loss of working ability. That may occur by a change of the working conditions, even if his/her disability was not made worse from a medical point of view (Council of State 1442/89, in EDKA 1990, page 212, Council of State 2229/88, in EDKA 1988, page 629, Council of State 863/88, in IKA Review 1989, page 281, Council of State 3944/88, in EDKA 1989, page 216, Council of State 4230/88, in EDKA 1989, page 277).

The legal notion of incapacity (disability, invalidity) has not much to do with the time of the corporal or mental disorder, but with the interruption of work and the claiming of insurance benefits. It has also been judged by the courts (*see* the StE Decisions 1630/89, in EDKA 1990, page 150, 482/88, in IKA Review 1989, page 121, 2509/88, in EDKA 1988, page 632 and 3322, 3984, 4012/86, in Law Tribune 1989, page 191) that invalid is also the one who continues his work with the same earnings but at an occasional or temporary job.

§2. The Concept of Permanent Incapacity (Disability)

140. The corporal or mental disorder of a person in such a duration and degree, that his/her bread-winning job is totally or partially impossible is defined under the term 'permanent incapacity or disability'.

A social insured person is defined as 'seriously disabled', if he/she cannot earn from a job, which corresponds to his/her strength, abilities and education, more than one-fifth of the amount that a corporally and mentally healthy person earns in similar conditions (i.e., incapacity rate 80% and more). The insured is considered as 'disabled', if he/she cannot earn more than one-third of the above amount (i.e., incapacity rate from 66.6% to 80%. He/she is considered as 'partially disabled', if he/she cannot earn more than one-half of the same amount (i.e., incapacity rate from 50% to 66.6%).

Among the criteria that somebody is characterized as 'disabled' or 'partially disabled' important are the earnings from the insured person's previous (usual) professional occupation. On the contrary, for the recognition of a 'seriously disabled', the incapacity of earning money from work, in general, is taken into consideration. Moreover, a decision of the Administrative Court has been revoked, which did not accept – as it ought to have done – the adaptation possibilities of the disabled to a similar profession in the labour market (StE 2062/86).

§3. The Amount of Benefits

141. The disability pensions level corresponds to the above-mentioned incapacity rates scale: The whole pension of a seriously disabled equals to the amount he would receive if he would have completed the conditions of entitlement of an old-age pension, i.e., the 80% and more of an old-age pension. If this amount is less than the minimum pension level, it is accordingly increased. If the insured person is judged as a common invalid, he receives three-fourths of the full pension or three-fourths of the minimum pension level. Finally, a partial invalid receives one-half of the full pension or one-half of the minimum pension level.

There are also some exceptions from the previous calculation rules. Thus, the insured, who has completed 6,000 working days and is judged as disabled with a percentage of 66.6% and more (common disability), receives the whole amount of the benefit. Furthermore, if the disability is due to neuropsychiatric diseases, and if the insured is judged as invalid to a percentage of 66.6% and more (common disability), or to a percentage of 50% up to 66.6% (partial disability), he/she receives the whole pension in the first case and the three-fourths of the pension in the second case.

142. About the duration of the benefit, there are various court decisions. According to one judgment, it depends exclusively on the anticipated medical diagnosis. Then, the insurance organs cannot decide a duration, which is not covered by the medical opinions (StE 556/1990, in EDKA 1990, page 353). According to another estimation, the insurance organs and the administrative courts can specify the duration, when it is defined on subjective (social) criteria of livelihood and not only on medical evaluations. Therefore, a limitation of the disability pension by the administrative courts is possible (StE 1333/1990, in EDKA 1990, page 538).

Chapter 3. Institutions for the Provision of Benefits

143. There are not any special institutions for the provision of the social insurance benefits in the cases of temporary or permanent incapacity to work. Nevertheless, there has to be a distinction between the benefits of the first category, which are usually provided by the sickness insurance branches and the benefits of the second category, which are provided by the pensions insurance branches.

From a systematic point of view, it is necessary to know the roles of several insurance organs, from the examination of applications until the provision of benefits.

The Centres for Certifying Incapacity (KEPA), established by article 6 of Law 3863/2010, medically assess the percentage of impairment and its consequences in the exercise of an occupational activity (health disability) for all insured and uninsured persons. The pre-existing Health Committees (HCs) of the former pension funds and the State were abolished and only the Supreme Health Commissions of the Army, Navy, Air Force, Police and Fire Brigade were retained.

The KEPA is required to give a reasoned opinion on the nature, causes, duration and degree of the insured person's physical or mental condition and its effect on the exercise of his/her usual or similar occupation and on his/her ability to regain his/her capacity to work. Where the insured person suffers from mental or other illnesses, the KEPA must indicate the primary cause of the disability because special pension provisions apply to mental illnesses. The KEPA bases its judgments on the Uniform Table of Determination of the Degree of Disability, which predetermines the degree of disability by percentages, in accordance with the findings of medical science, for each condition or impairment or impairment. This Unified Table covers all insured and uninsured persons and has been issued on the basis of the authorization of Article 7 of Law 3863/2010. The decisions of the KEPA are subject to an appeal before the Secondary KEPA to be lodged within ten days of the notification of the 'Disability Certification Result Notice' either by the insured person or by the competent administrative body of the insurance institution that referred the insured person to the KEPA.

Successively, the Director of the E-EFKA and, at a second degree, the Local Administrative Committee define the incapacity to work according to the personal characteristics of the insured (age, education, professional skills and so on) in relation to objective factors (work market in the same area). The social criteria, however, which are used by the insurance organs, cannot increase the medically ascertained percentage of incapacity by more than 15%. An exception is made for self-employed persons because the insurance bodies are not allowed to make their own judgment on incapacity for work and the decisions of the KEPA are final and subject only to judicial review.

If from the comparison with the average earnings of the healthy people in similar conditions occurs that the insured is unable to earn more than half of the wage of a healthy person, he is considered partially invalid. An insurance organ's opinion has to be cancelled, if it is only based on the medical percentage of incapacity, instead of including its impact on the actual living conditions (Council of State 141/89, in EDKA 1989, page 402).

Dependent on invalidity levels (of 50%, 67% or 80%) and kind of chronic illness, recipients are entitled to different levels of care provision. The degree of incapacity is evaluated by the Centres for Certifying Incapacity (KEPA).

Disability is distinguished into partial, ordinary, severe and total, depending on the extent of the inability to work. In particular:

- Partial disability is defined as the inability of the insured person to earn from work corresponding to his/her strengths, skills and education more than one-half of the amount that a physically, mentally and mentally healthy person of the same education normally earns for similar work, due to a physical, mental or intellectual ailment or impairment that occurred after the insured person became insured and, according to a medical assessment, has a duration of at least one year (disability rate of 50%).
- In the case of ordinary disability, the insured person cannot earn from work corresponding to his/her strengths, skills and education more than one-third (disability rate 66.6%).
- In severe disability, the insured person cannot earn from work corresponding to his/her strengths, skills and education more than one-fifth of the amount that a physically, mentally and emotionally healthy person of the same education would normally earn for similar work (disability rate 80%).
- In the case of total disability, the insured person is in a state requiring constant supervision, care and support from another person, as in the case of tetraplegia, for example.

The amount of the disability pension is graduated according to the degree of disability (Article 27 of Law 1902/1990).

Beneficiaries of invalidity pension have to be periodically examined by the above-mentioned bodies of doctors, in order to retain their right to the pension.

144. The contribution of the jurisprudence to the definition of the invalidity criteria is very important. Especially, it has been judged that the medical committees' opinions have to answer all the relevant questions without any vagueness or doubt (StE 3799/89, in EDKA 1990, page 279); then, they are binding for the insurance organs and the administrative courts (StE 484/89, in EDKA 1989, page 486, StE 1711/87, in EED 1989, page 866); if a judge is persuaded that the medical opinion is inadequately justified, he can either cancel the administrative act, which is based on it (StE 2830/89, in EED 1990, page 922), or ask for further clarifications (StE 4781/1988, in DιDικ 1989, page 579).

145. According to Articles 7 and 27 of Law 4387/2016 the national invalidity pension is calculated according to the invalidity level as follows:

Invalidity Level	*Percentage of the National Invalidity Pension*
Less than 49.99%	40%
From 50% to 66.99%	50%
From 67% to 79.99%	75%
From 80% or more and retired according to N 612/1977 (blind, paraplegic, etc.)	Full amount (EUR 384)

The National Invalidity Pension for twenty years of insurance is EUR 384 per month and is reduced by 2% for each year less than twenty years, with a minimum of fifteen years. For example, an insured person with an invalidity rate of 55% and six years of insurance will receive a national invalidity pension amounting to EUR 172.9 (345.60 x 50%).

The amount of the contributory pension under Article 11 of the Act will be regulated by a newer legal regulation which has not yet been introduced.

Part VI. Industrial Accidents and Occupational Diseases

146. Disability due to a labour accident or occupational disease is dealt by the social security system by introducing more favourable conditions in relation to disability from an illness or accident out of work.

§1. Beneficiaries

147. Historical reasons in Greece justify the facing of labour accidents and occupational diseases as separate social-insurance risks, but not as different social-insurance branches (Article 8 case 4 and Article 34§1 of the Law 1846/51). A special concern for the victims from work injuries has been indicated before the recognition of the social insurance as a legal institution (*see* Law 551/15 for the employers' professional risk, and also Article 914 of the Civil Code for the indemnification of the damages).

The dependent workers and their family members can usually claim compensation for health damage or death due to a labour accident or an occupational disease. Furthermore, a right is recognized to the civil servants and their dependents for a favourable calculation of the pension in case of accident, disease or death during the public service. The tradesmen and craftsmen are also entitled to claim benefits from their sickness or pension insurance branches. This is, however, not self-evident with all the independent professionals, for example, the farmers, the lawyers.

148. According to Article 34§1 of Law 1846/51, for the various benefits from the sickness or pension insurance branches, the victim of a labour accident or occupational disease is not necessary to have completed any insurance period. It is not even important, if he was already registered to E-EFKA (Supreme Court 704/75, in EED 31, page 1102). One day of insurance is enough, if an accident takes place during that day.

In cases of accidents at work or occupational diseases, either sickness benefits or invalidity pensions are granted.

§2. The Concept of Labour Accident

149. The elements of the 'labour accident' derive from legislation (Articles 8 case 4 and 34§1 of the Special Law 1846/51) and jurisprudence. The concept of such an accident has been considered as the corporal or mental health damage, which is caused by an external, sudden and violent event during the exercise of work or because of the work, and which causes financial repercussions to the insured or his family. Thus, it also included the fatal accident of the family supporter, while he was implementing his professional duties.

150. There are three basic conditions that must be satisfied in order to establish the concept of the labour accident:

(1) Health damage from external reasons. Sometimes an insignificant damage can cause an incapacity to work by aggravating the already troubled health of the insured. An external event, however, must have taken place. Therefore, the sudden manifestation of an abnormal pathological condition, i.e., the haemoptysis of a tubercular during work, is not a labour accident.
(2) Sudden and violent pathological or anatomical alteration. Here, for instance, are included the infection of a doctor from a common dangerous medical care, as well as the incidents caused by special labour conditions, i.e., the heart attack after an exhaustive occupation (*see* StE 490/89, in EP.IKA 1989, page 1009, StE 249/1989, in EDKA 1990, page 14, StE 2006/88, in EDKA 1988, page 625, StE 1119/87, in EED 1988, page 1136, StE 3602/86, in NoB 1989, page 193).
(3) The causality between the violent event and the health damage (incapacity to work), but also between the accident and the specific profession. The essential element of the concept of an accident at work is the existence of a causal nexus between the real event which caused the damage and the occupation, for the determination of which the timing, the causes and the results of the damage must be taken into account. The concept of the causal nexus and the criteria required for its determination have been mostly elaborated by the jurisprudence (AP 600/1996, StE 3250/1996). Not only a damage (e.g., the breaking of a leg) but also a disease can be considered to be an accident, provided that a causal nexus as described above exists, as long as it develops after a violent event, namely a sudden effect of an exterior event irrelevant to the health condition of the victim and caused by unusual, exceptional and unpredictable working conditions. A disease that develops due to the nature of work and under normal working conditions cannot be considered to fall within the meaning of the concept of an accident at work.

151. In cases of accidents at work or occupational diseases, either sickness benefits or invalidity pensions are granted. These relations are often estimated according to the prevailing – well known from the Penal Law – theory of the commonly accepted suitable reason (causa adaequata). Nevertheless, for a more effective protection, the jurisprudence sometimes accepts every (direct or indirect) causal relation.

Normally, the concept of a labour accident is not established, when the victim is responsible for the health damage. Thus, the death of a soldier during military exercises at the moment he had put his helmet off is not considered an 'unexpected event' (State Audit Council II Department, 334/79, in State Audit's Council Bulletin 1981, page 94). However, even a suicide can be due to a psychological disorder because of the unfavourable working conditions; then, the necessary causality can be recognized (High Court 853/79, in EP.IKA 1980, page 75, High Court 301/77, in EDKA 1978, page 23).

Interpreting the prerequisite of the harm 'during the work or because of it', one searches for a specific temporal and local relevance between the violent event and the professional occupation. Therefore, undoubtedly a causal relation arises when the accident is directly related to the work, even an illegal overtime work (Administrative Court of Kalamata 21/88, in NoB, page 1510).

Health damage, which would not have happened objectively, is also considered an industrial accident, provided that the insured was not obliged to some movements relevant to his professional duties. Following this interpretation, all accidents on the way to work and the return to the residence are considered industrial accidents. Especially, the deviation of a building worker for a sea bath during which he was drowned was actually considered unjustifiable (Administrative Court of Hania 264/1989, in EDKA 1990, page 102). In addition, the events during the leisure time at the working location according to an employer's order, etc., were characterized as labour accidents (*see* the following court Decisions: StE 1651/86, in NoB 1989, page 193, StE 4697/83, in EDKA 1984, page 350, StE 4000/83, in EDKA 1984, page 292); moreover, the violent event during the exercise of the right to strike is also considered within the concept of a labour accident (StE 4149/1988, in EDKA 1990, page 273).

152. Sometimes, the legal consequences of labour accidents (favourable prerequisites and higher amount of benefits) are extended to events which do not have the above characteristics, for instance, the health damages taking place during the vocational programmes in all kinds of educational units (work sites, factories, etc.) run and sponsored by DYPA (*see* Law 4504/1966 and the Legislative Decree 1104/72), moreover, the total incapacity to work caused by a terrorist or criminal action against the insured due to his working position or to the nature of his duties (Article 1§1 of Presidential Decree 195/89).

§3. THE CONCEPT OF OCCUPATIONAL DISEASE

153. The concept of an occupational disease has been defined as the intense or chronic illness of the insured caused by the harmful effect of the profession, which decreases his capacity to work. This social-insurance risk affects the human organism in an imperceptible and steady way, contrary to the labour accident. In other words, an occupational disease develops gradually, and it is not easy for someone to foresee exactly when the insured person is going to be affected.

154. These different characteristics justify the usual classification of the common prerequisites of the professional diseases, as follows:

(1) Typical symptoms of certain diseases. Here health damages from various contamination are included, e.g., from lead, from microbial infections, e.g., by tetanus, or from environmental pollution, e.g., skin diseases, according to the ILO Convention 42/1934 'on indemnification of occupational diseases', which is ratified by Law 2080/52. If a certain type of illness is not specified in the list of occupational diseases, or if it is not timely announced, there is not a guaranteed social security protection (StE 4055/88, in EDKA 1989, p. 84).
(2) Dangerous enterprises, occupations and professions. The professional activities, which lead to occupational diseases, are usually enumerated in an exhaustive way. For instance, the virus of hepatitis is considered an occupational disease only if the affected person belongs to the following professional groups: doctors, nurses, lab assistants, stretcher-bearers, cleaners in medical laboratories and hospitals.
(3) Minimum time of employment. This prerequisite is necessary for establishing the assumption that the disease has been caused by specific professional activity. The IKA Sickness Regulation anticipates a minimum exposure to the danger for each disease separately, while in other social-insurance schemes, a general minimum period is provided for all the chronic diseases. Given the gradual development of this insurance risk, a period of time is also covered following the eventual interruption of the professional activities. Such periods are normally estimated through factors provided in special lists of occupational diseases. For those diseases for which no provision has been made about the minimum time of employment at a certain profession or about the maximum time of affection after the work interruption, the IKA Sickness Regulation entrusts the competent medical committees with the task of judgment according to the internationally established practices and perceptions of the so-called medicine at work. Where inventories for occupational diseases are in force, providing for their nature and duration, the insured are relieved from the obligation to prove causality between the disease and the specific professional activity. Otherwise, the search for a causal relation between the disease and the health damage (incapacity to work) has to be preceded.

155. A disease that develops due to the nature of work and under normal working conditions cannot be considered to fall within the meaning of the concept of an accident at work. For the determination of the concept of occupational diseases, certain lists of diseases recognized as such are valid as regards IKA.

§4. Benefits in Case of Work Disability

156. The *insurance risks* do not necessarily correspond to the *social insurance branches* (i.e., the established means of protection for facing such risks). This differentiation is mostly illustrated in the cases of labour accidents and occupational diseases, which are separate insurance risks covered from the sickness or pension insurance branches, according to their consequences. The rules of common sickness benefits (in cash or in kind) and the rules of pensions also govern the risks of labour accidents and occupational diseases.

Exceptionally, if the insured has not completed the necessary number of daily wages during the former calendar year, the estimation of the benefits is achieved on the salary basis of the day of the accident or, in the case of occupational disease, on the wage of the last working day (*see* Law 321/76). Also, in such cases, the cash benefits are paid from the first day of notification of the health damage. Namely, the three-day waiting period is not applicable, provided, of course, that incapacity to work lasts for more than three days.

157. Moreover, in the cases of labour accidents or occupational diseases, the law provides for an obligatory minimum amount of pension. As far as the invalidity pension is concerned, this amount cannot be less than fifteen times of the presumed daily wage, which is determined by the beneficiary's insurance class and augmented with eventual family allowances (according to Law 997/79). In addition, there are no maximum pension limits in the cases of industrial accidents or occupational diseases. The general maximum limit of twenty-five times of the presumed daily wage, which is provided in Article 29§11 of the Law 1846/51, is not applicable here (Supreme Court 8/77, in DEN 33, p. 1133). This possibility – of exceeding the pension levels – is apparently in force also for the later introduced maximum pension limits (*see* Laws 1405/83 and 1902/90).

§5. Benefits in Case of Death

158. A lump-sum grant equal to eight times the reference pay of the highest insurance category is paid in the event of the death of an insured person who has accumulated hundred insurance days in the year before the year of death or over the last fifteen months (with the final three months not taken into account), or in the event of death of an old-age pensioner or a person receiving an invalidity pension or a death benefit. This compensation is not paid for the death of a dependant. The compensation is paid in principle to the widow or the person who paid for the funeral.

§6. Direct Actions for the Protection from Labour Accidents and Occupational Diseases

159. The Greek social security systems do not include an independent branch of social security benefits with regard to the social risk of accidents at work and/or occupational diseases. If an accident at work or an occupational disease causes a temporary health damage, the person concerned can be entitled to sickness benefits, whereas in cases of lasting health damages, the person can be entitled to an invalidity pension. If the cause of invalidity is an accident at work, there is no precondition of fulfilling insurance periods for providing the invalidity pension.

160. The occurrence of a labour accident and the symptoms of an occupational disease have to be notified to the social-insurance organization with reference to specific events and to certain persons (*see* Article 21 of the IKA Sickness Insurance Regulation, as amended with the Ministerial Decision from 1986).

Normally, the employer, the insured or his family members, as well as the administrative or medical authorities are obliged to announce the health damage to the competent social-insurance organ. The announcement to a private clinic, collaborating with the E-EFKA, is also considered as necessary notification, if the main characteristics of labour accidents are included in the medical attendance documents (StE 5106/88, in DEN 1989, p. 1124, StE 3245/81, in DEN 38, p. 796, StE 2606/78, in DEN 35, p. 706). A simple mention of the health damage symptoms is not sufficient (Decision of StE 870/89, in EDKA 1990, p. 419, StE 3014/82, in EDKA 1983, p. 148). If an announcement does not include the necessary external elements of the above-mentioned formal notification of labour accidents, it cannot be completed later on (StE 4618/88, in DEN 1989, p. 1123; *see*, however, the more lenient Decisions of StE 4618/1988, in EP.IKA 1990, p. 111, and 870/1990, in EDKA 1990, p. 418). Therefore, the decision of a social-insurance organ, which does not report in full detail what was exactly notified to the doctors, is subjected to appeal.

161. The announcement of a labour accident has to be made within a specific time limit.

A deadline of five working days is provided for the employer and the insured person, whereas the doctors and the administrative staff members of IKA must declare the accident within twenty-four hours from the knowledge of the relevant events. However, the head officer of the competent IKA branch could accept a notification of a labour accident within sixty days at the most, if he is convinced that reasons beyond the will of the interested hindered the announcement in due time. This sixty-day deadline is extended up to one year for the granting of a total invalidity pension and up to two years, if the labour accident was fatal.

The period, in which the accident has to be announced, starts from the following day or from the day of the appearance of the health damage symptoms. The above-mentioned time limits can only be overruled in cases of *vis absoluta* (StE 1915/88, in DEN 1989, p. 1122). It has been judged that the Local Administrative Committee of IKA, re-examining the entitlement conditions, can accept a delayed notification, if the failure is due to reasons beyond the will and the intention of the interested person (StE 870/1990, in EDKA 1990, p. 418).

§7. Who Is Obliged to Pay Reimbursement?

162. Provided that all the social-insurance prerequisites are fulfilled, i.e., the legal affiliation of the victim to a specific social-insurance scheme, the conjunction of the necessary events, and their announcement in time, the social-insurance organization is basically responsible for the reimbursement of the health expenses.

163. If the refusal of the health restitution can be attributed to the intention of a specific organ, then this organ becomes jointly responsible. As a general rule, in cases of social-insurance schemes organized as entities of public law, the provisions for the State's responsibility are applicable (*see* Articles 105 and 106 of the Introductory Law to the Greek Civil Code).

The employer's responsibility appears as follows:

> If the insured person or – in death case – his family members are entitled to labour accident benefits by the IKA, the employer and his authorized managers are discharged of any responsibility (according to Art. 60§3 of Law 1846/51), including the reimbursement of hospitalization and funeral expenses. Such discharge is applicable, even if the labour accident or the occupational disease is due to the negligence of the employer and his representatives (AP 461/79, in DEN 36, 873). In such cases, however, the victim could claim indemnity for mental distress against his employer (AP 401/87, in DEN 44, p. 830, AP 1916/86, in DEN 44, p. 238, AP 1803/85, in DEN 43, p. 352, Athens Court of Appeal 6650/89, in EP.IKA 1989, p. 942). No claim, of course, is provided, when the victim is exclusively responsible for his health damage.
>
> According to a provision of Article 34§2 of Law 1846/51 if the accident or the occupational disease is due to the intention of the employer or of his employed persons, the victim or in death case his family members can claim from the employer the difference between the health expenses reimbursement based on the regulations of the Civil Code and the total amount of the social-insurance benefits (AP 461/79, in the DEN 36, p. 873, Athens Court of Appeal 6650/89, in EP.IKA 1989, p. 942). In addition, the IKA is justified to ask for the employer the amount of the provided insurance benefits (AP 126 7/76, in DEN 33, p. 310). Thus, only in case of employer's deceitful behaviour the victims can finally hope for a complete reimbursement of their damage.
>
> The insured does not have any claim against the person who caused the accident. Only the E-EFKA is entitled to start a lawsuit against him for the covering of the expenses from sickness, invalidity, or death of the insured due to a labour accident or occupational disease (Article 10§5 of Law 4104/61, as it was amended by Article 18 of Law 4476/65).
>
> The supporting documents required for payment of the death grant are:
>
> – the deceased's health booklet;
> – the death certificate;
> – the deceased's insurance booklet (if he or she was still working) or certificate of cessation of the pension (for a pensioner);
> – the original funeral bills.

§8. Procedures

164. The social-insurance organization's competence in case of labour accidents or occupational diseases depends not only on the interpretation of specific legal rules but also on the evaluation of the particular events. For example, the nature of the health damage may lead to a decision of medical or hospital care and not to the recognition of a partial invalidity pension, which was eventually asked by the victim.

165. The process of offering benefits can be described as follows:

> The insurance organs have to find out the elements of a violent event and its causal relation with the insured person's work (Art. 29 of the IKA Regulation of Insurance Competence). The medical organs are competent to analyze the nature and the duration of the health damage in relation with the violent event (StE 242/89, in EDKA 1989, p. 405, StE 37, 3602/86, in NoB 1989, p. 193).

The recognition of a 'labour accident' is based on the place, the time and the reasons for the violent event, in relation to the health damage, as these conditions arise from the victim's notification and from the competent insurance organs' investigation. Different elements from those which are composed in the initial announcement are accepted only if they are ascertained by another public authority.

The Director of the E-EFKA branch of the place of work is competent for the characterization of an event or symptom as a labour accident or occupational disease. He has the overview of gathering the relevant proof elements (StE 4695/86, in EDKA 1987, p. 214), but he is bound by the justified report of the health organs, as far as the causality between the real facts and the health damage is concerned (Articles 21–26 of the previously mentioned Regulation, StE 2006/88, in DEN 1989, p. 1124).

A Committee of the E-EFKA branch of the place of the labour accident can re-examine the Director's decision. If there is some doubt left, the case is led to a Second Degree Committee, which cannot worsen the position of the insured, especially without sufficient reasoning (Article 30 of the above Regulation, Administrative Court of Piraeus 617/1990, in EDKA 1990, p. 566). The necessary elements cannot be first completed in the administrative court, if they were not taken into consideration by the competent insurance organs (StE 4618/88, in DEN 45, p. 1123).

The medical organs' opinion (KEPA) has a binding effect also for the administrative courts, which have to refer back to the case for clarifications or complete reasoning before their definitive judgment (StE 1129/89, in EDKA 1989, p. 610), otherwise their decision will be revoked as unjustified (StE 1124/89, in EDKA 1989, p. 678).

166. The procedures for claiming compensation or health care vary among the several social-insurance schemes. Relatively, for instance, to the victims during the military service, other organs and other procedures are anticipated. The Supreme Army Medical Committee (ASYE) is appointed as a competent organ for the ascertainment of the health detriment conditions before the provision of a military pension (State Audit Council 808/1983, in D.EL.SYN. 1989, p. 368). Therefore, the opinion of the ASYE is obligatory not only for the State, as a social-insurance organization, but also for the State Audit Council, as an administrative court, for resolving relative disputes (State Audit Council 1135/1983, in D.EL.SYN. 1989, p. 361).

Part VII. Unemployment

Introduction: General Questions

167. Since 1954, there is in Greece an independent SSI, which replaced former special branches within the main social security schemes and took the name of Dimosia Ypiresia Apasxolisis (DYPA, ministerial Decree No. 212/69). It should also be noted that great parts of the Greek labour force are not covered by such insurance against unemployment, such as civil servants, who, according to the Greek legislation, are permanent and, in principle, do not risk losing their jobs, the self-employed and farmers.

The legal regulation of unemployment in Greece is condensed in several texts: ministerial Decree No. 2961/54, Law 3464/55, ministerial Decree No. 2698/53, Law 3198/55, Law 1545/85, Law 1836/89, etc., as well as the special Regulation of Unemployment Benefits, set by the Decision of the Minister of Labour No. 37274/56, as subsequently amended. The provisions of Articles 11, 15 and 16 of the ministerial Decree No. 2961/54 define unemployment as the situation where a person capable of working loses his insured dependent employment and cannot find employment corresponding to his qualifications.

Chapter 1. Labour Provision

§1. Labour Mediation

168. The covering of the unemployment insurance risk with temporary cash benefits is not effective enough. It must be completed by appropriate social services. These services correspond to the employment policy at a certain period and often help the return of the unemployed to the labour market (*see also* the ILO Treaty 168/88 for the promotion of the productive occupation and the protection against unemployment).

In Greece, the employment policy is mainly supervised by the Ministry of Labour, Social Insurance and Social Solidarity with the collaboration of other Ministries in matters of education, financial incentives of job demand, etc. The realization of this policy with particular interventions in the labour market is the task of the Public Employment Service (DYPA).

The social services which are offered by the DYPA seem to exceed the framework of the social-insurance institution. However, they are examined with the other social-insurance benefits in kind because they have many common characteristics.

169. It has to be mentioned here that the Social Insurance Law, and the Social Law in general, are not only consisted in 'regulatory' rules of specific rights and obligations. They are also composed by the so-called institutional regulations, which entrust the solving of social problems to social services without specific legal conditions. This second method reflects in the labour mediation for the job demanding and for the career consulting, provided by the competent DYPA organs.

With labour mediation services aimed at fighting against unemployment, which is due to an inappropriate coordination between the offer and the demand for work. This situation is basically caused by two reasons: (1) the unemployed person's ignorance of the existence of jobs corresponding to his abilities and knowledge and (2) his difficulty in moving for searching suitable jobs.

The services we are examining refer only to the first reason. The second reason has led to the establishment of cash benefits, which are also offered by the DYPA.

170. The labour mediation by a public institution aims at promoting a full occupation policy with objectivity and far from profiteering. Apart from the prohibition of private mediation offices (*see* Articles 14 and 20 of Law 5288/31 and Article 9 of Law 3248/55, which have ratified the ILO Treaty 95/49), the Greek legislator has established special labour mediation offices of DYPA (*see* Articles 2 and 3 of Legislative Decree 2656/53 and Article 7 of Legislative Decree 212/69). The competence of their organs was later amended by the Law 4504/66, the Legislative Decree 763/70 and other regulations.

Specifically, the public mediation in the labour market is indicated by the employers' obligation to search their personnel among unemployed people who have been registered in DYPA. However, the immediate announcement of a free hiring is enough to save the employers from every penalty, if they do not follow the anticipated labour mediation procedure.

From the specific regulations, a triangle of legal obligations emerges: (1) the individuals' obligation to declare their unemployment to the DYPA branches in the district of their residence, (2) the employers' obligation to search for registered unemployed or to announce in due time the free employments, and (3) the obligation of DYPA to propose for employment qualified persons following the priority of their registration. As far as the specific social-insurance legal relations are concerned, the most important is the last obligation. The first one derives from the need for a general promotion of employment, whereas the second one indicates a rather small confinement of a third individual's development of personality.

For the fulfilment of the previously mentioned obligations and for the estimation of possible infringements, the organs of DYPA have been delegated (by Article 7§6 of Law 3252/55) to control the manpower policies at the places of work.

§2. Cash Benefits

171. The regular unemployment benefits will be examined in the following chapter. At this point, some other allowances will be presented, which are also offered by the DYPA. They concern persons who still work in enterprises with financial problems, or who are already unemployed and searching for a job.

In conformity with the EC Directive 80/987, for the protection of the employed persons in case of an employer's insolvency, the DYPA was appointed by virtue of Law 1172/81, as the competent organization for the guarantee of the workers' salaries. Later, under Law 1836/89 (Article 16), a Special Account was established in DYPA with an employer's contribution of 0.15% on the monthly wages. This account aims at the payment of the delayed wages because of the employer's bankruptcy. The protection cannot refer to more than the wages of three working months during the last six months before the bankruptcy.

172. Similar is the extension of the unemployment insurance risk, even in the case of a temporary suspension of the labour relation during the exercise of the workers' right to the attachment. The DYPA is competent for the workers' financial support (Article 5 of Law 549/77), though they are not actually unemployed. Specifically, according to Article 20 of Law 1836/89, an 'unemployment' subsidy is provided (up to three months per year), when the labour relation is suspended during a work attachment for financial reasons.

173. The DYPA can also pay (between 1/10 and 31/12 every year) special lump-sum benefits to persons working in Greece at seasonal jobs, for instance, builders, who are not yet entitled to the regular unemployment benefits (*see* Article 22 of Law 1836/889 and the Decision of the Ministry of Labour 30659/89, published in the Epith. IKA 1989, p. 488). Besides, Article 23 of Law 1836/89 regulates a special financial help (up to forty-five daily unemployment benefits) from DYPA in stoppages of work due to *vis absoluta*. One should also mention the financial assistance from DYPA to the unemployed earthquake-stricken builders, which was based on the Decision of the Ministry of Labour 32707/88 (published in KNoB 1988, p. 1396), according to the Article 17§3 of the Legislative Decree 2961/54 and the Legislative Decree 212/60.

In addition, the Minister of Labour is authorized (by Article 7 of the Legislative Decree 2961/54) to approve that the DYPA covers expenses for the moving of the unemployed and his family to a new place of work. Not only the travelling costs but also expenses for the transport of household, and a lump-sum amount of money, can be paid by the DYPA.

Relative is the case of the financial aid from DYPA to enterprises of the frontier areas (Law 1262/82), at a 4%–6% on the whole cost of salaries payment (*see* Article 21 of Law 1767/88, as replaced by the Article 32 of Law 1836/89, and Decision of the Ministries of Labour and National Economy 31730/88, in DEN 1988, p. 1289), moreover the case of financial incentives for the facilitation of the manpower's mobility (Decision of the Ministries of Labour and National Economy 32664/88, in DEN 1989, p. 123).

174. Regarding the health care, it should be noted that lately, young workers under the age of 29 entering the labour market, who seek and cannot find employment, are also included in the personal scope of application of the provisions on sickness applying to IKA (Article 1 of Law 1545/85, decisions of the Minister for Labour No. 31548/85 and 30663/86 and Article 18 of Law 2639/98).

§3. Vocational Training

175. The restructuring of the productive procedures – one of the economic policy targets – is often combined with the industrialization of the production and the abolishment of working positions. For the protection against the social-insurance risk of structural or technological unemployment, a whole range of social services and benefits is provided. The social policy measures, which contribute to the covering of this risk, are basically distinguished in career advising and vocational training.

The social security and the social-insurance institutions are overlapped, as far as the career advising services are concerned. The free and equal provision of these services to every citizen places them in the first institution. Their characteristic, however, as entitlement conditions for the awarding of unemployment benefits, relates them to the second.

176. In conformity with the definition of the ILO Recommendation 87/46 'career advising' is the social aid to a person for the selection of an appropriate profession or for his professional promotion, so that his specific abilities correspond better to the needs of the labour market. In such general terms, the social right for career advising is also formulated in Article 9 of Law 1426/84, which ratified the Council of Europe's Social Charter. Moreover, with Law 1856/1989, the ILO multilateral agreement 142/75 'on the role of the career advising and of the education to the exploitation of the work force' is ratified. Thus, some basic career advising programmes have to be established in the future. It is not accidental that in the same year, the professional rights of the graduate career advisers are formally recognized (Article 1 Presidential. Decree 50/89).

Career advising in Greece is exercised by central and peripheral services of DYPA (*see* Article 1§3 case a' of Legislative Decree 212/69 and Articles 24, 38 and 39 of Royal Decree 405/71). These services consist of the adviser and his assistant, a psychologist, a special doctor, a social worker and administrative personnel. In addition, with the so-called active career advising (Article 15§1 of Law 1346/83), introductive lessons and practice exercises for candidates of the educational units of DYPA are offered.

According to Article 4 of Law 1837/89, the under-aged persons (15–18 years old), if they apply to DYPA for a job, they have to attend at first programmes of out-of-school career advising, as they are enforced by the Organization. The unemployment cash benefits seem justified only after the failure of these social services. Therefore, career advising becomes not only a citizen's right but also an obligation for the facing unemployment.

177. 'Vocational training' is the complex of educative measures which develop the professional abilities of a person, proportionately to the chances of employment, for his profit and for the benefit of the society (*see* the ILO Guideline 117/62). The right to professional education, as defined in Article 10§1–3 of Law 1426/84, which has ratified the Council of Europe's Social Charter, is enforced to the extent that relevant social services are ensured.

178. Despite the generality of this definition, we have to differentiate the vocational training from the rest of the educational policy, which is coordinated by the Ministry of National Education and Religions. Here, we are interested in the first one, which makes a part of the employment policy under the supervision of the Ministry of Labour, Social Insurance and Social Solidarity.

Every attempt for the anticipation or the fight against unemployment is usually based on vocational training programmes concerning: (1) those who are first entered into the workforce, and (2) those who are further educated for a new job.

179. Services of the first category are offered in the so-called apprenticeship units of DYPA (Articles 10 and 14 of Law 1346/83). It is a combination of benefits in kind and in cash. The benefits in kind are courses of theoretical education and the benefits in cash are subsidies to the enterprises which undertake the practical exercise of the unemployed (*see* the AYE 101850/88, in DEN 1989, p. 60). In addition, the participants of vocational training programmes are financially supported for their education in the apprenticeship units or for their practice in the private or public sector (*see* the AYE 40130/89, in DEN 1989, p. 1165).

180. Schools, for quick, professional education function in DYPA, aiming the young persons' readjustment in new professions. In that case as well, the possibility of studying for some months is combined with a financial aid to the apprentices (*see* Article 11 of Law 709/77 and the AYE 40188/88, in KNoB 1988, p. 1255). Quick professional education, besides, can be provided to the confined in rural prisons (*see* Article 38§1 of Law 1836/89).

181. Furthermore, it is possible that public organizations or even private enterprises are asked by DYPA to organize vocational training programmes with reimbursement of the students' financial support (Articles 8–12 of Law 1836/89). These programmes, which are to a large extent subsidized by the European Social Fund, are guaranteed and controlled by the DYPA (Article 25 of Law 1262/82). The basic conditions of such educational programmes, organized by private enterprises, are provided in the AYE 40099/90 and AYE 112851/91 (published in DEN 1990, p. 751 and DEN 1991, p. 809).

182. Greek society has always been characterized by a strong demand for general education and university studies. VET held little appeal for young people and was associated with 'laborious' and 'inferior' manual labour; on the contrary, general education is associated with expectations of improved social standing. Today, young people continue to see vocational education as a last resort, despite unceasing efforts by the authorities to present it as an alternative of equal value with general education. The statistics show that those with technical and vocational qualifications have less trouble finding jobs than those with general education. Most youngsters (about 75%) still opt for the general upper secondary school giving access to university studies. Vocational education remains the second choice for most parents and children. It attracts low performers, who, for the most part, come from lower economic brackets. This tends to reinforce negative stereotypes and creates a vicious circle at the expense of vocational education. Low participation in VET seems to be directly associated with its inability to attract young people.

A crucial issue for the attractiveness of vocational education, both generally and in relation to specific specialities, concerns occupational rights. While the construction sector, to take one example, grew considerably, related specialities in vocational upper secondary schools have seen low participation. This is because there are no established occupational rights for technicians with low or intermediate level qualifications, even though these trades demand enhanced knowledge and skills (such as ironworkers, builders, aluminium technicians, metal structure technicians, carpenters, cabinet makers). In several other occupations, rights have not been secured, such as bakers, confectioners, butchers, cooks and tourism workers; needs are met chiefly by workers trained on the job. By contrast, establishing occupational rights in sectors such as plumbing and hairdressing has led to strong demand for related educational services.

Since 2000, four laws – on the national system linking VET with employment (Law 3191/2003), systematizing lifelong learning (Law 3369/2005), developing lifelong learning (Law 3879/2010), and restructuring secondary education (Law 4186/2013) – and numerous amendments have been enacted in an attempt to regulate the domain of VET and lifelong learning. This legislative activity is mainly due to the EU's post-2000 emphasis on creating a competitive Europe that is capable of meeting the new challenges of the knowledge-based society. But the Greek State also recognizes the positive impact that developing lifelong learning would have on the country's economic life and on social cohesion.

International surveys show that close links between vocational education and the requirements of the job market and economy are an essential precondition for an efficient, high-quality system that would make it easier to move from school to active life.

The new law on the restructuring of secondary – including vocational – education (Law 4186/2013), which came into effect in September 2013, opens the VET system to the economy and the job market and attempts to regulate the field from the perspective of lifelong learning. Nevertheless, the major issues facing the Greek VET system persist: closer links with the job market and economy, more vigorous involvement of the social partners, a sense of social co-responsibility and consensus on vocational training matters, decentralization and greater school autonomy, attracting more young people into vocational training, improving the quality of initial vocational training and linking it more closely to continued vocational training.

§4. Temporary Employment for Youths

183. For the assistance of young persons, who enter for the first time in the labour market, special programmes are organized by the DYPA and partially subsidized by the European Social Fund. They usually appear in the form of Minister of Labour Decisions (*see* Articles 29 of Law 1262/82 and 8 of Law 1545/85).

Among the programmes, which helped young people to find a dependent work, we mention the following:

(a) Special two-year programme for the promotion of employment, subsidizing social insurance contributions and aiming at the recruitment of 25,000 unemployed people.
(b) Subsidy Programme for enterprises to recruit up to 35-year-old unemployed graduates of university and technological Higher Education Institutes.
(c) Work experience programme for new labour market entrants aged 16–24 years.
(d) Special Three-Year Programme of Aiding Employers through a subsidy equalling the social insurance contributions' amount, aiming at recruiting 2,300 unemployed people with disabilities, ex-addicts, ex-convicts, young delinquents or young people at social risk, and Subsidy Programme for fifty jobs involving the Ergonomic Arrangement of Workplaces for People with Disabilities.
(e) Programme for new entrepreneurs of the year 2009 – Cycle B.
(f) Programme for 6,000 New Entrepreneurs – Young Scientists of the year 2009.

§5. Job Creation Programmes

184. Apart from the programmes for young unemployed, which have just been indicated, and persons with special needs, which will be examined in the following part, it is worthwhile to describe some social-protection schemes for unemployed of every age with full working ability. They also concern programmes of DYPA, which are usually specified with Minister of Labour Decisions and partially subsidized by the European Social Fund.

Some of the job creation programmes aim at the social reintegration of problematic individuals. Among them is the employers' financial support to create new working positions for people released from prisons or submitted to other corrective measures (AYE 30422/92, in EP.IKA 1992, p. 408 and 30147/89, in DEN 1989, p. 395). Here, also, belongs the employer's support from DYPA to create new jobs for cured drug addicts (AYE 30641/91, in DEN 1991, p. 618 and 30381/90, in DEN 1990, p. 514).

Other programmes aim at the regional economic development or the facing of the educated persons' unemployment, who risk to enter the threshold of new poverty. Such an example refers the subsidy concerning the creation of new positions for graduate executives in manufacturing and industrial enterprises in the frontier areas (Article 44 of Law 1563/85 and AYEO A/5516/E.907/88, in KNoB. 1988, p. 529).

Some programmes do not directly favour the job creation, but they contribute to the avoidance or the limitation of the personnel decrease, especially in the seasonal professions. Therefore, there is a subsidy to the hotel enterprises for the maintenance of working positions (AYE 33470/91, in DEN 1992, p. 111, 31205/89, in EP.IKA 1989, p. 825 and 31309/89, in DEN 1990, p. 52). Also, the maintenance of the personnel is aimed with Article 31 of Law 1836/89, which regulates a subsidy from DYPA to the Organization for the Financial Reconstruction of Problematic Enterprises.

185. The job creation programmes are sometimes combined with environmental policy measures, also for the promotion of long-run social targets. The financial support from DYPA to municipalities and communities for carrying out public interest projects, for example, irrigation works, is referred to as this kind of programme (AYEO 30406/90, in DEN 1990, p. 516, AYEO 32733/88, EP.IKA 1989, p. 171).

It is often possible that temporary work, financially supported by the DYPA, becomes later a permanent employment for specific workers. For instance, the Law 1874/90 anticipated that people employed – till 31 December 1988 – by the local self-government organizations with a limited-term labour relation of private law for the cover of temporary, seasonal and urgent needs, or through DYPA programmes, etc., is appointed to permanent working positions, if steady and continuous needs are serving according to the competent council's judgment.

Some job creation programmes follow the new production and working methods of an enterprise, preventing unfavourable consequences for the manpower and the businessmen. Among these programmes is the financial support from DYPA to the employers creating new working positions (at least for six months) after the introduction of the continual daily working hours in the retail trade (AYE 30028/89, in DEN 1989, p. 334).

186. The financial help to the employers for job creation is significant not only in relation with their labour charges but also with their social-insurance charges. The employer who hires new staff, among the special unemployment benefit receivers, is entitled to a subsidy for the total of the employer's contributions in favour of the employed persons' social-insurance organization (Article 34 of Law 1892/90).

The indisputable assistance to the employers, in developing their activities through the DYPA programmes, is somehow binding in relation with the newly created positions. Apart from the employers' obligation to return the amounts of subsidy, if they do not establish real and permanent working positions, they must follow specific entitlement conditions, which are continuously enlarged by the court decisions. Thus, it has been judged that the subsidies in the framework of job creation programmes refer only to new full-time labour contracts (Administrative Court of Athens 12194/1989, in EDKA 1990, p. 368).

Law 4929/2022 seeks to shift the emphasis of the country's employment policy from passive policies (granting benefits and facilities) to active policies (upgrading skills, entering the labour market). To this end:

- address issues related to the internal functioning of the Labour Employment Agency (OAED), which is renamed Public Employment Service (DYPA),
- resolving issues related to the benefits granted to unemployed persons who are actively seeking work, and in particular issues related to the precise definition of the conditions for granting benefits, the concept of active job search, and the modernization of the approach of the PESA towards job seekers,
- address issues relating to the governance of the system for upgrading the skills of the workforce, diagnosing the skills needs of the labour market and providing continuing vocational training for the workforce,
- regulate issues relating to the real estate of the DYPA, its schools and its seconded employees.

Chapter 2. Unemployment Insurance

§1. Beneficiaries

187. The protection against the social-insurance risk of unemployment is introduced by Law 118/45, where an unemployment fund was established for the protection of the workers in industrial enterprises. The Legislative Decree 1255/49 expanded the social insurance covering all dependent workers and two years later, the fund was integrated into IKA, as a separate social-insurance branch (Article 5 of Law 1846/51). With Legislative Decree 2961/54, this branch was abolished and in its place appeared DYPA, as a general employment policy organization. This entity of public law (*see* Legislative Decree 212/69) functions with other unemployment insurance organizations or insurance branches for special professional groups, e.g., the Unemployment and Sickness Fund for the Seamen (*see* the Presidential Decree 272/82).

'Unemployment', as a social-insurance risk, is the condition of a person, capable and willing to work, who lost without responsibility his/her job and who cannot find a working position corresponding to his/her education and experience.

188. The Greek Manpower Employment Organization (OAED), which by Law 4929/2022 is renamed Public Employment Service (DYPA), is the main instrument for the implementation of Government Policy on Employment. DYPA is a Legal Entity of Public Law and is directly accountable to the Ministry of Labour, Social Insurance and Social Solidarity. The task of the Directorate of Employment of DYPA is to provide the unemployed population with information about training and employment opportunities available in the labour market, as well as take active measures in creating new jobs. The social-insurance scheme of DYPA does not cover every type of unemployment, but mainly the short time unemployment of dependent workers. Affiliated to this scheme are people who, irrespectively if they are Greek citizens or foreigners, offer mainly salaried dependent work and are insured against the sickness risk from IKA or another social-insurance organization (Article 11 of Legislative Decree 2961/54).

The prerequisite of offering salaried dependent work, as a main profession, reminds the affiliation conditions to IKA.

The connection with a sickness insurance branch is necessary because DYPA does not cover this risk for unemployed people.

Nevertheless, as regards the most employed persons, this condition distinction does not have a real practical meaning. The offer of salaried dependent work causes affiliation to the general social insurance of IKA and, consequently, the sickness insurance protection. Only the professional groups, which are covered by special social-insurance organizations without sickness insurance branches, may be deprived of the unemployment insurance of DYPA. They have, then, to search for a prior affiliation to a special sickness insurance fund of public or private law (e.g., to the existing mutual funds), irrespectively of the extent and the protection level offered.

Regardless of the nature of the employment relation, affiliated to the unemployment insurance of DYPA are by law: the contractors and the subcontractors of building and technical works, the home workers, etc.

189. Moreover, Law 1545/85 permits the registration in special records of young unemployed (between 20 and 29 years of age) and the allowance of a short time (up to five months) unemployment benefit from DYPA, even without a prior insurance period.

§2. Conditions for the Payment of Benefits

190. The social-insurance risk of unemployment is related to the following events (Article 3 of Law 1545/85).

I. Involuntary Loss of Work

191. The termination of a labour contract of indefinite time from the employer or the expiring date of such a contract of definite time is decisive elements for the covering of the unemployment risk. The connection with an unemployment insurance branch or organization becomes inefficient, if the worker has contributed to the loss of his work.

The insurance organization controls with discretionary power, if there is any worker's responsibility, without proceeding to a legal judgment on the validity of the break of contract. The loss of the job can be characterized as involuntary when an enterprise has been moved unexpectedly to a very long distance from the worker's residence. It has been judged by the courts, that the payment of unemployment benefits to a person neither presupposes nor intimates, the validity of his dismissal (Appeal Court of Thessaloniki 277/90, in DEN 1990, p. 842). If the notice of the work termination is nullified, the employer is obliged to deduct from the salaries owed the amount of the unemployment benefits, which had been paid to the dismissed person, and to return it to DYPA.

The cases of under occupation, with reduced working hours and salary, as well as the temporary suspensions of the labour contracts, are not assimilated with 'loss of work', except if there is a different legal provision.

II. Work Ability

192. Capable of working, in the special legislation of DYPA, is the person who is able to gain at least one-third of the earnings of a healthy person with equivalent qualifications in the same region (Articles 15§1, 2 and 4 of Legislative Decree 2961/54).

The legislator's aim was probably a coordination between the prerequisites of the unemployment insurance and the insurance risk of invalidity, as it has been regulated in the general insurance scheme for dependent workers. So, the accumulation of more insurance benefits was avoided. After Article 27§5 case g' of Law 1902/90, where an incapacity to work of (at least) 50% is demanded for someone's recognition of invalidity, the already mentioned legislative scope would be satisfied, if 'work ability' is analogously interpreted, for the right to unemployment benefits.

If someone with reduced working ability can finally exercise his usual job, he must be protected from the unemployment risk. Otherwise, he would be treated as a total invalid. On the contrary, it is regulated (in Articles 1§4 of Law 1648/86 and 18§2 of Law 1836/89) that real invalids, 15–65 years old, with a limited working ability by reason of a chronic corporal or mental disease, are excluded from the unemployment insurance, if they receive benefits of a pension character in the same or higher level than the minimum-invalidity pension of IKA.

III. Availability to Work

193. This condition exists, if someone is ready to work, as soon as an appropriate job is offered to him/her. That means a job with a reasonable salary and perspectives of future evolution, which corresponds to his/her professional abilities and knowledge, furthermore to his/her experience and education, without any health danger.

Though the DYPA covers only the dependent workers, the person who rejects a self-employment is also excluded from the unemployment protection (Article 16§1 of Legislative Decree 2961/54). Moreover, some financial advantages are provided for those who are available for certain jobs of public interest. For instance, the unemployment benefit amounts more for people searching for jobs for the promotion of cooperative or local initiatives (Article 21 of Law 1836/89).

The availability, besides, is presumed when someone is taking part in a programme of professional readaptation, instead of waiting when a proper job is going to be offered to him/her by the DYPA.

IV. Insurance Periods

194. Unemployment benefits are available to those who have been insured by DYPA and lost their job through termination or the expiration of their work contract. Within sixty days after the redundancy, an application for benefits should be submitted to the local DYPA office. Once registration is complete, the unemployment benefit begins. Payments could take as long as eight weeks to process.

Those applying for unemployment benefits for the first time must meet the following criteria:

- in the two years prior to the application, completed eighty working days in each year;
- worked at least 125 working days in the last fourteen months, excluding the last two months;
- a request to DYPA that has to be submitted within sixty days after the termination of the employment relationship.

Those applying for unemployment benefits for the second time must meet the following criteria:

- worked at least 125 working days in the last fourteen months, excluding the last two months;
- applicants in the tourism industry, as well as those seasonally employed, must have worked hundred working days in the twelve months prior to application.
- a request to DYPA that has to be submitted within sixty days after the termination of the employment relationship.

In order to apply for unemployment benefits in Greece, the following documents are required:

- Written proof of termination or expiration of the work contract.
- Proof of unemployment contributions for the prior two years (such as a letter from the previous employer or the e-EFKA).
- Verification of insurance for the sickness branch of EOPYY.
- A recent tax clearance note provided by a KEP or a photocopy of the latest income tax declaration.
- For information from the Greek government on how to obtain a tax clearance note, *see* http://www.ermis.gov.gr/portal/page/portal/ermis/FullStory?sid=599.
- To find a local KEP anywhere in Greece, *see* http://www.ermis.gov.gr/portal/page/portal/ermis/KepIndex.
- The applicant's legal identity card or passport (and a photocopy).
- A completed application form (available from the DYPA).
- Proof that a Greek bank account is held, and account information.

Unemployed formerly waged and salaried persons in one EU country are able to transfer their unemployment entitlement to another EU Member State. Transferred benefits are available for up to three months. The following requirements must be met:

- The applicant must register for work with their national unemployment service before departure and be available for at least four weeks after the end of employment.
- The applicant must obtain a completed form E303 from their country of origin (from which they will be leaving).
- The applicant must register with the national employment service of the EU destination within seven days of arrival and present the form E303.

Applicants should notify the unemployment service in their country of origin two to four weeks before departure so that all administrative procedures can be completed.

§3. Cases of Exclusion

195. Except for the unemployment protection of dependent workers, even today, the loss of work is not considered as a social-insurance risk for many professional groups.

The competent Service of the Ministry of Labour, Social Insurance and Social Solidarity regularly announces valuable elements for the number of unemployed in the economically active population. However, the unemployment percentages refer only to the registered and controlled by the DYPA persons. So, the usually indicated unemployment of 8%–10% has to be understood with the previously mentioned reservation.

Among the groups which are not typically covered for the unemployment risk are the civil servants because they are protected by another legal institution – permanency.

Thus, a precise control of the labour market and an integral evaluation of the employment policy measures seem impossible.

196. As regards the unemployment insurance of scientists (e.g., lawyers, engineers, physicians, doctors, pharmacists), who work for a certain employer, the DYPA initially refused any affiliation considering that they do not face unemployment after their ‘dependent’ work. In fact, they are always allowed to exercise their independent profession (County Court 2730/61, in D.IKA 1961, p. 638). The refusal was later overcome by contrary decisions of the DYPA administration. Finally, after Article 20 of Law 1483/84, which kept in force other exceptions of unemployment insurance, it is accepted that also scientists can fulfil the affiliation conditions and be covered against the risk of unemployment (*see* DYPA Circulars 173/86, 48/87, in DEN 43, p. 367).

197. They are not insured against unemployment because they do not offer dependent work, though they are exceptionally affiliated to IKA, the following professional groups.

The administrative board members of the professional associations, the self-employed, who are economically weak without a professional roof (insured in former IKA through insurance cooperatives, the lottery-ticket sellers, the street market sellers, the litterateurs, the artists, the managers, co-acting counsellors and administrators of the anonymous societies (SA), the newspaper sellers, the tobacco experts, the fur workers of Kastoria, etc., who are members of handicraft cooperatives, the cleaning ladies, who are paid by the State or legal entities of public law, the private agronomists of OGA, the chartered accountants, the directors, subdirectors and presidents of the legal persons of public law and of public utility organizations, the employed with a work contract, the priests.

198. Cases of exclusion from the unemployment insurance, according to the DYPA legislation (Article 3§2 a’-st’ of Law 1545/85) or other specific regulations, are also:

(a) The young workers until the 15th year of age, and the students-technicians of the DYPA Schools (Royal Decree of 6 June 1952), who are aged from 14 to 20 years and placed in enterprises for an apprenticeship.
(b) The employer's spouse, the parents and the children, if they offer work in family enterprises contributing to the capital of the company with a share of more than 50%.
(c) The pensioners from public organizations, except pensioners in former OGA, who receive a main or supplementary pension from a direct insurance relation, i.e., the old age, invalidity or resignation pensioners, but not the survivor's pensioners, who offer a salaried dependent work and therefore can be affiliated to the unemployment insurance.
(d) The ordinary civil servants of the State and other public organizations, even if they have selected the IKA insurance, but not the extraordinary civil servants who, after five years of public service, move from the pension insurance of IKA to the same insurance of the Public Fund (Article 1 of Legislative Decree 874/71).
(e) The workers without a steady employer, who are insured to IKA through insurance cooperatives, e.g., the stevedore workers, the skinners, moreover the guides who are collaborating with many tourist offices or persons.
(f) The domestic helpers, the pedagogues, the kindergarten teachers, the cooks, etc., if they are fed in the employer's house, even if they do not stay overnight.
(g) The insured against unemployment in another public fund, than DYPA, as the seamen, etc.
(h) The employed in agricultural, forest and cattle-raising jobs, apart from the ones who are insured as employees.
(i) The employees in organizations of public utility, such as the personnel of the Greek Telecommunications Organization (OTE), the Greek Railway Organization (OSE), the Greek Post-Offices, etc.

§4. Amount of the Benefit

199. The unemployment benefit consists of a basic amount and some augmentations.

As a calculation base, the 'presumed daily-wage' of the social-insurance class is considered, where the unemployed person was classified according to his last salary, or if there are any doubts, according to the average salary of the last six months. The unemployment benefit for workers amounts the 40% of the calculation base and for employees the 50% correspondingly (Article 21§3 of the Legislative Decree 2961/54).

An augmentation of 10% is added for every family member who is supported by the unemployed person (up to 70% of the benefit calculation base). Special financial aid for Christmas and Easter holidays is provided, and also lump-sum subsidies are offered from DYPA to unemployed people who do not receive social-insurance benefits anymore (Article 19§§1 and 2 of Law 1836/89).

The duration of the unemployment benefits increases in proportion with the insurance period, which was preceded.

In the initial legislation (Article 19§§1–4 of Legislative Decree 2961/54, as replaced by Article 5 of Law 3464/55), the unemployment benefit lasted two months, if the person could prove at least 125–149 working days, and up to five months, if longer employment was accomplished.

Later, it was regulated (Article 6§1 and 2 of Law 1545/85) that the unemployment benefit continues two months for an insurance period of at least 125 working days, three months for 150 days, and five months for 180 days.

A recent, more complex, legislation (Article 37 of Law 1892/90) provided that the unemployment benefit continues for one more month in all the cases of the above regulation, as it was already replaced (Article 2 of Law 1874/1990). Two more cases are added: an unemployment benefit of ten months for 220 working days and twelve months for 250 working days. The duration of the same benefit is extended up to twelve months for more than 49-year-old unemployed (*see* Article 6§4 of Law 1545/85, as replaced by Article 2 of Law 1874/1990) and for those who have totally realized 4,050 working days.

200. The monthly rate of the unemployment benefit was reduced to 22% to EUR 359.97.

§5. Seasonal Unemployment

201. Seasonal unemployment benefit can be claimed if the insured, in the last fourteen months has at least 125 working days, but not including the last two months. Or, the insured has at least two-hundred days in the last two years, not including the last two months. For example, someone who has worked May to October 2009 and May to October 2010, with a minimum of hundred days 'stamps' for each of those years, is entitled to unemployment benefit from November 2010 (usually between April and May – i.e., for five or six months, depending on the number of contributions paid). The insured must have at least one hundred working days in the last twelve months. In some cases, the seasonal unemployment subsidy is foreseen for a shorter number of days (100 instead of 125).

To make a claim go to the 'DYPA' (Public Employment Service) office within sixty days of termination of employment, with the following documents:

- Tax Return E1 for previous year and a photocopy of this.
- IKA statement of 'stamps' paid for the previous two years.
- IKA health book and any dependants' health book, plus photocopies of these.
- Passport and a photocopy of passport.
- Residence certificate (EU citizens) and a photocopy of the residence certificate.
- A letter from the employer stating when work has been finished – when the business has closed at the end of the season or when the person interested was laid off.
- A copy of the bank book for a NBG bank account (of which the person interested must be the main account holder).

Part VIII. Pensions

Introduction: General Questions

202. Most of the employed and self-employed persons insured under the Greek social security legislation against the risk of old age are affiliated with two insurance schemes: with a main pension (kiria asfalisi) and with a supplementary insurance scheme, which, as the main pension, is mandatory and financed according to the pay-as-you-go system (epikouriki asfalisi). Therefore, the main and the supplementary pension are parts of the First Pillar. The insured persons are granted the supplementary pension, provided that they have completed the qualifying insurance periods laid down in the legislation. Moreover, a prerequisite for the entitlement to the supplementary pension is the award of the main pension. In order to calculate the benefit, the supplementary pension fund ETEAEP that since 2020 merged to e-EFKA, aggregates the insurance periods completed under the legislation of supplementary funds that merged to it, according to the rules of successive insurance.

203. The nature of a pension can be converted, if more than one insurance risks occur to the same person. For instance, the low invalidity pensioner who reaches 62 years of age, or the old-age pensioner who starts suffering from a serious occupational disease, could claim for a higher level of old-age pension. A pensioner takes also additional advantages in such alterations. In the first case, he/she is released from the periodical medical examinations. In the second case, there is a possibility to start the payment of the pension earlier.

Chapter 1. Pensions for Employees

§1. Old-Age Pensions

I. Beneficiaries

204. In Greece, old age was not a real social problem, as long as the family had the care of its old members. During the last decades, great socio-economic changes forced the productive family members to neglect this 'duty' moving into industrial areas. Besides, the older part of the population, i.e., people more than 65 years old, has increased very much.

In the terminology of the social insurance, 'old age' is the condition of the natural deterioration of the corporal or mental abilities, which is presumed with the completion of an age limit or a long period of working activity.

205. Workers (men and women) with a contribution record of twelve-thousand working days (forty years) can retire on a full benefit on the condition that they are 62. There are concessions for people who work in arduous or unhygienic occupations and for insured persons with dependant or disabled children.

Workers (men and women) with a contribution record of 4,500 days (fifteen years) can retire on the condition that they are 67.

Therefore the maximum age limit for an old-age pension is 67 years of age without any discrimination between men and women.

Many transitional legal provisions allow insured people to retire under more favourable conditions. However, these provisions do not apply after 2022.

206. Early retirement is possible. This usually entails a penalty with the exemption of certain cases including, very long careers (40 years – age 62) and employment at arduous and unhealthy occupations, where a full old-age pension is paid under favourable prerequisites. Late retirement is possible and no compulsory retirement exists with the exception of employees in the public sector. It is also possible to combine income from work and pension withdrawal, provided that the pensioner is no younger than 55 years of age. In that case, the part of the pension income that exceeds EUR 1,007 is reduced by 70% but there is an increment of six wages for dependent children.

II. Conditions of Entitlement

207. The three basic prerequisites for an old-age pension are: (1) the completion of an age limit that is already presented in the previous paragraph; (2) termination of the professional occupation and (3) the realization of a certain insurance period. In some cases, however, the end of the professional occupation must also be proved.

III. Insurance Period for the Award of Pensions

208. The time prerequisites for the establishment of a right to social-security provisions are formed, as it is known, according to insurance principles in a bigger or smaller duration according to the principality of the risks and the extent of the retrospective provisions. For the old-age retirement, many years of insured work have to pass.

209. From a socio-political point of view, in every case, such a duration of insurance and payment of contributions is imposed (in other words insurance time), as the one which is necessary from analogistic estimations for the financing of the provision of the insured. There are, however, other criteria for the escalation of the time prerequisites. The retirement of the civil servants depends on the cause of the termination of the service, so that if they are discharged for general reasons, twenty-five years of authentic service is needed, if they are dismissed twenty-year period will suffice, whereas if they are dismissed for a corporal detriment, then five years will suffice.

Exceptionally, the tendency of less time prerequisites has prevailed, if it is a newly established insurance organization, for the expansion of the insurance in new areas or professional groups, for insured with seasonal work, etc.

By establishing time prerequisites for the insurance provisions, the Greek legislator sometimes believes that a simple passing of a specific insurance period suffices and sometimes imposes a certain duration of insurance periods in accordance with another time or another event.

210. It has to be mentioned that the notions 'pensionable service' or 'pensionable time' are notions of genus in which the notions of kind, such as real service, fictitious service, successive service, are included.

For the old-age insurance for employees who reach the anticipated age limit, there is no examination of when the necessary time has passed.

211. With specific reference to the assimilation of certain time periods to insurance periods, it should be noted that the periods during which sickness benefits in cash and unemployment benefits are granted is assimilated to periods of insurance (Article 40, paragraph 1 of Law 2084/92). Furthermore, the times of military service, of leave for raising children and of leave for purposes of training without wages for up to two years are also assimilated to periods of insurance, according to the same provision. In particular, for establishing a right to a pension, all periods of granting sickness benefits in cash and regular unemployment benefits are assimilated to periods of insurance of a maximum limit of two-hundred days within the last ten years before the submission of the request for pension (Article 40, paragraph 2 subparagraph 1 of Law 2084/92). For establishing a right to pension and for the calculation of the pension's amount, periods of leave for purposes of training is to be assimilated to insurance period, after submission of a relevant application by the person concerned, who has to make payments of contributions (the so-called buying-off of time periods); such contributions calculated on the basis of the percentage for the calculation contributions of the employer and the employee and of the income earned at the time of the submission of the application (Article 40, paragraph 2 subparagraph 2 of Law 2084/92). For establishing a right to a pension, periods of leave for raising children is also to be 'bought-off'; the amount of the contributions to be paid is calculated on the basis of the percentage for the calculation contributions of the employer and the employee and the twenty-five times of the minimum day's wage of an unskilled worker, as valid at the time of the application's submission (Article 40, paragraph 2 subparagraph 3 of Law 2084/92). Furthermore, the period of granting an invalidity pension is to be assimilated to insurance period for the establishment of a right to old-age pension (Article 40, paragraph 3 of Law 2084/92). Previous provisions on the assimilation of time periods to insurance periods have been abolished since 1994.

For the establishment of the right to an old-age pension from the IKA, important is the way the necessary insurance period has been covered and not when it has been covered.

212. According to the widespread approach in our country, employment is not sufficient for the realization of the social security bond and for the beginning of the insurance time. The employment has to be announced within a reasonable time to the insurance organization, unless it is an insurance status, which determines an ipso jure beginning of the insurance. Thus, our jurisprudence has formed the principle of activation of the insurance bond (Decision of StE 911/1990, published in EDKA 1990, p. 422, Decision of StE 2498/88, published in EDKA 1988, p. 698, Decision of StE 2434–9/1988, published in Legal Tribune 1989, p. 1117, Decision of StE 4598/86, published in Legal Tribune 1989, p. 186). The meaning of this principle is the activation of the personal insurance bond at the obligatory insurance with registration in the records of the insurance organization and with the settlement of the contributions before the appearance of the insurance risk. The typical affiliation prerequisites for the obligatory insurance end up to become part and not only proving elements of the insurance ability and as a result of the work of people, who neglected or were forced not to maintain the relative formalities, remains uninsured, despite the obligatory character of the social-insurance law (*jus cogens*).

213. In case of exercising more than one job which is affiliated with different organizations, if there is not a different legislative regulation, Articles 17 and 36 of Law 4387/2017 provide that the insured person pays contributions on the total amount of his earnings. However, he is not entitled to a second pension, although he pays contributions for his entire income. The insured person will eventually be entitled to an increase in the pension.

214. The typical insurance favours the person, the employee who thinks that he is affiliated with a specific insurance organization and he/she is in good faith and also fulfils his/her obligations, though the legal prerequisites are not actually in force. The insurance organization, which has borne, this situation without any doubt cannot refuse the passing of time and the offering of provisions.

The legal ground of the typical insurance has not been made clear. The juridical decisions are usually based on the analogous application of the principle for the retraction of the administrative acts, more rarely of the principles of fair administration, of good faith or of mutual trust. The theory of the formation of de facto insurance relations worth of protection is correct.

If the prerequisites of illegal affiliation in the insurance have been fulfilled, the passing of time, good faith, collaboration of the organization in the creation of the insurance bond and the existence of a legal gap, the legal consequence is the contribution of the retrospective time in the pensionable time.

215. For the estimation of the real insurance periods of the employees, the maintenance of the employment contracts and of the labour or service relations, in general, is important (*see* Decision of StE 176/77, published in EDKA 1977, p. 268, Decision of AP 879/72, published in EDKA 1972, p. 723).

This interpretation does not seem to be compromised with the character of obligatory insurance, which should not depend on private agreements and on other forms, but on the simple appearance of specific real events.

The preference of the criterion of ‘the real working condition or of the real working event’ is advisable, without being neither the only nor the most important instrument in favour of the interpreters, when the insurance periods are calculated. Sometimes, the employment stops, justifiably or not, though the legal working relation is maintained.

More correct solutions derive if one depends on the duration of the insurance relation of the employees on the continuation of their ‘salary’ (Decision of StE 2681/1989, published in EDKA 1990, p. 427).

However, the characteristic of the salary is not always enough, for the control of the insurance time. According to the Decision of StE 4207/88, published in EDKA 1989, p. 86, the paid contributions have to be analogous to the provision of insured work, i.e., in a real event which has to be fulfilled justifiably. Then, according to the correct opinion, the reference to the real occupation is additionally imposed.

Therefore, the real insurance periods of the employees are estimated without interruption, as long as there are no periods of stoppage of work with deprivation of salaries. For reasons of leniency, even small periods could have been added to the insurance periods where a demand for salary, for instance, a strike is not justified. There is a principle of insurance law that the insurance days which correspond with a reasonable time of omission of contributions’ payment (Decision of StE 2069/78, published in EDKA 1978, p. 468).

216. Reasons of general interest (national, social) impose to the legislator the expansion of the insurance periods in periods of profession or other activities, even unemployment, which would not justify the maintenance of an insurance relation. Then there is a matter of fictitious insurance.

The acknowledgement of the time usually depends on four prerequisites, three substantial ones and a typical one: The following have to be fulfilled by: (1) a specific time of fictitious insurance, (2) interruption of the social insurance relation from a legal reason, for example, military service, (3) payment of contributions of the acknowledged time, the total of the contributions on the salary and (4) submission of an application from the beneficiary, if there is a right and not an obligation of the insured.

217. When the beginning, the continuance or the extent of the social-insurance relation is based on the declaration of the interested person's will, then there is voluntary insurance.

In the legislation of several insurance organizations, there is an anticipation of special prerequisites, according to the form it appears. There are three forms: (1) at the voluntary insurance in *stricto sensu* there is a legal right to uninsured persons to be affiliated with their simple declaration in a common or in a specially formulated social-insurance status; (2) with the voluntary continuance of insurance, the need, for not being helpless those who lose the prerequisites for obligatory insurance, is fulfilled. The legislator, when the obligatory insurance is ceased from a specific time, permits the continuance from the interested person, with his own exclusive charge and (3) the legal form, which offers to the obligatorily insured the possibility of quality and quantity protection improvement with the payment of additional contributions, is called additional voluntary insurance.

218. Every change of professional occupation in countries with multiple social-insurance systems, as in Greece, raises a problem. The problem is the establishment of the insurance expectation, which was caused in the past.

Therefore, a peculiar institution was established, so that the insurance periods (in several insurance regimes) will not get lost, in cases where the change of profession is accompanied by an alteration of the competent insurance organization. The successive insurance allows the counting in of the periods of affiliation in previous insurance organizations, when a right for insurance provisions is going to be established or augmented.

Successive insurance within the e-EFKA (Article 19 of Law 4387/2016).

After 2017 and the distinction of the pension into a national and contributory pension is limited to the contributory pension. The national pension funded by the state budget is granted once, even when the insured person independently establishes two pension rights.

Within the e-EFKA, successive insurance is defined as insurance that has been carried out until 31.12.2016 at successive intervals and in different organizations that were subsequently integrated into the e-EFKA.

Successive insurance is not compulsory and is applied at the request of the insured person. The application at the time of retirement for the inclusion or exclusion of the period of successive insurance is binding on the insured person. For this reason, it shall not be allowed to be taken into account after retirement.

The competent authority for examining the pension application of persons who have been successively insured with several organizations or the State is the service of the OKA (Organisation of Social Insurance) that has been integrated into the e-EFKA or the State to which the insured person was affiliated at the time of submitting the pension application.

The total time spent in the insurance of the e-EFKA and of the organizations that have been integrated to it shall be taken into account, provided that he/she is not insured in the e-EFKA for an activity covered by the insurance of the corresponding former OKA whose time he/she does not wish to be counted.

In the case of parallel time that is not counted in the successive insurance, the provisions of Article 17 of Law 4387/2016 (for the increase of the pension) apply.

These provisions apply to all applications submitted after the entry into force of Law 4387/2016. Special arrangements for persons who have been insured with the State before 1 January 1983 continue to apply.

As regards the applicable legislation for the establishment of the pension right:

(a) The legislation of the last former organization integrated in the e-EFKA to which the insured person was insured before the risk materialized shall apply, provided that:
   - In the case of an old-age pension, he/she has completed 1,000 HA, of which 300 HA in the last five years before the cessation of insurance or the date of application for an old-age pension.
   - In the case of an invalidity or death pension, he has completed 600 HA at any time in the aforementioned OASI before the cessation of employment or the date of submission of the application for a pension for invalidity or death.
   - In the case of those who have established entitlement with at least 15 EA and at the age of 67, the competent service does not examine whether the above conditions are fulfilled, thus facilitating their retirement.

If the insured person has either not completed the above periods of insurance in the last OKA to which he/she was insured before the risk occurred or has not fulfilled the time requirements required by his/her legislation for the granting of a pension, then he/she is entitled to a pension from the OKA in which he/she completed the longest period of insurance (except the last one). In that case, the legislation of the awarding institution is applicable as regards the conditions for the award of the pension, except for the age limit and the rate of disability, for which the legislation of the latter institution is applicable if:

- they have reached the retirement age for old age pension or have the percentage of disability provided for by the social security scheme to which they were subject at the time of their last employment; or
- they satisfy the conditions for retirement laid down by the legislation of the social security institution of the activity in which they have completed the greatest number of years of insurance.

If these prerequisites are not fulfilled, competent is a former organization, to which the insured was affiliated when the most working days were realized.

IV. Calculation of the Pension

219. In order to understand the difference between the system that existed before and the new system introduced by Law 4387/2016, we briefly describe the previous system. The main pension until 2011 replaced the income and was calculated as a percentage of 2% per year of contributions on the average monthly income based on the earnings of the last decade before retirement. For the insured after 1993 with thirty-five years of insurance, this resulted in a replacement rate of 70% (35 years

X 2%) and for those insured before 1993, the replacement rate was even higher, which was 77%. The pensioner also received an extra amount from supplementary insurance. Most of the pensioners had a total replacement rate (from both main and supplementary pensions) of more than 90%. Furthermore, if the total amount of the pension was inferior to the minimum pension, defined by law, the pensioner was entitled to receive the difference between his pension and the minimum pension. In short, until 2010, pensions and minimum pensions were generous.

220. From 1 January 2017 and based on Law 4387/2016, the pension consists of two parts:

(1) *The basic part of the pension* is defined by the State and aims at combating poverty and social exclusion. It is financed by the State budget. Persons who have been permanently and legally residing in Greece for at least fifteen years, after the completion of the fifteenth year and before reaching the pensionable age, are entitled to the basic (flat rate) part of the national pension. The conditions are the same as those required for permission of permanent residence to be granted to third-country nationals (from outside the EU).

The basic pension amounts to a monthly sum of EUR 384 if contributions were paid during a twenty-year insurance period. This amount is reduced progressively by 2% for each missing year of residency, and amounts to EUR 346 for a fifteen-year insurance period, which is the minimum time required to receive benefits. Moreover, the national old-age pension is reduced by 1/200 for each missing month in cases where old-aged persons apply before their pensionable age. Thus, for example, a pensioner who has settled in Greece at his 40th birthday and is seeking a pension at the age of 67 will receive a basic pension of EUR 233.28 (with fifteen years of insurance, he will receive a basic pension of EUR 345.60 and this amount will be decreased by 13/40 because he is missing thirteen years of residence in the country out of the forty laid down by law).

(2) *The contributory part of the pension* aims at maintaining previous living standards and varies according to the incomes or salaries submitted to social insurance contributions; and to a percentage (replacement rate), which increases in accordance with the insurance periods during a person's working life. The contributory part is calculated as a percentage of pensionable earnings on the basis of the insurance period and the replacement rate for each year of insurance according to the scale indicated in Table 1.[1] The rates provided for in the original law have been modified by Law 4670/2020 in compliance with the jurisprudence of the Council of State, which ruled that they were too low for those with many years of insurance and did not result in adequate pensions.

1. For example, for 24 years of insurance the replacement rate is calculated at (0.77 x 15 years= 11.55%) + (0.84 x 3 years = 2.52%) + (0.96 x 3 years = 2.88%) + (1.03 x 3 years = 3.09%) and this sums to 20.04%.

Table 1 Years of Insurance Replacement Rate

From	*To*	
0	15	0.77%
15.01	18	0.84%
18.01	21	0.90%
21.01	24	0.96%
24.01	27	1.03%
27.01	30	1.21%
30.01	33	1.98%
33.01	36	2.50%
36.01	39	2.55%
39.01	42 and more	0.50%

221. Generally, all future pensioners will see a reduction of up to 30% of their main pension in comparison to the pension they would receive according to the previous system. This considerable cut is due, first, to the new method of calculation (the calculation base will extend to the entire working life and not to the last ten years for employees or the last salary for public servants) and, second, to the new reduced replacement rate (40.7% for forty insurance years).

222. In calculating the pensions of civil servants and employees, the average monthly earnings of the insured person for which pension contributions were paid during his working life is taken into account. The yearly incomes are adjusted by the annual salary change, as calculated by the ELSTAT. For the calculation of the pensions of self-employed and liberal professionals, the income, which is subject to contributions during their working life, is taken into account. The yearly incomes are also adjusted by the annual salary change, as calculated by ELSTAT.

223. Insurance periods for which higher contributions have been paid than that of the Common Scheme, for example, due to Heavy and Unhealthy Work, are calculated at an annual replacement rate of 0.075% for each percentage point of the extra contribution. This provision applies for pensioners after 13 May 2016.

224. Transitional Articles 8(3) and 28(3), as amended by Law 4488/2017, stipulate that the calculation of the contributory part of the pension applications submitted after the entry into force of Law 4387/2016 shall take into account the average monthly salary – income derived from the year 2002 until the submission of the application. From 2017 this reference period increased annually by one year. This arrangement demonstrates the difficulty of finding retirement benefits in the absence of computerized data for the whole insurance period.

225. The final pension amount is increased by several supplements, e.g., percentages for disabled children, or doubling of the pension for blind or dependent recipients. There are also pension increases for family members (following a marriage or a cohabitation agreement) and eventual family and child welfare allowances.

The final pension amount has been decreased, as of 1 January 2016, by 6%. Namely, all retired persons have to pay a contribution for medical treatment provided by the EOPYY. For persons eligible for retirement but who decide to continue working, pensions are paid at a rate of 60%, as long as the 'retirees' maintain their work or professional activity. If this work or activity belongs to the so-called public sector, the pension is totally suspended. Two months after submission of the pension application, formerly employed or self-employed persons receive, as an advanced pension payment, approximately 50% of their definitive pension amount. This advance payment is calculated on the basis of the average salary or income of the twelve months prior to the application and cannot be less than 80% of the basic pension.

226. The introduction of new entitlement conditions for all insured and retired people presumes a pension recalculation under the latest rules, with a provisional maintenance of acquired rights. As of 1 January 2017, the new legislation introduces an automatic mechanism for the adaptation of benefits. The Minister of Labour and the Minister of Finances decide on the percentage of the pension adjustment within a percentage frame set by two indicators: the GDP and the Consumer Price Index. Every three years, the National Actuarial Authority issues compulsory actuarial studies, which have to be ratified by the Economic Policy Committee of the European Commission. These studies, among others, estimate the volume of the main pension (basic plus contributory parts) and supplementary pensions, which should not exceed an increase of 2.5% of GDP by the year 2016 (with 2009 as a reference year). This way, the sustainability of the social security system will be regularly controlled and maintained.

There is great concern as to how to finance pensions, in order to avoid further pension cuts. The legislator focuses, along with the resources for the social-insurance system, on revenues collected from the assets management, on the amounts received from penalties in case of violations in paying contributions, etc.

227. Supplementary pension and lump-sum benefits are administered by the two corresponding insurance branches of ETEAEP that, since 2020, merged to e-EFKA. Both insurance branches resulted from the merging of several pre-existing funds for supplementary social insurance and lump-sum benefits. ETEAEP follows the pay-as-you-go system with defined contributions and individual notional accounts.

§2. SURVIVORS' PENSIONS

228. The survivors' pension aims to protect the members of the family of the insured or the pensioner, who has died. Initially, it has to be defined that it is a provision, which is established in an autonomous legal relation from the Social Insurance Law and is provided separately from the rest of the heritage property. Therefore, the prerequisites of the insurance provision are peculiar and limited to: (1) the death of the family protector, (2) the specific insurance bond and (3) the existence of protected persons.

Death is an objective event without any need for a special legal definition. The reason for death is not important; it is possible that it has also been due to a suicide of the family protector. Only in case that the death has been caused because of a protected member of the family, he/she is excluded from the protection (*see* Article 28§13 of Law 1846/51), without any consequences to the rest of the family members. The insurance risk of death is classed with other cases of loss, even of temporal loss of the family protector. The same insurance risk is considered to be in force when somebody is declared missing (Article 40 of Civil Code).

229. The time insurance prerequisites for survivor's pension after Law 1902/90 (Article 27§6) were partly adjusted to the prerequisites for the provision of invalidity pension (Circular IKA 85/90, published in the Syndicalistic Review 9–10/ 1990, p. 91). Thus, for the distribution of survivors' pension to the assignee family members, it is necessary that the insured had completed the number of working days which are defined by Article 27§4 case a' in Law 1902/90 for the retirement because of invalidity (300 working days until the 21st year with escalation 4,200 working days until the 54th year), as previously mentioned by examining the assignee beneficiaries in case of continuous incapability for work, or 1,500 working days and at least 300 during the last five years before the year of the death.

230. The circle of the protected persons is formulated by the legislator with the criterion of the real needs which is caused by the loss of the family protector. Beneficiaries are especially: (1) the widow or the widower. The legislator assimilates the party of a cohabitation agreement with the widow or widower; (2) the children until their 18th year and if they study until their 24th year, unless they are incapable of working before the completion of the age limits, at which case the pension is paid until every kind of invalidity is removed, the orphans from father and mother, the grandchildren and the stepchildren if they were supported by the dead man or woman; (3) the parents, if their support was covered by the dead man or woman. From the enforcement of Law 1902/90 (17 October 1990), the retirement of the divorced daughter of the insured or the pensioner was abolished.

(a) According to Article 12 of Law 4387/2016, the pension amount which the widow or the widower is entitled to is equal to the 50% of the pension that the insured was receiving.

    However, if the marriage or cohabitation agreement has taken place after the award of the deceased's old-age pension and if the difference in age between the deceased and his or her spouse is less by ten years than the duration of their marriage or cohabitation, the survivor's pension, for each full year of difference, is reduced to:

- 1% for the years from the 10th to the 20th year.
- 2% for the years from the 21st to the 25th year.
- 3% for the years from the 26th to the 30th year.
- 4% for the years from the 31st to the 35th year.
- 5% for years from 36th and above.

If the surviving spouse is disabled at a rate of 67% or more and if the invalidity occurs at the time of the death of the insured, then he/she receives the entire amount of the pension (i.e., 50%).

(b) For children, the remaining 50% of the pension is equally distributed. If the child is an orphan child by both parents, this percentage is doubled unless the orphan child is entitled to a pension from both parents.

(c) For divorced, if the marriage lasted ten years until termination by an irrevocable court decision, the amount of the pension to which the widow or the widower is entitled is shared by 75% for the widow or widower and 25% for the divorced. For each marriage year beyond the 10th and up to the 35th year of the marriage, the widow's pension is reduced by 1% and the pension of the divorced is increased by 1%. If a marriage lasted more than thirty-five years, the widow's pension is shared equally between the widow/widower and the divorced. If the deceased does not leave a widower, the divorced person is entitled to the same percentage as the widow. In the case of more than one divorced beneficiary, the amount of the divorced is divided equally among them. These provisions apply also in the case of the cohabitation agreement.

§3. Disability Pension

231. The right for disability pension is established in cases of continuous disability, which derives from the insurance risks of invalidity, labour accident or occupational disease. On the contrary, the incapability from a common disease is covered with insurance allowances in kind or with benefits in cash of limited duration (allowances) which we have already mentioned. The basic prerequisites for invalidity pension (*see* Article 25 of L. 2084/92), in brief, are: (1) the invalidity risk, (2) the specific recent insurance bond and (3) their capability for work, and also with the amount of disability pension we have already dealt with in the chapter for the subjects of continual incapability for work.

Chapter 2. Pensions of the Civil Servants

232. The social security scheme for civil servants is one of the oldest in Greece. It was established in 1852 (for military officials) and 1861 for civil servants in general and was covering the risk of old age. Those falling under the scope of the scheme are the regular (e.g., permanent) public servants of ministries, the Parliament, the prefectures, municipalities and communities, the State hospitals, universities and technical universities, all teachers, the judiciary, the military personnel, priests, invalids of war and of national assistance, those who have been awarded the so-called honour-pensions, and the members of their families. The basic legislature regulating the social security scheme of civil servants is the Code of Civil and Military Pensions (Presidential Decree No. 169/2007). Accordingly, the Supreme Administration of Greek Civil Servants Trade Unions or (as abbreviated in Greek) 'ADEDY' covers, as a union, all civil servants occupied by the State and legal entities of public law and, in particular, civil servants occupied in the fields of central government (ministries), municipalities and communities, education and health.

233. Civil servants who receive their salary from the State and, in particular, the State budget are entitled to a lifelong pension granted by the State. One of the most important general reforms of the Greek social-insurance system, including the pension scheme for civil servants, was achieved by means of Law 2084/92. Law 2084/92 (Article 18 paragraph 1) divided civil servants into two categories: (1) the so-called formerly insured, namely civil servants who were recruited by the State for the first time until 31 December 1992 and (2) the so-called newly insured, namely civil servants who are recruited for the first time by the State after 1 January 1993.

A similar distinction was made by the same law for all insured persons, depending on their being subject to a social-insurance scheme. And the aim of this division, for all insured as well as for civil servants, was the harmonization of insurance modalities (calculation of contributions, the preconditions for acquiring a right to pension and the method for the pensions' calculation) for both categories. In this respect, the provisions governing the insurance of the 'newly insured persons' were less favourable than those applicable to the 'formerly insured persons'. In particular, the preconditions for the retirement of newly insured men and women were harmonized and the percentage of the pensionable income, expressing the amount of pension, was limited. Moreover, Law 2084/92 was also important for civil servants because it introduced the notion of 'contributions' into their pension scheme – until 1992, no contributions were abstracted from civil servants' salaries as a means to finance their pensions. Rather, their pensions were entirely financed by the State budget or, in other words, paid by the employer who is the State. From 1992 onwards, contributions were deducted from civil servants' salaries and were also paid by the State-employer, in order to finance their pensions. On this basis, we shall be referring to 'formerly' and 'newly' insured civil servants from now on. Let me clarify that my intervention shall be confined to the basic principles governing their pension insurance and shall not refer either to the regulations regarding the military personnel not to specific regulations regarding specific groups of insured persons (i.e., university professors).

234. When civil servants retire from service, they are entitled to the following benefits:

(a) 'main' pension;
(b) 'supplementary' pension.
(c) a lump-sum benefit.

235. According to Laws 3863/2010 and 4387/2016, civil servants are insured with E-EFKA for the main pension and to ETEAEP for supplementary pension and lump-sum benefits, in 2020, ETEAEP has merged with E-EFKA. However, their regime remains different from that of employees as the Code for Civil Servants and Military Personnel's Pensions is applied and the competent court is the State Audit Council.

236. The pensionable income of civil servants and employees is the average monthly earnings of the insured person for which pension contributions were paid during their working life, increased by the annual salary change calculated by ELSTAT.

237. Pensions are granted as survivors' pension to the family members of the insured (mostly spouse and children) after their death. Finally, as a basic rule, it should be mentioned that only one main pension may be granted by the State to a civil servant.

Chapter 3. Income Inadequacy and Concurrence of Pension with Income from Work and Other Benefits

238. There are no regulations, which impose income inadequacy, for the establishment of a right to pension or the calculation of the amount of pension that is received by the self-employed workers.

On the contrary, the stoppage of the insured profession (e.g., the bankruptcy or the legal transfer of the insured enterprise) is necessary for the applicant for pension provision. The transfer of the commercial business to persons who are consisted of the economical unification of the pensioner's family can lead to the suspension of the retirement allowance from the E-EFKA.

Some professions seem incompatible among them. That is the explanation of the anti-accumulative regulation, which prohibits the affiliation in OGA and subsequently the retirement as farmers of the persons, who are directly insured for main social insurance as civil servants (*see* Article 34 of Law 1140/81 and Circular of OGA 6/81, published in EGA 1982, I, p. 84). Subsequently, the existence of a pension both from the Public and from OGA is not possible. The Lawyers' Code, which defines the exercise of the trade as incompatible with the function of a lawyer (*see* Article 63§1 of Law 3026/54), then results in the inability of a lawyer to receive both pensions from the Tradesmen Insurance Fund and from the Lawyers' Fund.

Chapter 4. Optional Supplementary Pension

239. Self-employed professionals usually resort to private insurance in order to supplement their social-insurance pension. Nevertheless, after the introduction of Law 3029/2002, they are also entitled to establish occupational pension funds.

When the insurance sector is anticipated for the completion of the main pension with a supplementary pension, that is not a provision with an optional character; see the supplementary insurance sector for the supplementary pension of the lawyers from the Lawyers' Fund. We have also already mentioned that in Greece, the institution of supplementary insurance belongs generally to the public law sector.

240. The institution of the voluntary insurance is also anticipated for the self-employed professionals. It is yet useful either for the voluntary continuance of the insurance of persons who have stopped the profession, such as, for instance, the bankrupted tradesmen after five years of real insurance or either for the affiliation in the insurance of persons, who have not such right, as, for instance, the craftsmen who exercise their profession in villages less than 2,000 inhabitants, where the insurance for craftsmen has not been expanded.

With the application of the regulations of voluntary insurance, we are not actually directed to the taking of a voluntary complementary pension, but we are facilitated to the completion of the retirement prerequisites or the augmentation prerequisites of the main pension from the social insurance. For example, an obligatory insured in the Craftsmen Insurance Fund can claim for his optional classification in an insurance group bigger than the one, which is justified from his annual income and thus, he can establish a future right for the 'completion' of his pension 'at a voluntary base'.

Chapter 5. Procedures for the Granting of Pensions

241. For the beginning of the legal administrative procedure, a former application of the beneficiary is necessary with a declaration of his will for the realization of the benefit. It is steadily accepted that the application has to be submitted in writing. However, the pension application is acceptable even if all the necessary justifying documents, which have to be submitted in a reasonable time, are not attached.

As far as the content is concerned, the application has to be explicit, i.e., the necessary real events have to be declared (legal affiliation in the insurance, insurance risk, time prerequisites) and to conclude to the sufficiently defined claim, for example, survivor's pension from a labour accident, without any reservations.

From the submission of the application, the anticipated (for the specific insurance organization) administrative procedure starts for the ascertainment of the retirement prerequisites and the competent organ is obliged to the issue (approving or refusing) pension decision. This is declared in writing and it should correspond to the regulations and to the types of the administrative acts, as they have been formed from the jurisprudence of our administrative courts.

Part IX. Disabled Persons

Chapter 1. Health Care

242. It has been observed that in Greece, the social-insurance regimes do not usually consist of especially organized units for the health care of the disabled. The special insurance branches for facing disability risk are limited to the pension provision.

Yet, the cases of health rehabilitation of the disabled are faced, as it is possible, from the medical care services of the health insurance branches. Within the medical care services from the social insurance, the ensuring of the necessary spa-therapy (in private or contracted spa-therapy centres) for the rehabilitation of the ability to work of the disabled pensioners is, for instance, included, as well as the necessary special therapeutic means and limbs (artificial bulbs, artificial limbs, etc.).

The social-insurance organizations, instead of organizing proper health care units for the rehabilitation of the disabled, are confined either in benefits in cash of limited duration, as the readjustment allowance from IKA up to two years (*see* Article 28§2 case b' of Law 1846/51), which was abolished, because its purpose had not been fulfilled, or in the best case in expenses reimbursement for the health care of the disabled from a third person.

In the second case belong, indicatively, the incorporation in the notion of medical and hospital care from the IKA (1) the health care of the insured in asylums of incurable diseases (Article 31 of Law 1846/51), (2) the health care of corporal or mentally disabled or maladjusted children insured in special institutions (Article 6 of Law 861/79 and 22 of Law 997/79), (3) the health care and therapy, as the tetraplegia and the paraplegia (Article 42 of Law 1140/81), (4) the transplantation of kidney (Articles 6 and 9 of Law 1383/83), though special regulations are anticipated for the sanatorium care or the medical treatment of the tubercular at home.

In 1999, however, a detailed law concerning the evolution and the modernization of the services of mental health was voted (Law 2716/99). It includes provisions about the organization of the mental clinics and the units of mental health. Furthermore, by virtue of this law, a special committee is established in the Ministry of Labour, Social Insurance and Social Solidarity, having as an aim to control the protection of the rights of persons with mental problems.

243. Moreover, there are special programmes for the health care of the disabled within the framework of the social welfare institution. Such is the rehabilitation programmes (diagnosis and partial facing of invalidity) of the people with special needs, i.e., the persons who are in a condition of chronic detriment or deterioration of their corporal, psychological, mental functions or the systems of the organisms resulting to the decrease or loss of their ability for their self-reliant performance in the society.

The social assistance aid from the Medical-pedagogical Stations and Services belongs here (*see* Article 7 of Law 1143/81), where mainly diagnostic and social work services are offered. Within the same group, the social assistance aid from the Centres for Children Care of PIKPA belongs also (*see* Article 1 of Presidential Decree 332/87, Article 1 of Presidential Decree 469/85), where ergotherapy, physiotherapy, temporal medical care and closed protection are offered to persons with emotional problems or mental retardation, if they already face serious family and social problems.

Chapter 2. Education

244. In the social-insurance sector, the employment policy in general, educational programmes are organized by DYPA, in collaboration also with other educational organizations.

There are special rehabilitation programmes for people with less abilities (*see* Law 963/79), professional education in certain specialization, for example, building trades (*see* Article 14 of Law 1414/84) and so on. Lately, the legislator has started to become sensitized to such matters. Interesting are, for example, the regulations of Law 963/79, for the special programmes of educational rehabilitation of persons with decreased abilities and the regulations of Law 1836/89, for the education and employment (professional rehabilitation) of persons with special needs. The payment of educational allowance is also anticipated (Article 2§1 of Law 709/77) to the ones who follow such educational procedures.

245. In the social assistance sector for the education (elevation of the abilities and skilfulness of the disabled) belong to the broader programmes of special and professional education (Article 32§4 following Law 1566/85, Article 1 following Presidential Decree 603/82), and also other special programmes, as the ones referred to the blind education (Article 2 of Presidential Decree 265/79, Article 1 of Presidential Decree 448/82, Articles 1, 2, 12§4 of Royal Decree 158/15.2/9 March 1973).

From the expression of the relevant texts, it does not derive clearly, whether the social administration is bound to ensure general or specialized educational services. Only indirectly from the aim of these programmes derives which are these services alternatively, for instance, the possibility of attending special courses in regular schools and how obligatory is their organization finally. Therefore, the acknowledgement of a right to social assistance for some educational activities could be accepted with enough reservations, unless they are necessary services, for instance, the learning of an international acknowledged writing system for the blind.

Chapter 3. Provision of Work

246. After the ratification of the European Social Charter of the Council of Europe by Law 1426/84, the international obligation of Greece was made official to take the proper measures for the rehabilitation of the disabled in the society. It is also a fact that as anticipated in Article 15§2, the relevant measures for the encouragement of the employers to employ the disabled have been more realized (*see also* Articles 6 of Law 963/79 and 9 of Law 1346/83).

According to Articles 1–5 of Law 1648/86, the employment of a percentage of deficient persons in private enterprises and in public services is acknowledged as obligatory (also *see* the Decision 4365/88, published in EDKA 1989, p. 33, Decision of AP 335/88, published in the Legal Tribune 1989, p. 251). The DYPA subsidies the enterprises which have more than fifty employees to decrease the relative burden of the personnel's payment of salaries cost (*see* Article 2§1 of Law 1648/86 and Ministry of Labour Document 31031/87, published in IKA Review 1989, p. 831).

Also, with the same piece of legislation (Law 1648/86), the employers can ask DYPA for a subsidy for the reformation of the place of work for the facilitation of the employment of persons with special needs (*see* Decision of Minister of Labour 30040/90, published in DEN 1990, p. 513, also the Decision of the Ministers of Financing and Labour 30136/90, published in DEN 1990, p. 458 and Decision of Ministers of Financing and labour 32852/89, published in DEN 1989, p. 396, for the employment of persons with special needs).

247. In the social assistance measures of employment (finding or creation of employment positions for defective persons) belongs the preference – between applicants with the same abilities – during the appointment, the employment (Article 32 of Law 1324/49, Article 7§1 of Law 4471/65) or the professional establishment (Article 2, 10§1 of Law 1043/80) of persons with special needs (*see* the Decision of StE 2375/88, Plenary Session, not published, for the right to professional exploitation of a specific place from a disabled).

They are measures which help the most difficult rehabilitation of the disabled, the professional one. With the administrative act, where the control of the prerequisites of such a social privilege is completed and the relevant license is provided, i.e., the permission for exploitation of a kiosk, then an integral and legally actionable right to social assistance is acknowledged on behalf of the disabled.

Chapter 4. Income

§1. Beneficiaries and Conditions for Benefits

248. Within the framework of the social insurance, we have indicated that the replacement of the permanent or temporal loss of income from the inability to work for the disabled is faced by the provision of disability pensions or readjustment allowances from the insurance organizations.

Beneficiaries are the ones from the insured who have gathered the relevant prerequisites (legal affiliation in the insurance of the organization analogously to the profession, appearance of the insurance risk of invalidity and completion of the anticipated insurance time).

249. Within the framework of the social assistance institution, we can indicate between the programmes of direct financial aid (subsidy) and the programmes of indirect financial aid (of financial deprivations or social privileges) for persons with special needs. Some programmes, however, aim simultaneously the direct and indirect financial aid.

250. In the first group, several monthly financial subsidies are indicated, according to the form of invalidity. Indicatively the subsidy of the blind (Article 3 of Law 958/79), deaf-mute, the heavily mentally retarded, the persons who suffer from tetraplegia, paraplegia, the heavily maimed, the absolutely invalid with a weakness of self-servicing, the seriously ill for two years after their coming out from Institutions and Hospitals (*see* Article 1 of Presidential Decree 286/88, Article 2§1 case b' of Presidential Decree 108/83) and so on. The second group is indicatively classified as the discount from the income of the taxpayer is invalid (*see* Article 8§1 of Legislative Decree 3323/55, Article 4 of Law 12/75, etc.), the immunity from the tax for the first residence transfer (Article 1§1 of Law 1078/80) and the tax exemption for import for the personal needs of the disabled (Article 1§1 of Law 490/76, Article 16 of Law 1798/88).

251. The circle of the beneficiaries is indicated in the several assistance programmes, according to the covered 'social' need and sometimes by the condition of the financial (income-property) inadequacy of the disabled. The more general prerequisites of assistance protection are going to be dealt with in the following part. Especially it has to be mentioned that the abolishment of the criteria of the financial weakness for the provision of the social assistance allowances to persons with special needs (*see* Decision of the Minister of Health, Social Assistance and Social Insurance GG4b/F. 32/oik. 591/7 February 1989).

252. Among the general prerequisites for the beginning, but also for the maintenance of the disabled protection, the sometimes self-evident collaboration of the citizen with the administration is also placed. Such is, for example, the readiness of the disabled to undertake an offered occupation relevant to his abilities. Such an obligation of the beneficiary towards the competent (insurance or assistance) organization can be broad, but not unlimited. The refusal of a benefit in cash to the invalid is not easily accepted because of the so-called unjustifiable rejection of a simple, but irrelevant occupation, according to the prohibition of the obligatory work (a contrario interpretation of Article 22§1 of the Constitution).

§2. Procedures and Institutions

253. The former variety of the income support programmes for the disabled within the framework of the social insurance and the social assistance do not favour the systematization of the types and the organs that provide the benefits.

However, we once again underline the obligation of submission of a written application from the insured, in order to control the prerequisites and to issue a decision for disability pension (*see* Article 10§1 of the IKA Insurance Regulation), though for the health care services to the disabled, from the disease insurance branch, the ex officio diagnosis of the need from the competent (insurance and medical) organs could be enough. From the social assistance beneficiary's point of view, an application is needed, and only in special cases, the ex officio administration activity is enough. It is also possible that it is not clear when an application is a fundamental prerequisite for the enacting of the relevant right or a simple procedural action, so the administration is aware of the extent of the needs before it offers ex officio social services. From the legal expression and the aim of the specific legal rule will depend, if the content of the application is of a component or of a probative character, and then it is an alternative way of beginning the procedure for the confirmation of the necessary prerequisites.

The submission of an application is, in any case, useful, so the doubts regarding the extent of the administrative control of the case and of the juridical control of the 'right' of the invalid are concerned, so that they are limited, when the administration refuses implicitly to perform its duties (*see* Article 19§2 case b' of Presidential Decree 341/78).

There are no special (first or second degree) organs for the provision of supplementary provisions towards the disabled from the various social-insurance regimes. So, a special dealing with the subject is protracted.

On the contrary, the competent organs of the social assistance or other organizations, which provide analogous benefits, show a great variety, see the former competencies of tax, customs or other administrative principles, so that every limited enumeration of them is unsafe.

Chapter 5. Institutional Care and Attendance

254. While examining the health care subjects of the disabled, we have met some cases where the social-insurance institution contributes to the relief of their problems with the cover of their expenses for staying in asylums or in homes for incurables.

Yet, in Greece, the most basic programmes of institutionalized health care and protection of the disabled function within the framework of the social assistance institution.

The institutionalized health care is basically offered to those who suffer from chronic ailments, i.e., to persons confined to bed, semi-confined to bed or who are moving with mechanical means, if they are not totally or partially self-serviced because of an insurable lifelong disease.

According to the basic legislation of Articles 1 and 2 of Legislative Decree 162/73, the protection of the persons, who suffer from chronic ailments, is expressed either as 'institutionalized' health care, or as a social aid at home, offered with a form of ethical help, economical aid or other material help, as especially defined to the several social assistance programmes. By virtue of Article 10§1 of a Draft of Law (1992), for the 'Regulation of the profession of the specialized technician of supplementary and erecting constructions and other relevant regulations', natural or legal persons can establish therapy and rehabilitation centres for the provision of health and medical care services to internal or external diseased, who need natural rehabilitation. In these centres, guesthouses can function for the rehabilitation of the diseased who need re-control.

For the understanding of the type of the relevant services, we resort to two indicative examples of established institutional health care and to an experimental programme of health care at home.

255. By virtue of the Presidential Decree 332/87 in the village of Lehena in the Prefecture of Ilia, a Centre for Children Rehabilitation was established, as a decentralized service of PIKPA, aiming at the health care of children from 6 to 18 years old, who suffer from a serious mental deficiency and who also face a social problem. The health care is offered free to persons who have been characterized as economically weak after a decision of the competent Prefect, or with payment of the medical expenses which is decided by the Administrative Council of the Centre. Such a Centre usually consists of an Administrative Section, a Health Care Section, a Section of Creative Occupation, a Physiotherapy Office and a Social Work Office.

256. Representative for an institutionalized health care of adults with chronic mental or emotional disease and with the inability of self-service is the C' Athens Health Institution of Chronic Diseases, established as an entity of public law (by virtue of the Presidential Decree from 1985). According to its establishing Organization, this provides sanitary housing and nutrition, proper clothing, medical care, physiotherapy and ergotherapy, though it takes care of the entrance of the needy into a proper medical institution. Moreover, the psychological encouragement and the social rehabilitation of the hospitalized are pursued with various recreational and educational programmes. Within the entrance, prerequisites are the Social Research

Report, a medical certificate for the reason of the chronic ailment and for the possibility of living together with other people. The hospitalized contribute to the medical expenses according to their financial abilities, based on a price list which is defined from the Administrative Council of the Health Institution, unless if there are prerequisites of acknowledged financial weakness.

257. The programme 'help at home' is directed to adults without social and economic discrimination, who have lost permanently or temporarily their autonomy because of health problems, etc., and they need special care. Its personnel consist of a physician, a psychotherapist, a nurse, a social worker, a cleaner-domestic helper and volunteers. Within the offered services, some practical favours are consisted, as invalid's wheelchair, etc. The programme has concrete beneficial results and, among them, a decreased possession of hospital beds.

Part X. Minimum Income Benefit

§1. Beneficiaries

258. The existence of a predefined person (subject), who can claim the necessary social aid or action, is a substantial prerequisite of the right to social assistance. The circle of the beneficiaries is defined in the several assistance programmes relatively with the covered need; see the people who have many children, the war victims, the defected persons, etc. The importance of the residence, the nationality and other defining factors of a person are not usually mentioned.

Two are the tendencies – the first confines the social assistance protection to the citizens or to the permanent inhabitants of the country, which organizes the specific social services. The other broadens the protection in every person or family, if they face needs covered from an assistance programme. The arguments in favour of the confining tension are the initial aim of the social assistance institution for the establishment of a specific public order, the difficulty of satisfaction of massive claims of the foreigners, even from the socially developed countries, and furthermore, the importance of the permanent stay for the better estimation of the need. On the contrary, the broadening tension is justified by the modern social assistance conceptions, which are centralized, to the human being regardless of his special characteristics. Consequently, the principles of territoriality, nationality or other restrictions have to be applied with the most possible flexibility in favour of humanity.

The first tension, which uses important regulative grounds, is the most prevailing in Greece. According, for example, to Article 1§1 of the Legislative Decree 57/73, the social assistance protection is clearly confined 'to the Greek citizens who permanently stay in Greece', whereas within Article 5 of the law, there is a delegation for a gradual expansion of the protection to homogenous who stay temporarily or to foreigners who stay permanently in Greece.

259. The various social assistance programmes are not in any case coordinated between them regarding the issue, which we are examining. Sometimes the circle of the beneficiaries is analytically defined in relation to the nationality, descent, permanent stay, etc., without special reasons, and sometimes the importance of these abilities is doubtful for the provision or the exclusion of a person from the social services.

Irrespectively of the international bindings of Greece, a doubt prevails today, whether the provision of social assistance benefits only to Greek citizens, who live in Greece and to some foreigners, in relation with their descent, their arrival conditions or the duration of their stay in our country, is harmonized with the Constitution of 1975.

The aspect that the social rights have to be consolidated also in favour of foreigners, if they have permission to stay and work in Greece, has also been expressed. Moreover, it has been stressed that the legislator has to adopt the proper measures for the realization of this consolidation. Yet, in the crucial Article 21 of the Constitution for the social assistance protection, there is an impression that the State concern (for health) refers only to 'citizens'. According to the main social assistance benefits, the legislative possibility for exclusion of foreigners does not derive from the expression of the Constitution.

260. According to the most correct opinion, the former doubt has been overcome with the help of some more general constitutional orders. Therefore, the social protection, which would prevent the destruction of human value (*see* Article 2§1 of the Constitution) and the insult of human dignity (*see* Article 5§§1 and 2 of the Constitution), is acknowledged as imperative to every person. According to these regulations and the modern conceptions of the social legal state, the confinements of 'Greek nationality' had to be effaced in every extent in which they exclude the State aid of foreigners, who face, for example, existential needs or they are victims of calamity (according to Article 1§1 of the Legislative Decree 57/73). On the same grounds, some 'staying' confinements should be revised, such as the obligation of 'at least two year permanent residence in the area of the competent Prefecture', before the acknowledgement of a homeless, uninsured and financially weak lonely Greek, from 67 years old and more, as a beneficiary of a residence allowance.

261. Until the realization of the corrective legislative intervention, the protection of foreigners, provided that they have the special characteristics, which were indicated in the former examples, would be ensured with the gathering of reflective rights from the more general social assistance administrative activity. The possibility of juridical control of the social administration exists also in these cases, even if it is weakened. This derives from Article 47§1 of the Legislative Decree 170/73, which permits the exercise of a petition for annulment at the Council of State and for cases of simple insult to the legal interests of every private individual. This solution is not less effective than the other ones, which are given to other countries. Most of the time, the social assistance protection, which is provided by stretching the principles of nationality and territoriality, generally depends on the discretionary administrative power. It does not correspond to a genuine and actionable right of the person.

Many significant arguments are in favour of the former expanding reformation and the relative temporal solution. However, some distinctions have to be made in relation to the various social assistance types of protection.

262. A main characteristic of the contemporary types of social assistance protection is not the elimination of the risks, which threaten to reverse a specific public order. The aim of the social assistance institution consists in ensuring persons or groups from possible deprivations of the necessary means of subsistence. The need for social assistance cover is safely bound with the conditions of residence, which explains the termination of the social assistance benefits, if the interested person is unjustifiably absent. The enforcement of long-life residence prerequisites for ensuring protection is not compromised by the individualized and urgent character of the social assistance services. The criterion of the permanent residence would be useful for the social assistance aid from the diplomatic authorities in favour of the Greeks, who were abroad and exposed to a great social or economical need.

263. It is known that the receipt of social assistance benefits refers to an absolute personal right. This does not mean that the family, as an integral whole, leaves unaffected by the extent or even the provision of social services. From the circumstances of the family environment, the exclusion of the social assistance protection is possible, according to the principle of subsidiarity or this principle can be expanded, according to the principle of individualization. Sometimes the family members acquire special rights for benefits, which belong to the object of the social assistance right. In addition, the whole family is possible to become an object of such right.

There are namely indications that in the social assistance law and in the relative jurisprudence, significant elements have already been located, so that it is supported also by science that social assistance does not protect a person only as an individual, but as a family member which, theoretically sometimes, suffers with him.

The 'parallel programme' of the government for the support of the poor and excluded

In 2014 the Greek Parliament approved the government's 'parallel programme', a package of social welfare actions meant to soften the negative social impact of the austerity policies agreed upon by international institutions under Greece's third bailout programme. To this effect, a specific law enabled 2.5 million uninsured people, who were unable to enter the public health care system without incurring a hefty financial charge, to be fully covered (Law 4368/2016). In the framework of the EU-financed 'humanitarian aid', free electricity and water have been provided to many households, and previous debts have even been erased. In addition to offering free transportation to the unemployed and free supermarket goods to 148,000 people, the government offered hot meals to 200,000 school students while also setting up a KEA project in thirty municipalities nationwide.

§2. Benefits

264. This very broad subject is better analysed, if a former more general presentation of the 'social services' in Greece and a more special reference to partial 'social assistance programmes' is carried out, to any extent in which there was not any reference about them.

265. Under the term *social services,* we mean the organized activities of public or private social policy organizations, which usually aspire – with procedures of income redistribution – the maintenance, the improvement or the rehabilitation of the ability of persons, groups or economical problems from the continuously changeable living conditions.

Among the social services under a broad meaning, one can place the benefits (in cash, material commodities or personal services), which ensure bearable living conditions in society, such as the ones for the prevention of criminality and the cleansing of the environment, and also the provisions, which improve the living conditions, as the ones for professional occupation, medical care (diagnosis or therapy), education and social care (insurance or social assistance). Since the contemporary social and financing problems are complicated and the resources are usually limited, the provisions of amounts and material commodities are not as effective as the personal social services from people with special education, such as the social workers, psychologists, pedagogues. The social services, to this extent, are only bound by an institution of social protection. The services are offered within the framework of a health, social insurance, social assistance working, civil servant, procedural or other legal relation.

Social services *stricto sensu* belong mainly to the personal services, which aim at the completion of a legally established or socio-politically obliged social assistance aim. In the first case, one can speak of social aid with a possible retrospective personal right, whereas in the second case, for social action, with simply favourable results for the person.

The two conditions are not yet dogmatically elaborated in Greece, though they appear quite often in legal texts and within the administrative practice. While tracing their fundamental characteristics, one can observe the following.

266. The social aid is a basic expression of the social assistance institution in its narrow sense, within the more general framework of the administration, which offers benefits. It is usually evolved by especially organized public services, which fulfil social assistance aims with predetermined methods, means and procedures of social protection. Specifically, the question of whether the competencies of the social assistance bind substantially the administration, depends on the application prerequisites of the several social assistance programmes, i.e., if they correspond to a right of the social services' user. The social aid is provided for the individuals and with a supplementary character, after a research of the personal and family conditions of the interested person and after the discovery that there is no other way for the cover of a serious social or economical need.

267. The social action functions also in the social assistance area, but it does not have the characteristic features of a special legal institution because the pursuit of its socio-political aims is not regulated obligatorily by legal rules. It is an integral system of continuous and various personal services from the public of private sector. The services within the framework of a social action have fluid content, since they appear occasionally so as to be evolved and be established as social aid measures, provided that they have been effective or to be terminated atypically, as they are usually established. Contrary to the activities of simple charity, the services of social action seem to be offered uniformly to every person who needs them, without controls of economical insufficiency. They do not apparently correspond to genuine personal rights because of the generality of the pursued aims.

Referring to the typical (legislatively or regularly specialized) social aid or to the atypical regularly social action, the social services promote the mission of social assistance with various methods or techniques. The most important of them is social work.

268. Social work is the method (applied social science, psychological technique, function or profession) of providing individualized services from properly educated persons (social workers) for the ascertainment of the conditions which caused a basic (social or economical) need and for helping a defected person (as a person, member of a group or community) to face his problem, by evolving his adaptation abilities against the unfavourable conditions and by developing every available form of social protection.

With the previous definition, an attempt is made to determine the social work services not only in the cases of the traditional social work for the ascertainment of the prerequisites of the application of social assistance programmes but also in the contemporary cases of social aid and action with educational, therapeutical or sociological models.

From the same definition also derives the question of how broad can the extension of the social assistance social services be, provided that they promote the social solidarity and the human dignity.

269. A discreet, but important, discrimination of the personal social services is among those, who aspire to the fulfilment of a specific need, analogous with the 'reasons' which caused it and to those which facilitate a specific 'result', as its elimination.

In the first case, the social services are differentiated from the viewpoint of form and content, according to the social or economical consequences of an event (i.e., calamity) or of a condition (i.e., invalidity) for the specific person. In the second case, usually uniformed social services for the prevention of a risk or for the fulfilment of an aim are organized (e.g., social rehabilitation of the released from prison), so that there is a substantial limitation or the elimination of the social assistance protection. Actually, the social services are finally offered analogously to the available means, but the examined discrimination does not lose its value. When personal services are anticipated for the confrontation of consequences for predefined events or circumstances, it would be impossible for the social assistance organization to refuse them, without a specific justification, provided that the interested person suffers truly by its unfavourable consequences. In case of social services from private social assistance organizations, such refusal would constitute anticontractual behaviour. On the contrary, where personal services for the pursuit of a general aim are established, the person would claim an available form of protection, if the organization has a broad authority to choose the type of means which lead to the beneficial result. Apart from this, interpretative problems emerge usually regarding the effectiveness of an aim or the coincidence of more, even contradictory, social assistance aims (*see* the difference of opinion for the medical care of the disabled in their family environment).

The social services are distinguished into primary or secondary services according to their organizational structure.

The first are offered by specially constructed organizations (*see* the KAPI) or from independent specially educated professionals (*see* the speech therapists), though the second are offered from integral sections of other organizations such as OPEKA. In the first case, the legal nature of the social assistance organizations prevails or the normative rules of the professionals, while in the second case, the variable provisions' regulations or the managerial right of the competent organizations are important.

270. With reference to the time of provision and at the dependence rate or cooperation of the person, the social services are systematized in preliminary, such as the information for the most proper social assistance programme and in final ones, such as the affiliation to a special rehabilitation action, temporal ones, as the emotional support of the victims from disasters and permanent ones, as the domestic help to people confined to bed.

A discrimination of the social services of diminishing importance is their division according to their special regional conditions, where they are offered, namely in open (i.e., of consultative character) and closed (i.e., of an institutional character) services.

Despite the theoretical value of the classification of the social services, for the resolving of common legal problems from various social assistance programmes, in action, this is not always maintained. Analogously to the extent of the need, the social administration can accumulate more types of social services, as in the case of the invalidity from the birthday of a financially weak. Theoretically, it is possible that needs, which do not correspond to a granted system of social services, can emerge.

We, therefore, conclude to the question of whether, parallel to the systematization, a general stipulation for the provision of every available social service is to be examined, so that cases of atypical need are also covered by the administration.

According to the most correct opinion, beyond the organizational and economical difficulties, for the verification of such a vacant hypothesis, a very broad administrative discretionary power had to be established for the estimation of 'every kind of needs'. The free choice of the proper means could prohibit the legal control of the decisions of the social assistance programmes. This could be compromised with the orders of the modern state of justice and the established principle of legitimacy. Sooner or later, the general rule would result in a simple wish. The same end would have the acknowledgement of the consequent administration obligations, from the legal relation of social assistance, for 'every necessary' supplementary protection. Searching for common characteristics of the social services, analogous to the organizational forms of the social assistance organizations or to the profession of the social assistance organs, we approach the same aim indirectly; and this is due to the fact that the analogous application of the social assistance regulations is made easy even in atypical cases of need, which would otherwise remain uncovered.

There is an indicative reference on the most important social assistance programmes later on, so that the most representative claims would be better defined within the State social assistance. However, this description is indirectly useful for the definition of the social assistance aid from private organizations. It is obvious that the administration, by providing the necessary licenses for the specific social services from the private sector, aims to guarantee the more general prerequisites for achieving social assistance work.

271. From the first years of the national reformation, after the revolution of 1821, the State concern was consequent to take care of the occasional protection of the disabled and the war victims, the abandoned children and also the suppression of epidemics and of the rehabilitation of the refugees (1867, 1906). More systematic social assistance measures – of institutional character – were taken by the Church and national benefactors, though the public organizations were confined to services of public interest. These social services, which covered unexpected and exceptionally urgent needs, did not correspond to every kind of personal claim. They were passive recipients of the charity activities. Even after the establishment of the first social assistance organizations, i.e., the PIKPA (1914), the social aid and action aimed mainly at the cover of exceptional needs. The limited resources did not permit the predetermination of the social services, which would have made easy the acknowledgement of the retrospective rights.

After the Second World War, there was definitely a more organized provision of social assistance benefits for the cover of isolated risks and for those facing poverty in general.

In the various social assistance programmes, the social services are sometimes defined in such detail, so that the persons would know, which type of social assistance service could be offered to them, as long as the anticipated prerequisites are satisfied. A claim for a specific protection is founded, when it is justified by the available means.

272. During this period, the following State social assistance programmes are inductively detected.

Towards family members, as persons or as a unified whole, the following are offered: (1) social advantages (*see* the services at the same place, at an absolute priority, of spouses of teachers and the rest of the public servants (Law 2087/252), (2) child allowance (Article 214 of Law 4512/2018) and (3) immunities from financial burdens (*see* the decrease of the juridical expenses and taxes for people having many children (Law 1910/44). Moreover, in the maternity and infancy programmes, the following are also placed within: (1) the financial aid of the women during maternity, if they are uninsured and they do not have a sufficient level of living conditions (Law 1302/82, which ratified the International Labour Agreement 103/52), (2) the genetic advice from the Stations and the Centres of Family Programming and the consultative support from the Infants' Centre 'THE MOTHER' towards unmarried mothers, from the pregnancy until the social adaptation and the professional rehabilitation (Presidential Decree 830/80) and (3) the services from State Infancy Stations (Law 1431/84, Presidential Decree 160/86) and Baby Homes for babies abandoned, illegitimate or other unprotected infants (Law 4227/62, Royal Decree 814/62). In the social aid and action for the children, i.e., for persons from 3 years old up to 15 usually, belongs the monthly financial aid, when they are unprotected and they 'stay' with their natural family or with a relative one (Presidential

Decree 286/88, Presidential Decree 147/89), the services of indication of work chances from the National Social Assistance Organization (Legislative Decree 572/70), the camping or staying at the country for children (Law 749/48 and Royal Decree from 24.6/2.7.49), and also the centres of children concern (ex orphanages) (Law 2851/22, Royal Decree 273/73).

The protection measures for people with special needs have already been analysed in the former Part.

The social assistance protection for the old aged evolves in two pivots: The direct State concern with special programmes and the State guarantee of a specially accessible and effective private enterprise action.

The first pivot consists of, among other services, material or other support for the stay of the old aged at home (see the applied programmes of housing contribution with the form of rent to lonely persons and couples and especially the Centres of Open Health Care for the Old aged) and services of institutionalized health care for the old aged which are not self-serviced (*see* Legislative Decree 162/73). The second pivot, which was prior chronically and affects more than 80% of the medical care places, is analysed in two partial guarantees – the ensuring of the establishment and function conditions of private profiteering enterprises for the medical care of the old aged (Legislative Decree 1118/72, Law 877/79) and the definition of the prerequisites and function conditions of the non-profiteering private Old People's Home and Hospitals of Chronic Ailments (Presidential Decree 631/74, Legislative Decree 162/73).

273. The programmes for public aid are of special importance because they refer to the minimum survival protection.

Aspiring to the established structure of the central social services (Articles 12, 15 of Presidential Decree 112/89) and to the discrimination of the §§ 3 and 4 of Article 21 of the Constitution, as provisions of public interest, we would regularly mean the social assistance services to the financially weak, to the frail and socially unacceptable groups or to the victims of exceptional social needs, except for the cases of accommodation aid, which show organizational integrity. However, the persons, who face accommodation problems, are almost identical to the previously mentioned users of services of public care, and it is simpler and more human to relate the accommodation with the various forms of public care.

274. The very developed preventive social action in other counties, though it is not totally unknown in Greece (see the services for the pre-announcement of tempest or severe heat wave), it has not been organized in systematic preventive services of public care.

Referring to the suppressive social aid or action, in matters of public care, the following discrimination is proposed: (1) services of economical rehabilitation and (2) services of social rehabilitation. In both cases, the adaptation of the person in the natural, family, professional and social environment is pursued. In the first case, the social assistance services refer to the fundamental facing of poverty (from every reason) with financial means, whereas in the second case, they aim at the elimination of the social consequences (from predefined human abilities or events) with any kind of mean. Actually, there is a reference to the rights of the poor and to the rights of the suffering.

In the services of public care for the economical rehabilitation belongs every benefit to the financially weak. Here belong, especially, the lump sum or the periodical temporal allowances in cash to the poor from credits of the 'Account for the First Social Aid' by the Ministry of Health, Social Assistance and Social Insurance at the capitals of the Prefectures (Articles 1§1 case a' and 7 of the Legislative Decree 57/73), the offer of using residences without auction to homeless citizens with the one-fourth at least of the current value (Article 191§1 of Law 1065/80), the benefit of being poor (*see* Articles 194–204 of the Civil Procedure Code, 2§5 of Law 1649/86 and 37 case a' of Legislative Decree 170/73, as it was amended by Article 25 of Law 702/77).

275. The group of public care measures, which is examined, consists mainly of benefits in cash. This helps to a considerable degree their affiliation in the subject of a retrospective right to social assistance. The unreserved expansion of such a right to an indefinite circle of persons, for facing of their poverty for any reason, would cause an excessive absorption of the social assistance resources. That is why the legislator depends, correctly, on the extent of the right from additional indefinite legal notions and its exercise from detailed diagnostic procedures. The allowance in cash in case of 'poverty' can, analogously to the available means of the organization, mean gradual financial aid for the coverage of needs either because of sordid poverty or by shortage of corporal, mental and social well-being or from a shortage of a definitely dignified level of life.

276. The services of public care for the social rehabilitation are divided into two sub-cases: the services to the so-called frail groups and to the services to the victims of unexpected events.

In the first sub-case, the economical or other support measures of the repatriated and migrant refugees are detected (*see* Law 358/45, Royal Decrees Code 330/60, Legislative Decree 4377/64, Article 1§1 of Law 1736/87, Article 7 of Law 1807/88) of the beggars and tramps (Article 7§1 of Legislative Decree 57/73), of the drugs addicts (Article 1 of Law 1729/87), released from prison (Article 41, 95§§1 and 2, 113 of Law 1851/89), etc. The needs of such frail groups seem to be serviced by the social allowances from Article 23§1 case c' of Law 1622/86, which are consisted in the competencies of the prefectorial local authority and generally refer to the 'persons who need special protection'. In this way, the network of social assistance benefits can also be expanded to atypically frail groups, which the established public care could possibly leave without any protection.

To the second sub-case belong all the types of social aid and action from social assistance organizations, for the facing of urgent social needs, such as the disasters from earthquakes (Law 867/79, Law 1668/86, Law 1190/87), the disasters from unfavourable weather conditions (Article 2§1 Royal Decree 775/64, Article 1§1 of Law 1331/83, Article 3 of Law 1807/88) and the detriments from fires or other unexpected events (Law 6072/34, Law 857/71).

From their nature, these services cover very fundamental needs of support and health care. According to the definite delegation from Article 1§1 case c' and §4 of the Legislative Decree 57/73, it is possible that a whole network of social assistance benefits for the victims of the 'unexpected events' with social administration actions is created. Such services of public interest can be defined in detail at a legislative level. A sufficient specialization at a regular administrative level is observed, which logically poses social assistance law, provided that it considers that the necessary aid measures exist.

277. The legal position of the victims of such disasters would be supported *de lege ferenda*, if the administration would follow a legally established indicative enumeration of public care measures instead of the former more general delegation. The reference of Article 2§1 of Legislative Decree 857/71 to a social aid 'with all the available means of the area', after the 'available supplies and means of every kind are used', is concerned extremely abstract for the contemporary organizational and socio-political data. Such vague legal rules echo opinions of other ages, when the person was only a passive recipient of social charity in cases of absolute misery. In the legislative will therefore lies the definition of a more specific measure or height of social aid. The proposed regulation does not derive from our Constitution as an integral object of State concern. It is, however, referred to as an obvious expression from the established principle of the social legal State.

§3. Control of Financial Insufficiency

278. A legal regulation, which depends on the social assistance benefits on the shortage of economical means, is logically possible to mean either a simple emphasis on a defined element of 'need' or the establishment of an additional social assistance condition.

Systematic reasons strengthen the second version. In such regulations, the fundamental social assistance principles of subsidiarity and individualization are expressed. The utility of an independent economical criterion (an economical prerequisite) for facing every 'need' is obvious. The real abilities of the citizen for self-protection are revealed and the choice of the more proper assistance is made easy from the organized social solidarity.

Vividly one could say that the type and the extent of the social services depend on the nature and the size of the protection vacant, which derives, if one contrasts the condition of social need with the ability of self-help of the persons. Actually, there is a general and substantial prerequisite of social assistance benefits, with such a great theoretical and practical interest, which is worth preceding an integral analysis.

279. The prerequisite of 'economical inadequacy' neither concerns exclusively the social assistance institution, nor is it defined uniformly in the various social assistance texts. The science is called to answer in at least five main subjects, if they remain unregulated or undefined:

(1) For how long there has to be a condition of economical need and at which rate is it affected by legal conditions?
(2) How bound is the social administration by controlling the available means for the cover of a specific need?
(3) Which family members or third persons are considered to contribute to the protection of the interested?
(4) Which income excludes the offer of social assistance benefits?
(5) Which fortune excludes the offer of social assistance benefits?

According to the first matter, it is obvious that the more limited the unit of the crucial time, the bigger is the number of the beneficiaries. The economic deficiency, however, in cases of shortage of the minimum means of support, cannot be expanded in big time periods. It would cause, inevitably, either a kind of self-protection or the extermination of the person. Where a legal gap emerges, the month is concerned regularly as a reasonable time for the consolidation of a condition of economic need from temporal fluctuations, for example, from using up self-protection savings, from the exploitation of help from third persons. Exceptionally, the drawing of financial resources from a former time period could prove important, when it is possible that they were enough for the effective cover of the specific need.

280. In relation to the second subject, one should examine how much independence the social assistance organs have by estimating the conditions of financial need and how the criteria of financial deficiency coordinate among them in the various social assistance programmes.

According to the fundamental stipulation of Article 1§2 case b' of the Legislative Decree 57/73, the 'inability of coverage of a specific need with their own means (of the financially weak) and of their family members' is a prerequisite of social protection. Therefore, a more special subject arises with regard to the legal importance of the notion of 'means'. According to our opinion, it is a vague legal notion with composite (empirical and notable) content. The means for the coverage of a specific need are adequately defined, only if the knowledge of the daily common experience is combined, i.e., for the facing of expenses of basic needs, together with technical judgments, i.e., for the inadequacy of specific self-protection methods. Nowadays, it seems that finally, the values of importance prevail, especially when the adequacy of the economic means is bound with psychological, sociological and other abstract factors. On the contrary, some initial tensions have retreated for the regulative differentiation of the inadequacy and for the standardization of the criteria in the same matter. Consequently, the wide discretionary administrative power at the estimation of the 'economic deficiency' of the social assistance protection recipient is almost obvious.

However, in a few social assistance programmes, specific criteria for the deficiency of means for the cover of a need are defined. The special criteria apparently prevail over the former general criteria from Article 1§2 case b' of the Legislative Decree 57/73, even if they apparently derive from inferior sources of law. This derives from §4 of the same Article, which delegated the administration to regulate with regulative acts (ministerial decisions) 'and the criteria, in general groups, for the affiliation in the familiar programme of those who need social assistance protection benefits'. A special prerequisite of financial deficiency, adjusted to these conditions, has to be analogously interpreted, as far as the housing allowance is concerned for uninsured, financially weak and lonely persons more than 65 years old. The inadequacy of the 'means' of Article 1§2 case b' of the Legislative Decree 57/73 is specialized here as an income shortage from every kind of source and as a shortage of immovable property for facing housing needs. Thus it would be possible to support that the enforcement of a person to sell pieces of movable property, for instance, pieces of art, for renting temporarily a proper residence, exceeds the marginal lawful limits of the discretionary authority of the social assistance organs.

281. Regarding the third issue, the persons, who have to contribute first for the coverage of a specific need, are still searched for. If the help will be effective, then a negative prerequisite arises (reason of exclusion) of the social protection (*see* Article 1§2 case b' of Legislative Decree 57/73).

When the relevant social assistance regulation refers vaguely to family members, the persons, who have a legal obligation for support, which covers basic needs, are apparently meant by the Civil Code. For the settling of disputes, sometimes the committal to the obliged to support derives clearly from special laws, for instance, from Article 3§1 of Law 4051/60, which defines prerequisites for the assistance of unprotected children. The application of regulations of the Civil Code is characterized by simplicity and consistency to the need for exploitation of the whole legal order. However, there are some reservations whether with this way the scope of the better possible organization and distribution of the limited social assistance resources would be fulfilled. Sometimes the coverage of a need derives from living together and the support from persons, who do not belong to the established (from the Civil Code) notion of the family or they have been released from a support obligation. If, in such cases, we acknowledged a social assistance right, then the shortage of a real need would be ignored and the people, who were not interested to validate their family relations, i.e., with acknowledgement of paternity, would get rich. The interpretation of the notion of 'family', in the extent which is given for the 'households', so that beyond the father, the mother and the dependent children it consists of persons, who are active members in the broader family community of the defective person. The proposed opinion shows technical difficulties as far as the ascertainment of the de facto cover of needs. Analogous difficulties emerge after the verification of the real income transfer from persons, who have a legal support obligation. The social assistance organs have to be supplied with a broad discretionary power, so that a possible real cover of a need is distinguished from every person before the social assistance mechanisms move. However, the accession to broadly established research units of the 'rest protection means' corresponds to the undoubtful need for multidisciplinary elaboration of the social assistance legal rules. Therefore, under a broad interpretation of Article 1 of the Legislative Decree 57/73, the refusal of medical provision or other benefits would be valid, if financial enforcement is ascertained 'on behalf of every kind of children of the applicant'. Even if the coverage of needs was from illegitimate children, who neither belong to the legal family nor they have a duty of support, the possible negative administrative action would not be cancelled for a shortage of adequate reasoning. It is considered advisable, for the elimination of the control difficulties, the establishment for all the members of the household of a legally rebuttable presumption of support.

Relevant is the matter about which obligations or real assistance from third persons are estimated, for the legal judgment by the social assistance organization that a person can face a specific need.

The mature and safe claims of third persons for the coverage of a specific need from them can also be considered as counted assistance. The demands from natural or legal persons under private law also belong here, when they are founded under contractual conditions or legal regulations, as in the case of payment of insurance rate or reimbursement. In addition, claims from other public authorities had to be added, if they substantially contribute to the facing of the need, as possibly the demand for a tax return. The coverage of a need absolutely from the assistance of a third person, without a former contractual or legal obligation, is not excluded.

282. With reference to the fourth matter, the establishment of a (readjusted) amount of income is theoretically possible, under which the person would be in a condition of poverty and that would require social assistance protection. Finally, in Greece, such an inelastic way of income estimation was not established. Therefore, the social assistance organs remain free to define, with the rule of the principle of individualization, which assistance to the family of the economically weak would be 'income' and which expenses would be obligatory income 'decreases', which cannot be used for his self-protection.

The discretionary power of the social assistance organs seems to be enacted within lawful limits, when they contribute to the income the earnings from work, before the completion of the necessary time for the social-insurance coverage (a contrario interpretation of Article 1§2 case a' of the Legislative Decree 57/73). Moreover, the social assistance organization seems to be able to claim from the applicant that social assistance benefits the undertaking of every kind of work. The job does not have to be contrary to human dignity, his health status and his family conditions. There are no special restrictions regarding the suitability of the offered job, according to his professional abilities and other criteria, as in force in the social insurance against unemployment (*see* Article 3§1 of Law 1545/85). In the notion of income, the regular or irregular net earnings from every kind of property elements have to be affiliated, since there is no discrimination by the law or by the social assistance programmes. The unnecessary income from ownership occupancy had also to be added, according to the market value of the rent of the private residence. Had this not occurred, we would possibly have infringements of the social protection with a false increase in the housing needs.

On the contrary, the expense for the renting of a proper residence, the expenses of obligatory support of family members, the maintenance of the necessary property elements, the fulfilment of previous commitments to third persons, etc., have to be deducted from the total amount of the income. The special individual conditions and the social environment of the interested person depend, on how much the income can decrease in advance, beyond the amount of which 'the financial deficiency' is being accepted. The discount on a necessary expense for the free evolution of the personality would be advisable, for instance, an amount for contribution to fundamental educational activities.

283. Relatively to the fifth matter, we repeat that all the property means have to be composed in the measures of the self-protection of the person, if they are not used for his and his family support. The social assistance organs, by applying the principles of proportionality and of fair administration, estimate with discretionary power, when there are possibilities of substantial coverage of the specific need with a proper exploitation or even with sale of a property.

In the content of the 'property', amounts in cash and generally every movable or immovable object with objective value are affiliated. It suffices that the person has a legal and real authority of offer, i.e., a mature demand from available debentures of the bearer. Only then a financial deficiency could be effectively neutralized. The estimation will be expanded in less or more pieces of property, if only the need for subsidence will be covered or simultaneously other needs for expensive social services.

On the contrary, due to the nature and the aim of the social assistance institution, property objects which are useful for the daily survival are excluded from its notion, i.e., pieces of furniture, heating devices, etc., or for the organization of self-protection measures, i.e., professional utensils, orthopaedic devices, etc. However, the interested person could avoid the estimation of a simple amount in cash, if he justifiably sticks out that this is a saving for the same amount of obligatory future consumption, i.e., the provision of professional utensils he has already ordered.

Thus, the administration has a very broad discretionary power to estimate the available resources for the coverage of every kind of need. When, for instance, specific productive exploitation or sale of the pieces of property is not ascertained, it is possible that the refusal of the administration to enter into a loan with his property as a guarantee can be considered as an unjustifiable shortage of cooperation.

§4. Conditions

284. The necessary conditions for the provisions of social assistance benefits and especially of minimum subsistence benefits are the existence of a legally protected person, the condition of social need and the ascertainment of the economic deficiency. The content of the second prerequisite is still to be evolved and we proceed to this task as follows.

The abstract notion of 'need' is not only a basic prerequisite of provision but also a measure of social assistance benefits estimation.

An objective approach of need, however, would lead to its notional standardization, since every now and then a social protection for new conditions of need or for old needs, which emerge with more intensive social or economic consequences, is imposed. The need has to be faced as an abstract legal notion, during which the administrative organs give the content, which better responds to the social assistance pursued aim. With such a consideration in the social assistance law at least the broader framework of 'need' can be impressed, as the real condition of a person, who is short in an absolute way or relative of the subsistence resources or the measures for the facing of specific social risks.

By Article 1§1 case a'–c' of the Legislative Decree 57/73, a relatively simple method of defining need has been chosen. The social protection is offered alternatively to the one, who is generally in financial weakness (poverty) or the one who is presumed to have a decreased working ability (invalidity, old age, etc.) or to the one who faces unfavourable consequences from unexpected events (disease, calamity, etc.). Therefore it suffices when somebody is deprived of the necessary supporting resources, so that the worth socially protecting for, the notion of need occurs. If there are no financial problems, 'need' for social assistance exists only in very specific cases of inability for facing unfavourable conditions or events.

The definition of need, as a prerequisite or as a measure of the social assistance benefits, is first located in the loss of the necessary means for tolerable support. In the minimum living resources, some fundamental amounts are included, as well as a specific income in cash and every other benefits from public or private resources. Especially, the means which are objectively needed for the cover of basic living needs are calculated, such as housing, nutrition, fundamental clothing, health. Such a catalogue can only be indicative. Important is how serious the poverty is under the specific conditions.

According to an opinion, the absolute financial need could be estimated with financial criteria, i.e., analogous to the real or presumed family income for every person. This quantitative estimation of poverty, which would derive from statistical elements, is not considered satisfactory because it does not simultaneously reveal the degree to which the persons feel the specific deprivation. Thus, the searching for a qualitative dimension in the problem of economical need seems necessary.

According to the most prevailing opinion for defining the notion of poverty, the special personal and family living conditions of the person have to be taken into consideration, in relation to the nature and the type of the specific financial problem. It is obvious that the priority of the subjective criteria for the choice among legal solutions, and the administration is supplied with a very broad discretionary power.

According to an intermediate opinion, the need from the shortage of support resources would initially be judged objectively, so that the human dignity of the interested is not insulted. The shortage, i.e., of 'sufficient' resources, according to Article 12§1 case a' section 3 of the Presidential Decree 112/89, will be justified, only when the exceeding of the previous limit is jeopardized, since all the persons have the tension to consider their resources inadequate. According to the most correct opinion, the poverty of a person derives from the objective comparison between the real economic situation and the given conditions in the social environment, if his dignity is not finally insulted.

285. The relevant scientific discussion about poverty seems to be orientated in coordination between objective and subjective criteria. Though abstract economic sizes are used for the engraving of the so-called poverty line (i.e., the half of the medium income per person), as personal poverty one defines the shortage of income from the fulfilment of fundamental needs, knowing that they are affected from a changeable social environment and from a different every time living model. Though the notion of poverty is formed from two at least changeable facts (the minimum income and the basic needs), in its relevant form appears narrower than the 'need', which is examined here, though in its absolute form, it does not differ from the notion of 'poverty', which is anticipated in Article 1§1 case a' of the Legislative Decree 57/73.

286. Apart from the economic need or weakness (poverty), two important groups of need are distinguished, i.e., difficulties of social and professional adjustment of the person: The ones who are connected with specific abilities or deficiencies of human nature and the ones which can happen to everyone from special events.

In the first group, 'the needs of the persons with decreased social, corporal or mental condition' are placed by the legislator (*see* Article 1§1 case b' of the Legislative Decree 57/73). Within this framework, more specialized needs are also placed, such as the needs of maternity, family, childhood, youth, the old aged, the invalid and some frail groups. The needs of these persons, who belong to this group, could be characterized as special and it is possible they occur with the more general support need of every poor person. Though the satisfaction of the special social assistance needs could regularly be realized with specialized social services, we ascertain that in the various social assistance programmes it is usually pursued with every available means.

In the second group, the temporal or permanent 'needs from unexpected events' are placed among them by the legislator, as inductively the disease, the calamity, etc. (*see* Article 1§1 case c' of the Legislative Decree 57/73). The characteristic of these special needs is that they are caused by extraordinary and imponderable events.

287. Apparently, the 'seriousness' of the social risk does not have integral value, if all the rest social assistance prerequisites occur. With this interpretative version, all the persons, who come to a condition of economic weakness and shortage of protection measures because of any event of an act of God would have the right to claim social aid. Despite this, and the advisability of more decentralization of the social services, Article 192§2 of Law 1065/80 confines the municipalities and the communities to provide subsistence and medical care species only to the financially weak residents, who face an urgent and 'serious' need. The prerequisites are made more difficult, and therefore, it is possible that someone will be excluded from a social assistance programme of local government; in this case, he has to invoke 'a special condition of emergency' and appeal to a possible special State help or by invoking 'poverty' to confine himself to our known prefectorial aid (*see* Article 1§1 case a' of Legislative Decree 57/73). However, help from the prefectorial government could be asked by Articles 21§2 and 23§1 case c' of Law 1622/86, since they cover more generally the persons with 'need of special protection', without any discrimination.

The social assistance protection is judged justifiable, only when real, present and direct needs occur. These three characteristics could be proposed also as necessary criteria for the 'social character' of this condition of need.

288. *Real* is a need, when it is ascertained in an objective way, irrespectively of the reasons, which caused it. The objective estimation of the need is not contrary to the principle of individualized social assistance protection. On the contrary, it is harmonized with it by providing necessary guarantees that the unfavourable occasions or the special deficiencies would be covered from the social assistance with indiscriminate consideration of more general and financial factors. The daily needs, for example, of an invalid, even if they seem insurmountable to him, acquire a 'social dimension' and justify the social assistance protection, from the moment they cause broader psychological problems of insecurity, isolation, etc.

289. Present is a need, when its unfavourable consequences continue to affect a person or a group at the time the social aid or action is provided. Consequently, the retrospective cover of needs is excluded, unless if responsibility of the social assistance organs is intermediated. These facts and the personal character of the right for social assistance exclude the claim of an heir for social assistance allowances, which have not been paid illegally before the death of the recipient. After the hereditary succession, the need can be characterized as present. This feature contributes, that all the social assistance provisions have a temporal character.

Direct is a need, when there is a causal nexus between the defective condition, which is covered by the social assistance provisions and the social reason for such a protection. An accident, i.e., without important causality with the condition of war of a certain period, does not lead to the establishment of a right to social aid in the form of a war pension.

Facing the condition of social need as a 'total' problem, not only as a simple material or other 'detriment', the resort to more effective social assistance measures is made easy. With the static consideration of the condition of social need, as a detriment, the social assistance protection would be confined to the reimbursement of the detriment, and the social services would be the target. On the contrary, with the functional notion of this need, as an expression of a problem, the social assistance benefits appear as a means for activation of the person or of the group, so that they would responsibly contribute to their family, professional or social replacement.

§5. Procedures

290. For the definition of the time starting point of social assistance, we have to examine, which is the legal importance of social assistance demand.

Tracing back to the various social assistance programmes, we form the impression that the procedure of offering social services starts with the application of the interested and only in exceptional cases with an ex officio administrative function.

In the application, the person usually declares his will for a specific type of social aid, but also the occurrence of the real events, which they prejudge it. The necessary justifying documents are also attached, i.e., confirmations and experts' opinions, for the verification of the content of the confirmations. With the help of the social assistance organs, the file is finally created, and the effective enacting of the right to social assistance depends on its complicity.

According to a widely accepted opinion, the social administration has to be activated, when it will be informed that the legal social assistance prerequisites occur, regardless of the submission or the content of the applications. The social assistance organs usually function ex officio, when they organize preventive services, and also when they control the effectiveness of the already provided benefits. Then an application makes easy the verification of the social assistance prerequisites. According to the same opinion, the object of a social assistance right does not change with the application, if it is, for example, submitted to incompetent organization or if it concerns an irrelevant social assistance benefit. It is yet natural that the application for social services, which are considered inappropriate or inexistable, does not have a de facto value.

291. However, a timely beginning of the procedure can be fulfilled, with an ex officio administrative action, since the usually justified ignorance or hesitance of the interested people is skated over. Later on, usually detainment is caused because of the reasonable doubt as far as the time point, the crucial real events of the protection prerequisites were perceivable, is concerned. The obligatory application for the use of social services with unfavourable consequences, i.e., institutional medical care, decreases theoretically the possibilities of infringing on personal rights, such as, omission of administrative hearing. Actually, the limited offer, in relation with the increased social assistance benefits, obliges the social administration to choose among suspended applications, since it is impossible to satisfy all of them. There are no adequate means for the ex officio search of the problems from social assistance organs with proper knowledge of the given social and financial needs.

Therefore, the opinion that every application has a proving character is absolute.

292. On the expression and the aim of a social assistance programme, it will depend, if the content of the application has a constituent character, and in this case, the application refers indirectly to a fundamental typical prerequisite of social assistance benefit or if it has a proving character, then it constitutes one of the ways of the beginning for the verification of the substantial protection prerequisites. In the first case, the submission of an application defines the ulterior time of the retroactive provision of a benefit. In the second case, it constitutes a simple contribution in the diagnostic procedure, before the issue of the administrative act, which would possibly approve the benefit. It is not impossible that the protection will be expanded to a prior period, which would apparently start from the time point when the administration had the knowledge for the type and the extent of the situation of 'need'.

The ex officio administrative intervention results to be obligatory, when the fulfilment of the social assistance aim runs the risk of being cancelled permanently, as, for example, when a systematic molestation of a minor is ascertained in a family. In such cases, the submission of an application for social assistance aid is not to be claimed, since hesitations for the type and the extent of the personal and social interest are not justified.

293. In the necessary contribution of the administered with the administration, apart from the provision of information and the subjection to diagnostic examinations, the contribution of the person or obliged to support his family members to the expenses of social assistance protection is usually included. Such an 'economical collaboration' with the administration is confined to the principle of proportionality. The partial economical charge for expensive and specialized social services would be tolerable, but not for every benefit of public interest. Moreover, serious reservations are expressed if the 'principle of contribution' of the guests in the expenses of the social services from the special charity institutions is permanent, though it seems to have atypically prevailed in Greece. It is, for instance, remarkable, how the law of supply and demand, as a general principle, has weakened the rights of the defective persons arising from Article 3 of the Legislative Decree 1111/72, which prohibited the payment of board fees, hospital and medical expenses or other exchanges to the charity institutions!

294. Which are the consequences of the violation of the procedure for social assistance benefits?

The cancellation or not of specific social services would depend on the pursued aim and the extent of the protected rights. When, for example, some persons behave antisocially and refuse to cooperate with the social workers for the programme against begging and vagrancy, then probably the temporal financial help for them and their families is imposed (by Article 7§§1 and 2 of the Legislative Decree 57/73) until the more effective organization of the specific social work. When the beneficiary of a social assistance benefit always keeps, for instance, vacant a social residence, instead of covering his residential needs, then the loss of his right is justified, as anticipated in Article 9§1 case c' of the Royal Decree 775/64.

The social assistance law applicant has to distinguish, when the temporal or permanent social services' deprivation would compose the legal consequence for the loss of establishment prerequisites, for illegal exercise (beginning or continuation) or for abuse of the social assistance right.

§6. Social Solidarity Income

I. Minimum Guaranteed Income Provisions

295.

(1) Income support
(2) Supplementary social services, benefits and goods if the members of the 'beneficiary unit' meet the criteria for the integration of each of the following programmes:
  - Free medical insurance for uninsured persons.
  - Referral and inclusion in social care and support structures and services.
  - Integration into programmes and social structures to tackle poverty.
  - Integration into the actions implemented under the Operational Programme of the European Aid Fund for the People.
  - Special Social electricity tariff.
  - Special Prices for Water Supply.
  - Social Prices for Municipalities and Municipal Enterprises.

(3) Members capable of work: members of the 'beneficiary unit' activation services to promote their integration or reintegration into the labour market and these services may include, among others:
- Covering a proposed job.
- Participation in welfare projects.
- Participation in vocational training programmes.
- Participation in professional experience acquisition programmes.
- Integration or return to the education and second chance schools.

(4) Members incapable of work: those who are unable to work are considered to be household members belonging to the following categories:
- People with disabilities who, according to the Disability Certification Committee's opinion, have been judged incapable of work.
- Full-time students, trainees of vocational schools or those practising in the context of a vocational training programme without an employment relationship.
- Job-seekers: they are the beneficiaries of the age of 18 to 65 who do not work and who do not belong to the above categories.

II. Eligibility for the Programme

296.

(a) One-person household: any adult person who lives in his own home and does not belong to the age group of up to 25 years attending university or national or foreign schools or institutes of vocational education or training.

(b) Multi-person household: all people living under the same roof including: (i) hosted persons or family, provided that the hospitality was declared in the latest income tax statement; (ii) adult children up to 25 years of age attending university or vocational training schools or institutes; or training, irrespective of their place of residence; (iii) homeless people: people living on the street or at inappropriate accommodation, provided they have been registered by the social services of municipalities or Community Centres.

Programme exclusions: the following categories are excluded and are not considered as members of the household:
- Persons who are housed or cared for in closed care units or on residential living roofs or in hospitals for transitional homeless hosting.
- Persons who are housed in psychological rehabilitation units (boarding houses, hostels, etc.) or are beneficiaries of the Protected Apartments programme of No. 9 of Law 2716/1999.
- Persons hosted in monasteries.
- Persons detained in prisons.

III. Guaranteed Amount

297. The amount guaranteed by the programme for each household depends on the number and age of its members, and the payment of minimum guaranteed income. The guaranteed amount is defined as follows:

- For single-person households: EUR 200 per month.
- For each additional adult member of the household: an increase of the guaranteed amount by EUR 100 per month is provided.
- For each minor member of the household: an increase of the guaranteed amount by EUR 50 per month is provided.
- In a single-parent household, the oldest member is counted as an adult.
- In a household with an unprotected child, for the purposes of calculating the guaranteed amount, each unprotected child is considered an adult.

The maximum guaranteed amount is EUR 900 per month, irrespective of the composition of the household.

The declared income does not include: (a) the allowance of the provision of Article 9 of Law 2082/92; (b) non-contributory invalidity allowances granted by the State; (c) the financial support granted under paragraph 1(c) of Article 1(1) of the Legislative Decree No. 57/1973 (d) and the allowance paid to unemployed persons under paragraph 5 of Article 5(1) of Law 57/1973 (A '149) to those who are in a state of emergency as a result of natural disasters and other natural disasters (Article 30 of Law 4144/2013 (A-88).

IV. Eligibility of Households

298. (1) Income criteria:

The declared household income, as calculated for the purposes of joining the scheme, during the six months preceding the submission of the application, may not exceed six times the guaranteed amount for each type of household.

For each additional member, six times the corresponding guaranteed amount is added. The declared earnings may not exceed EUR 5,400, irrespective of the number of household members.

299. (2) Property Criteria:

(a) Real Estate:

The total taxable value of the household's property may not exceed the total of EUR 90,000 for the single-person household, increased by EUR 15,000 for each additional member and up to EUR 150,000.

(b) Mobile property:

- The objective cost of private cars (private cars), mixed-use cars (HX) and/or household bicycles may not exceed EUR 6,000 in total.

- The total amount of household deposits and/or the current value of shares, bonds, etc., as derived from electronic crossovers, may not exceed the limits in the table below for each type of household, up to and including the amount of EUR 14,400.

(c) Asset presumption:

The total amount of interest on deposits of household members in all domestic or foreign credit institutions as declared in the latest income tax statement (E1) must not exceed annually the amount resulting from the following mathematical formula:

Annual interest = deposit limit for each household type * average annual interest rate for deposit/100

The year of calculation of the average deposit interest rate is defined as the latest income tax statement.

No claims are received from households whose members, on the basis of the latest income tax statement:

- fall under the provisions of the luxury tax;
- declare costs for crew pay for recreational craft;
- declare costs for tuition fees in private schools;
- declare expenditure for domestic helpers, drivers, teachers and other staff as identified in the corresponding codes in Form E1.

300. (3) Residence criteria

Households reside legally and permanently in the Greek territory.

Income support is paid monthly by credit to a beneficiary's bank account, which is mandatory for a credit institution operating in Greece participating in the programme, within the last five calendar days of each month. The aid is not paid if the applicant has not stated in the application for membership of the CRL bank account number to which it is the beneficiary or co-beneficiary. In the event that the total amount paid is equal to or greater than EUR 100 per month, 50% shall be spent exclusively by using a payee's prepaid bank card, which may be used without any limitation on any purchase (including e-pet purchases) or payment.

There is no possibility to withdraw cash from the prepaid bank card. For the remaining 50%, it is possible to withdraw cash from ATMs of credit institutions via a bank branch of the credit institution that the account holder holds a bill and/or a debit card.

The entitlement to the payment of the income support is valid from the first day of the month following that in which the application was made. The minimum amount to be paid is EUR 10 per month.

After six months from the adoption of the authorization, the beneficiary may re-submit an application for inclusion in the programme.

V. Procedure

301. The supporting documents submitted, as appropriate, to the Municipalities or Community Centres in accordance with the provisions of Article 4 herein are:

(1) If the permanent residence of the household is different from that shown by the results of the electronic crossings, it is required: (a) for accommodation in a private residence, the presentation of a contract documenting the ownership and the public utility (DEKO) account, (b) for accommodation in a rented residence, the production of a copy, (c) for a stay in a free-of-charge residence, to be declared in the latest income tax return statement and the presentation of a DEKO account.

In the case of homeless people, a certificate of use of the services by a Dormitory is required or certified by the Social Service of the Municipality or the Community Centre.

(2) If the composition of the household is different from that shown by the results of the electronic crossings, it is necessary to present any supporting documents substantiating the change (e.g., birth certificate, death certificate).

(3) If any asset has changed in relation to what appears from the results of the electronic crossings, it is necessary to present to the Municipality or the Community Centre any documentation substantiating the change (sale or purchase contracts, donation or seizure). It is not possible to provide supporting documents for evidence of a change in household interest.

(4) If the applicant or adult member of the household is a foreigner, a residence permit in force or a certificate of filing a renewal application is required.

(5) In the case of a household with minor children for whom the conditions for attending compulsory education, as defined in the applicable legislation, are met, a certificate of enrolment/attendance at the school is required to certify that this requirement is met. For each subsequent application in the programme, after the completion of the first aid period approved under the present conditions, a certificate of attendance of underage children is required for compulsory education. These certificates may be provided either by the head teacher or by the Head of the School Unit or electronically via the interconnection of the CEA's IT systems and the Ministry of Education, Research and Religious Affairs.

(6) The next E1 tax form should include all changes reported during the application process. Otherwise, provision is made for discontinuation of the programme, in accordance with Article 9, and the repayment of undue payments.

Social Income of Solidarity is tax exempted, is not subject to any detention, is not credited or offset by already established debts to the State, individuals or credit institutions and is not added to the income for the payment of any social or welfare benefits.

§7. Minimum Pension for Uninsured Persons

302. To all uninsured people over the age of 67, a generalized means-tested monthly welfare benefit is granted, which is entirely financed by the State. It is the so-called social solidarity benefit for the non-insured elderly. This amounts today to EUR 360 and can be updated through Ministerial Decisions. The entitled persons should not have other pension rights or receive other insurance or welfare benefits from Greece or abroad. They should have legally and continuously resided in Greece for at least fifteen years before applying. Their individual yearly taxed income should not exceed EUR 4,320, and their family taxed income should not exceed double that amount. Furthermore, the value of their taxable real estate should not exceed EUR 90,000, and the value of their mobile property should be the amount of EUR 6,000. Once the entitlement conditions have been fulfilled, the solidarity benefit is fully paid for those who have resided in the country for at least thirty-five years. Otherwise, there is a reduction of 1/35 for each missing year of residence.

§8. Organizational Structure

303. From the organization of social assistance, services depend not only on the extent of the discretionary power of the people who offer them but also on the effective legal protection of persons who need them. In fact, the latter can claim a quantitative and qualitative sufficiency of the services only from organizations and organs, which are recipients of the social assistance benefit. Despite the need for clear organizational structures of the social services, so that their various types are promoted from the most proper organizations, usually complicated organizational forms evolve in practice. Therefore, it is natural that an important shortage of coordination among the various organizations of social policy is accused and also gaps or overlapping of competencies are taking place.

304. Let us proceed with the evaluation of the usual organizational forms of the social assistance organizations in Greece.

The social assistance organizations, i.e., the organizations of the persons and means with integral administration for the realization of the social assistance aims, are distinguished in organizations of public or private social services. The first consist of central and peripheral public services, entities of public law and local authority organizations, whereas the second consist of charity institutions or associations, labour unions, cooperatives, as well as enterprise or business organizations (*see* L. 2345/95 concerning the organized welfare services by the institutions of social assistance). In addition, the social assistance work of the church evolved to a great extent from entities of private or public law, which are supervised by the Athens Holy Archbishopric and the Holy Bishoprics.

Social assistance is directly offered by the public administration and by the organized private initiative, as their main or additional mission. It can also be offered indirectly, and then usually contracts with third people, who are regarded as capable of its realization, are constituted. When a form of social protection is evolved, one cannot refer to an integral social assistance organization, if the specific social aid or action is offered occasionally and temporarily or on behalf of an organizational group which did not correspond to the basic characteristics of the social assistance institution.

305. The structure of the fundamental organizational social services depends on their type, i.e., social work services, services for family protection, etc. Advantages and disadvantages from every one of these choices emerge, but the second one seems more effective. In fact, the modern social and economical needs are so complicated, that their interscientific facing seems absolutely necessary. Therefore, it is not necessary for the social assistance organizations to emphasize only the ensuring, i.e., the special social services. The simple reception of defected persons, before they are sent for individualized care is of great importance. Thus, not only the professional specialization starts to come first, during the facing of urgent cases of need, but also the coordination of the various professions, which have to collaborate obligatorily. Therefore, the organization and the function of the integral social assistance organizations had to be gradually directed towards this direction.

306. With centralized, organized social assistance organizations, a uniform social action of performing character sufficiently evolves, as in the low-levelled social services from no specialized executives (see the provision of calamity victims with material surviving means). On the contrary, with a decentralized organization, the offer of the services for facing poverty is made easy. Since they are usually local cases, the local organizations are facilitated to control the income or fortune deficiency. As far as the high-levelled social services are concerned, there is a limited demand, so their provision in broader peripheries is justified. They are, actually, provided with implicit contracts, according to the supposed free will of the contracted persons. Since they are actually accession contracts, with conditions, which are imposed unilaterally by the organization of social services, they have to be interpreted basically according to the protection of the person. In that way, some guarantees of effective social assistance cover are established in the cases where the intense dependencies are not inevitable, as in the institutionalized care.

307. After an estimation of the peculiarities between the various organizations' forms and the threatened interests of the defective persons, the diagnosis of 'need' is *de lege ferenda* proposed to be entrusted to public organizations with guarantees of objectivity, whereas the provision of benefits to public or private organizations according to the importance of the equal distribution or quantitative sufficiency to the specific social services. Some isolated applications of this opinion are located, as with the competence of the Prefecture to characterize a calamity as 'catastrophe' so that 'every suitable mean' for the salvage of the area will be activated, according to Articles 2§1 and 3§1 case a' of the Legislative Decree 857/71.

The effectiveness of the benefits in cash depends almost exclusively on the emphasis, which is given to the social policy of allowances (with retrospective assistance of the social assistance accounts), regardless of organizational structures. On the contrary, the definition and the evaluation of the organizational forms, which promote better personal social assistance services (i.e., in the consulting centres), is difficult. The public social assistance organization facilitates the approach to these services of a big part of the population. However, there are risks of shortage of protection in periods of decrease in the social expenses, then the social assistance organs have to face social problems using more economic criteria. The functional cost plays an important role in the systematic social assistance benefits from the private initiative. In that case, guarantees are legislated, that the benefits offered will be at least of medium quality (*see* Article 289§2 of the Civil Code).

Consequently, it is emphasized that the epoch of competition between the social services from the public or private sector is towards its end. The public social assistance organization acquires competition elements by entrusting partially the completion of its mission to unavailable social services, though the last ones are usually based on a State subsidy to be maintained approachable to the general public.

308. It is, however, worth mentioning that regarding the field of the organizational structures of social assistance in Greece, important progress was made in 1998, when Law 2646/98 was introduced regarding the organization and function of the national system of social assistance. By virtue of this law, a system for social assistance was actually established in Greece for the first time. Under the aforementioned law, with the aim of a simplification in the field of social assistance, *inter alia,* institutions of social assistance were merged and a legal entity of public law was founded, having as a goal the realization of programmes of the services, which were unified.

Finally, according to Law 4520/2018, OPEKA was established and provides welfare benefits and social services for economic and social support and integration to vulnerable groups of the population and implements the welfare actions and programmes of the Ministry of Labour, Social Insurance and Social Solidarity.

Part XI. Claims and Adjudications

§1. Administrative Dispute Settlement

I. In Social Insurance

309. The directors of the E-EFKA (since 2020, ETEAEP merged with E-EFKA) issue administrative acts concerning the affiliation to insurance, award of benefits, payment of contributions. They act either ex officio or after an application. They can convey a part of their competencies, with their reversible decisions, to other organs of their services. If a remedy application is not exercised against these administrative acts for possible flaws of the decision, in a specific deadline from its legal notice, then it becomes final.

310. Against the former acts, an administrative appeal can be exercised, in three months, if it is for a right to pension, at the Local Administrative Committee (TDE), which resides in every E-EFKA Office and it consists of representatives of the State, of the insured and of the employers. The Local Administrative Committee looks into the case but the administrative act is not obligatorily suspended. The whole case is transferred to the Local Administrative Committee and its real and legal part is judged from the beginning, without, however, being possible to conclude a worse decision. The meetings of the committees are not public, but their decisions have to be completely justified.

More special procedures are anticipated in several pieces of legislation. Thus, the arising disputes between the insured and the insurance organizations or between the insurance organizations for the application of the successive insurance regulations (Legislative Decree 4202/61) are solved with decisions of the Minister of Labour Social Insurance and Social Solidarity after an opinion of the Social Insurance Council which resides in the same Ministry.

II. In Social Assistance

311. For the timely prevention and the administrative resolving of the disputes from the social assistance, regulations of supervision and control of the various social assistance organs have been established and also regulations of re-examination of their decisions. However, the complete enumeration of the cases would exceed the limits of our research.

In the measures of administrative supervision, the replacement (with a common Ministerial Decision) of the members of the Administrative Council of a public welfare institution can be placed among (Article 99§3 of the Legislative Decree 2039/39), when they violate their obligations, so they indirectly make difficult the establishment or the exercise of the social assistance rights. In the initial stage of the receipt of mutual rights and obligations, it is possible that the appointment of an administrative council at the Specially Acknowledged Charity Associations (Article 14 of the Legislative Decree 1111/72) and the anticipation of an administrative council in the Old Aged Homes and in the Hospitals of Chronic Ailments (Article 11 of Legislative Decree 162/73) it is possible to contribute to the prevention of serious disputes.

By historically estimating these two supervision measures, we conclude that they were more established for the promotion of a doubtful public or social interest rather than for the establishment of a continual collaboration between the administration and the administrated for the prevention of the disputes.

312. The internal control of the public social assistance organizations is caused by all the established forms of administrative appeals, which are expressions of the fundamental personal right to appeal (Article 10§1 of the Constitution). The administrative appeal from Article 8§1 of Law 3200/55, which is exercised against decisions of the Prefecture before the competent minister, is of great importance because of its generality and juridical character. This appeal is confined to a nullifying legality control of the social assistance decision. Due to its nature, this appeal has, however, to be preceded so that the exercise of a relative nullifying application before courts will be admissible, we stress the steady jurisprudence version, according to which the public administration has an obligation to inform the citizens (Article 20§1 of the Constitution) for the possibility, the deadline and the legal consequences from the omission of an administrative protection mean.

313. Sometimes, the possibility for re-judgment of a specific prerequisite of the right to social assistance is anticipated, for example, the existence of the necessary type and invalidity degree. The person either appeals by himself or he is ex officio sent to an anticipated regulative procedure of a second-degree judgment, for example, to a second-degree health committee. So perspectives of a new substantial judgment of all the tension points between the social administration and the recipient of social assistance benefits.

The regular or irregular review of the social assistance protection actions is not actually a control mechanism, but a re-establishment of the right to social assistance to new legal or real facts. Such a re-establishment cannot be equated with common therapy applications. The later change of the circumstances has contributed so that the same case cannot be judged again. On the contrary, the revocation of a social assistance administrative action, for example, for reasons of the illusion of the competent organs, can be characterized as an administrative appeal, with the form of a simple reference, so then it is possible to be placed among the methods of out-of-court resolving of the social assistance disputes. However, the various cases of review cause confusion, so their regulation with special procedural rules is advisable.

314. Among the specialists, who deal theoretically with social services, some methods for more effective out-of-court protection are starting to get crystallized and be proposed.

Referring to the organization of procedures for the avoidance of creation of disputes, measures are proposed for supporting the supervision and the contribution of the representatives of the interested people to the taking of decisions and also measures for the evaluation of the services in the stage of programming.

With reference to the procedures for the resolving of real disputes, the unified or different, first or second degree, forms of optional intervention and arbitration from personal or collective organs with increased virtues of impartiality are proposed as necessary. Moreover, the establishment of special and clear procedural rules is supported for the examination of the administrative appeals with more guarantees of objectivity.

Which types of intervention and arbitration and which types of administrative appeals would finally prevail in Greece, that is a matter of social policy, which exceeds the framework of this research.

315. The juridical resolving of the conflicts between social insurance and social assistance has common characteristics, granted that it is mainly a resolving of the administrative disputes which is realized according to the administrative justice rules (*see* indicatively Law 702/77, Presidential Decree 341/78, Law 1406/83, Presidential Decree 18/89 and Law 1868/89).

In the following, we are confined to some subjects, which show a special theoretical and practical interest in our opinion.

§2. Legal Appeals

316. Before the appeal at the courts, the interested person has to use up all the margins for timely administrative settlement of his dispute, as it is defined in Article 7§3 of Law 702/77. It has also acknowledged an obligation of the social-insurance organizations (from Article 20§1 of the Constitution) to inform the interested in the possibility of exercising an administrative measure, its deadline and the consequences of its omission (Decision of StE 3168/88, published in EDKA 1988, p. 763). The administrative court rejecting an appeal as inadmissible – for not exercising an administrative measure – it controls ex officio the possible omission of information of the interested person and offers a reasonable time for its exercising, which starts from the legal notice of the juridical decision (Decision of the StE 3163/88, published in DEN 1989, p. 805).

317. The juridical resolving of the dispute for the offering, the type or the extent of the benefit from the social insurance or from the social assistance is a matter of the regular administrative courts. These initially control the substantial and legal validity of the claims in the two degrees. After the exercise of an appeal or a legal reimbursement action, the Administrative Court looks into the case and after an appeal, the Administrative Court of Appeal, if it is an administrative dispute of substance. At the last degree, the legality of the claims is judged by StE after an exercise of the juridical measure of cassation application. The same court judges at the first and last degree, after the exercise of the juridical measure of the nullifying application, if it is an invalidating administrative dispute.

So then a question arises, when does the judge has the power to simply nullify the illegal actions or omissions of the social administration, by contributing indirectly to the formation of the relevant right and when he is able to change them and also convict the competent organization to materialize the acknowledged content of the right and to compensate the caused detriment.

318. Expressis verbis, the characterization of an administrative dispute as substantial or nullifying, finally depends on the possible necessary techniques and scientific judgments, and also on the possible broadened hierarchical administrative control. Where such judgments have to precede the existence of a substantial administrative dispute and the burden of the judge to control substantially the real events would be futile to be acknowledged. The broader the hierarchical control of the social administration is anticipated, the greater the difficulty for re-estimation of the dispute within the framework of a substantial juridical judgment. Even, when a dispute is acknowledged as nullifying, i.e., subjected to a limited (only nullifying) administrative control, it is not actually cancelled, the actionability of the relevant social right is simply decreasing.

319. So, there has to be indicated that in the competence of the State Audit Council as an administrative court, the judgment of disputes, relatively with the establishment and the extent of the right for pensions for civil servants, according to the regulations and the legislation of the civil servants after the exercise of special juridical means, is affiliated (Decision of StE 481/1989, published in EDKA 1989, p. 594, Decision of the Athens Administrative Court 4523/88, published in EDKA 1989, p. 543).

The juridical measures which are anticipated by our legislation differ analogously to the type and the extent of the juridical protection. It is admitted that if they are exercised according to Law 702/77 before the Administrative Court of First Degree as appeals, instead of being exercised before StE as nullifying applications or controversially, they are not rejected as appeals which do not lie, but they are sent to the competent court, so that confusions or delays are not caused from their variety (Decision of StE 1300/90, published in EDKA 1990, p. 532, *see also* Articles 2 of Law 702/77 and 4 of the Presidential Decree 341/78).

The offended or his legal representative can enact an appeal against the competent organization, with the submission that 'an owed legal action' is omitted when there is no answer to a specific protection claim (Article 19§2 case a' of the Presidential Decree 341/78). The so-called social appeal is enacted in sixty days from the refusal of the organization to satisfy the demand. If three months pass from the submission of the relevant application, the inertia of the administrative organization is regarded as implicit refuse. If the omission of the administrative organ is nullified, the court sends the case to the administration for the promotion of the issue of the proper administrative act (Article 56§3 of the Presidential Decree 341/78).

The offended has the right of social appeal when clear refusal of the organizations to fulfil a specific benefit is ascertained or when the organizations proceed to its false performance. For the reverse of the negative administrative act, the defendant has to submit specific reasons: incompetence, violation of a substantial type or of a substantial legal regulation, false estimation of the facts, false use of the discretionary power or abuse of power. Then also, the deadline of sixty days is in force, but it starts from the following day the infringed act was legally notified or published (Article 21§1 case a' of the Presidential Decree 341/78).

If the appeal is accepted, the content of the right to benefit is defined by the court, by nullifying or amending the relevant administrative act. The extent of the juridical control is an object of discussion also in these cases. Finally, a discrimination is done, so that the independence of the Executive is not violated by the administrative courts: if the refusal or the deficient offer of benefits which belongs to the binding competence of the administrative organs is judged illegal, then it is abolished and properly amended by the juridical decision. It is enough, if it is such a specialized demand, that a simple material action or omission of the administration (for the provision of a specific insurance benefit or for the cover of a specific social or economical need) would be enough. But if the illegal administrative behaviour belongs to its discretionary power, the court only nullifies it and follows a new – substantially independent – administrative judgment.

The court has usually the power to nullify the illegal administrative act or omission, if it is a nullifying administrative dispute and the juridical control has been caused by a nullifying application from Article 45 of the Presidential Decree 18/89.

320. Apart from the appeal, the offended can ask for the reimbursement of a possible material or other detriments from violations of the social legislation, by filing before the regular administrative courts the legal measure of the reimbursement action (from the regulations of Articles 7§5 of Law 702/77, 1§2 and 24 following of the Presidential Decree 341/78 and 19§1 of Law 1868/89, in combination with Articles 105 and 106 of the Introductive Law of the Civil Code for the civil responsibility of the Public and Article 297 of the Civil Code). The juridical control is then expanded to the acknowledgement of the violated right, of the definition of the detriment, but also the conviction of the administration to reimburse it.

321. It is obvious that the demand of the recipient of insurance or social assistance benefit for the compensation of a specific financial detriment is materialized without a special – at least theoretical – problem of administrative coercion. On the contrary, the demand for the provision of specific social services for the actual compensation of another (abstract) detriment meets with some problems. These can be insuperable, when, for example, they are sick assistance benefits, which are offered exclusively by the public or from the private sector, with prohibitive prices. So the juridical, administrative coercion to compensate the in natural detriment of the recipient, is not only dependent on the degree of the specialization for the protection but also on its type and its aim. The social services lose their meaning, when the administration, after some time, is convicted to satisfy surviving meets without the possibility of enforcement.

322. Initially, with the reimbursement action, only the detriment exceeding the one covered by the appeal could be compensated. Demands which were satisfied with an appeal could not be an object of reimbursement action (Decision of StE 4403/88, published in EDKA 1989, p. 224, Decision of StE 2238/88, published in EDKA 1988, p. 690, Decision of the Athens Administrative Court of First Degree 14126/88, published in EDKA 1989, p. 621). After Article 19§1 of Law 1868/89, the reimbursement action before the administrative courts was established as an independent juridical measure in relation to the appeal, the nullifying application or other juridical measures against the administrative acts or omissions from which the claim for reimbursement can be enacted unilaterally after a free choice of the interested person.

The reimbursement action can be regularly enacted within five years from the illegal act or omission of the administrative organs (*see* Article 250 case 17 of the Civil Code). In cases of refuse or delay of the protection, the prescription starts from the clear refusal or from the reasonable waiting time after the application, though in cases of false fulfilment, from the moment which the offended is informed of the extent and the response of the detriment (Article 937 of the Civil Code).

Relative to the proving procedure, it has been judged that the witnesses before deciding organs of IKA are legal probating measures from the administrative procedure before the deciding organ and the Local Probating Committee. The administrative courts are also taken into consideration evidence according to the special procedure of Article 49 of the Presidential Decree 341/78 (*see* Decision of StE1379/88, published in EDKA 1988, p. 507). In addition, the administrative courts owe to claim for experts' opinions, especially justified and to possibly send the cases to the known committees for further clarification justification. In no case, the insurance organs and the administrative courts cannot express their own judgment on subjects of medical nature (Decision of StE 490/89, published in the IKA Review 1989, p. 1009).

323. When there are, at the verification of the prerequisites or at the provision of an illegal benefit, responsible violations, the interested can bring a charge against the competent civil servant for 'duty violation' before a penal court (Article 259 of the Civil Code). According to this regulation, there has to be the intention of the civil servant not only for the duty violation but also for the additional effects of the 'illegal profit' or of the 'detriment' of the other people's fortune. So the practical importance of this drastic measure of juridical protection is substantially decreased. However, the refusal of the competent insurance organ to comply with a court decision for the distribution of an insurance benefit has been correctly characterized as 'duty violation' (Order of the Piraeus Magistrates' Committee 677/82, published in EDKA 1982, p. 681).

324. It is a fact that in daily practice, illegal administrative actions are juridically reversed (they are nullified or amended) because of omission or insufficiency of legal reasoning most of the times. When the clear regulations for the reasoning of administrative acts are not maintained, for example, the rules for the reasoning of permissions of establishment and function of Private Old Aged Homes or Hospitals of Chronic Ailments, the juridical control is located in the complaint of the omission of a substantial type. When there is no reasoning which suits the nature of the act, for example, in the case of the financial aid of poor people, the control concerns the relevant violation of substantial law (*see* retrospectively Article 53§2 case b' and c' of the Presidential Decree 341/78 and 48§§2 and 3 of the Presidential Decree 18/89, in combination with Articles 7§3 of the Legislative Decree 162/73 and 1§2 case b' of the Legislative Decree 57/73). It has also been accepted that the substantial judgment of the administrative court as far as the acknowledgement of the insurance invalidity is concerned is not reversed with a cassation before the StE, unless if the proper reasoning is omitted (Decision of StE 4206/88, published in DEN 1989, p. 868).

From the former general forms of judicial resolving of the disputes, it finally arises that the control of the social administration is taking place in every extent is imposed from the substantial and legal validity of the complaints and the special nature of the specific case of need.

§3. Jurisprudence on Pension Cuts

325. Decisions on the constitutionality as well as on the compatibility of international treaties that the country has ratified in relation to pension cuts have been issued by the State Audit Council (having jurisdiction over civil servant pensions) and the Council of State (having jurisdiction over all other pensions).

Both the Council of State and the State Audit Council have not actually examined the pension cuts on the basis of equality, legal certainty, protected trust, proportionality, etc. They have stood only in the absence of actuarial studies and of studies on their economic and social impact. The Council of State jurisprudence on this issue even presents an ambiguity, as explained below.

326. The first in chronological order is the decision 668/2010 of the Council of State (Plenary Session), which accepts the constitutionality of the cuts in the laws of 2010–2011 on the grounds that they are temporary measures that serve the public interest, that the State did not have much time and was obliged to respond immediately. The European Convention on Human Rights (ECHR), examining *ADEDY and Koufakis v. Greece,* makes reference to this decision, reproduces its rationale and therefore 'validates' it.

327. Subsequently, the decisions of Council of State 2287/2015 (Plenary Session) were issued. They accept that the measures of Law 4093/2012 (pension cuts) are unconstitutional, as they have been issued without actuarial and economic and social impact studies. In particular, the Council of State considered that pension cuts as a fiscal measure are unconstitutional unless they are accompanied by an economic study of their consequences for the 'impoverishment' of pensioners, taking into account all the taxes and burdens that pensioners have suffered because of the economic crisis.

The decision states that: 'In the first two years of the crisis (2010–2012), the State has taken a series of measures to reduce public spending, including cuts in pensions. These provisions are not contrary to the Constitution and the ECHR. On the other hand, the arrangements introduced after 2012, after two years have elapsed since the initial surprise of the economic crisis and the planification of the measures to deal with it, are not in line with the Constitution, because the legislator did not, as he should, an assessment of the factors that caused the problem, nor did he evaluate the advantages and disadvantages of these measures. This was necessary because the measures the legislator had taken did not work and the economic recession intensified. Even if these measures were justified, the legislator had to decide on their necessity by examining the existence of alternatives and comparing the benefits and disadvantages of each one with the aims pursued. The legislator had to consider whether the impact of the cuts on the living standards of those affected, combined with the impact of tax burdens, led to an unacceptable reduction in their standard of living. The legislator is required to adopt the necessary measures by documentation, planning and in accordance with the principles of fairness, equality, proportionality, solidarity and reciprocity. This rationale is linked to decisions by international organizations against Greece and the findings of the National Commission on Human Rights.'

328. Shortly thereafter, the Council of State, with the decision (p. 734/2016), which refers to the cuts in lump-sum benefits, accepts that: 'Because the disputed cuts are based on the law and, together with the cuts in primary and supplementary pensions, are part of a wider programme on the one hand to restore the country's fiscal balance and, on the other hand, to reform the social security system, for its viability, a reform which finds its foundation in Article 22(5) of the Constitution, the introduction of such cuts serves public interest purposes and not just the cash interest of the State and the social insurance institutions. The macroeconomic data (both financial and non-fiscal) set out in the explanatory memorandum that the viability of the Greek social security system for workers, which also includes lump-sum retirement benefit providers, would be impracticable without the adoption of medium-term budgetary and without the long-term structural reform of the institution. Therefore, the specific legislative choice, which was manifested in the above provisions and forms part of the financial and structural aspect of the insurance reform (as opposed to the purely structural one), is duly justified, and otherwise falls outside the scope of judicial review, which is only to overcome the extreme logical limits of the concept of the public interest' (Council of State 1094, 2289/1987). The minority's position is largely identical to the decision 2287/2015 and the reasoning of the Council of Europe.

The plenary session of the State Audit Council follows the same reasoning as the Council of State and it is clear that the above actuarial studies and economic and social impact assessments regarding the wider fiscal planning are required. (*See* plenary decision No. 244/2017, minutes of its 2nd Special Session of 8 May 2017 and the minutes of the 1st Special Plenary Session of 20 April 2016, p. 46).

329. On 6 October 2017, two sets of applications for annulment against Law 4387/2016 were discussed in the Council of State (Plenary Session). The first concerns the cuts and recalculations of pensions and the second concerns the change in the method of calculating contributions especially for self-employed, liberal professionals and farmers. The basic argument of the Ministry of Labour, Social Insurance and Social Solidarity in these trials in relation to the argument that no actuarial studies were made is that they are not required to be made on the basis of the most recent decision of the Council of State 734/2015. In relation to the economic and social impact studies, the Ministry claimed that pensions are much higher than the minimum pensions provided for in the international conventions ratified by the country, and therefore, there is no question of the impoverishment of pensioners.

The Ministry of Labour, Social Insurance and Social Solidarity also argued that the pensioners are less affected by poverty than other categories of the population during the crisis. The Ministry also stressed that the principle of social solidarity requires poorer pensioners to be more protected and that wealthier pensioners only should suffer pension cuts.

Decisions were expected to be adopted in early 2019. The very long delay must be observed. However, before the publication of the decisions, the government amended the legislation on self-employed, liberal professionals and farmers' contributions under the aforementioned Law 4578/2018, accepting in practice the applicants' allegations of unconstitutionality.

With the Decision 1880/2019 of Plenary, the Council of State accepted that since the self-employed and liberal professionals do not have an employer charged with paying part of their contributions (in particular employed and civil servants pay just one-third of their contributions while the State or the employer pay the rest), they must pay the whole contribution, i.e., three times more than the employed or the civil servants, for access to social insurance. This is contrary to the principle of equality because both categories (employed and non-employed) have the same pensions and benefits.

In compliance with this decision of the Council of State, Law 4670/2020 redefined the contributions for self-employed and liberal professionals, from 1 January 2020, amending the relevant articles of Law 4387/2016.

Law 4670/2020, by amending Article 36 of Law 4683/2016 and adding Article 36A, bifurcated the categories of employed/civil servants, on the one hand, and non-employed/liberal professionals, on the other, and introduced insurance categories with different characteristics for the latter. The employed and the civil servants still pay one-third of their salary in order to contribute to main and supplementary pensions, health care, lump-sum benefits and insurance in case of unemployment. However, the self-employed, liberal professionals can currently select any of the insurance categories provided by law depending on the characteristics they prefer and pay the whole contribution specified for the particular category.

With the Decision 1880/2019 of Plenary, the Council of State accepted that further, with the Decision 1892/2019, the Council of State ruled that the replacement rates for over thirty insurance years should be increased and that the compensation rate for forty years of work cannot be less than 50% of the pensionable earnings. Hence, the calculation of the contributory pension needed to change. Law 4670/2020 finally increased lightly the replacement rates.

330. Regarding pensions recalculation, in December 2018, the government introduced Law 4583/2018 entitled 'Repeal of provisions on the reduction of pensions, etc.'. According to this law, 'From 1st January 2019, if the amount paid of these pensions (already paid pensions until the entry into force of Law 4387/2016, as of 31 December 2014 in accordance with the provisions in force at that time) is higher than that resulting from their calculation in accordance with paragraph 1, the additional amount shall continue to be paid to the beneficiary annually and until it is set off by the increase in retirement pensions due to the supposed improvement of the economy'. The law does not cover pensions issued after the entry into force of Law 4387/2016 and thereafter.

According to the explanatory memorandum to that law, the reduction of pension is a budgetary and not a structural measure. Based on the principle of protected trust and in view of the fact that the governmental fiscal targets have been achieved and in the future, the state's budget fiscal surplus is expected in the future to increase due to the supposed improvement of the labour market and economy, this reduction of pension should not be implemented. However, if the reason for introducing the reduction in pensions was simply budgetary, then the question of the viability of the insurance system still remains. Especially if there is no actuarial study that guarantees its viability and the employment data kept by the ERGANE system demonstrate that both the average and the median earnings are falling, the labour market converges to the minimum wage and the jobs created are low productivity, low-skilled and in low-wage sectors (*see* BSE Special Report on Economy and Enterprise, Future of Work, November 2018, p. 22). In fact, the system is not viable by itself but it is supported and funded through harsh taxation and contributions, which in turn impede economic development leading the country into a vicious cycle. If, on the other hand, the reduction of pensions was a structural measure (as we believe and Law 4387/2016 explains in its explanatory memorandum by referring to the need for equality, especially among those who have retired before the entry into force of the law and those who retire later), then the measure of non-implementation of pension reductions in view of the informal election period in the country and the international circumstances raises further questions.

Selected Bibliography

Bibliography in Greek

Social Insurance

Agallopoulos Chr. *Social Insurance Schemes*. 1955.
Amitsis, G. *The Judicial Establishment of Subsistence Standards Within the Greek and International Legal Order*. 2001.
EPIKAYP. *Pandect of Social Security Case-Law* (2 volumes). 1997.
EPIKAYP. *Simplification and Systematisation of Social Protection Rules* (in English). 1996.
EPIKAYP. *Social Security Clauses in Collective Labour Agreements and Social Dialogue*. 1996.
Hatzidimitriou Fot. & Psilos, G. *Insurance Legislation*. 1991.
Hatzidimitriou Fot. & Psilos, G. *The New Legislation of Social Insurance*. 1993.
Kalantzopoulos, K. *Social Security – General Principles*. 1965.
Kartsonas, G. *Pension Law*. 1991.
Katsadoros, K. *The Social Security Protection in the Liberal Social State*. 1979.
KEPE. *Social Insurance, Reports for the Programme 1988–1992*. 1990.
Koukiadis, J. *Lectures of Social Policy and Social Legislation*. 1981.
Karakatsanis Al. *Social Insurance as an Institution*. ed. Ministry of Social Services 1985, 35ff.
Katrougalos, G. *The Social State in the Post-industrial Society*. 1998.
Koukiadis, I. *Social Policy and Social Legislation*. 1981.
Kremalis, K. *The Social Insurance of Dependent Workers*. 1982.
Kremalis, K. *Social Security Mixed Benefits*. 1984.
Kremalis, K. *Social Insurance Law*. 1985.
Kremalis, K. (ed.). *Case Law on Social Security Issues*. 1996.
Kyriakoulakos, P. *Social Policy* (General Notions of Social Insurance). 1971.
Kyriopoulos, J. *Social Insurance Schemes*. 1990.
Lanaras, K. *The Social Insurance in IKA*. 1998.
Leventis, G. *The Social Rights of the Citizen*. 1976, 176.
Manassis, N. *Draft for the Establishment of a National System of Pension Protection* (in the Social Insurance Sector). 1991.
Manassis, N. *The Accession of Greece in the European Communities and the Greek Social Insurance*. 1979.
Metallinos Al. *The Successive Insurance*. 1991.

Mitsopoulos, P. *The Foundation of Social Insurance*. 1940.
Nikolakopoulou-Stefanou, H. *Convergence of National Social Security Systems*. 1992.
Paparrigopoulou-Pechlibanides, P. *Supplementary Social Insurance in Community Law of Competition*. 2002.
Paparrigopoulou P. *The Evolution in Social Security Law. More Market and More State,* 2004.
Paparrigopoulou P., *Social Security Law,* ed. Nomiki Bibliothiki, 3rd ed. 2019.
Patras, L. *The Fundamental Problems of Social Policy*. 1965.
Petroglou Ant. *Social Insurance Law*. vol. A' and B'. 1974.
Provopoulos, G. *Social Insurance*. 1987.
Provopoulos, G. *Yfantopoulos Joan. Special Subjects of Social Policy.* 1990.
Psilos, G. *Social Insurance Law*. vol. A' and B'. 1977.
Rombolis, S. *Social Insurance, The Continual Crisis and the Perspectives*. 1990.
Robolis, S., G. Romanias & B. Margios, *An Actuarial Study for the Greek Social Insurance System, Labour Institute*. 2001.
Sakellaropoulos, Th. *European Social Policy*. 1993.
Sakellaropoulos, Th. 'In Search of the New Social State'. In *The Reform of the Social State*. ed. by Th. Sakellaropoulos. 1999, 23–67.
Skoutelis, G.D. *Social Insurance. Evolution and Crisis*. 1990.
Stergiou Agg. *The Constitutional Consolidation of the Social Insurance*. 1994.
Stergiou Agg. *The Protection of Motherhood in Social Insurance Law*. 1989.
Stergiou Agg. *Family Allowances*. 1996.
Tinios, P. *Society, Economy and Pensions*. 2001.
Tsotsorou, T. & SkliKas, N. *Community Social Security Law for Migrant Workers*. 1997.
Vakalopoulos, G. 'Minimum Pensions after the Introduction of Law No. 2084/1992'. *Social Insurance Law Review* (1992): 745–747.
Zarras, J. *The Social Insurance Institution*. 1929.

Health Services

Alexiadis Ar.-Dim. *Introduction to the Health Law*. 1999.
Anaplioti-Vazaiou Ir. *International Acceptances in Health and National Systems*. 1987.
Anaplioti-Vazaiou Ir. *National Health System (ESY), Amendments – European Community Law.* 1988.
Anaplioti-Vazaiou Ir. *General Principles of Health Law*. 1993.
Androulidaki-Dimitriadou Ism. *The Obligation to Inform the Patient*. 1993.
Chortareas, K. *Doctors' Responsibilities and Health Legislation*. 1975.
Dimopoulos, K. *Medical etiquette*. 1986.
EPIKAYP. *Pandect of Social Security Case-Law* (2 volumes). 1997.
Gana An. – Zervou Theof. *Medicines: Level and Price Policy*. 1984.
European Social Security Institute/Greek Section. *The Health Services, Organization – Administration – Planning*. 1990.
KEPE. *Health, Programme of Development 1976–1980*. 1976.
KEPE. *Programme of Peripheral Development*. Peripheralisation of Health Services, 1970.

Kotsianos Stef. *The Medical Responsibility, Civil – Penal*. 1977.
Koutselinis Ant. – Michalodimitrakis Man. *Medical Responsibility*. 1984.
Kremalis, K. *The Right to Health Protection*. 1987.
Kremalis, K. *Health Law: Legislation, Case Law, Templates*. Nomiki Vivliothiki, 2011.
Kriari-Katrani Ism. *Biomedical developments in the Constitutional Law*. 1994.
Madianos Mich. & Zarnari Olg. etc. *Health and Greek Society*. 1988.
Mekos Zaf. *National Health System*. 1988.
Niakas, D. *Health and Regional Development; the Regional Health Policy in Greece*. 1993.
Paparrigopoulou P. *Public Law of Health*, ed. Nomiki Bibliothiki, 2nd ed. 2017 (in Greek).
Varka-Adami A. & Androulidaki-Dimitriadi, I. *The Law of Transplantation*. 1993.

Social Welfare

Aggelis, J. *Social Welfare*. Special Part, I–III, 1976.
EPIKAYP. *Pandect of Social Security Case-Law* (2 volumes). 1997.
Georgiadi Effi (coordin.). *The Old-Aged in the Community – the Old-Aged in Life, Ministry of Health and Social Insurance*. 1985.
SKLE. *3rd Panhellenic Congress of Social Workers*. 1987.
EKKE. *Code of the Provisions of the Social Services Organizations*. 1986.
Kanellopoulos, K. *Means of Income and Poverty in Greece, Defining Factors*. 1986.
Kanellopoulos, K. *The Old-Aged in Greece*. 1984.
Karagiorgas Sak. (coordin.). *Dimensions of Poverty in Greece*. 1990.
KEPE. *Social Welfare, Reports for the Programme 1988–1992*. 1989.
KEPE. *Programme of Regional Development*. 1980.
Kontiadis Xen. *Welfare State and Social Rights*. 1997.
Kremalis, K. *The Personal Right to Social Welfare*. 1991.
Kremalis, K. (coordin.). *Social Welfare, Research and Evaluation of a New System*. 1990.
Lixouriotis, J. *Social and Legal Conceptions about the Child*. 1986.
Mardas, G. *Organization and Financing of the Social Administration System*. 1993.
Mastrojiannis, J. *Social Welfare*. 1969.
Matthaiou Andr. *Interaction Between Social Insurance and Social Assistance Rules on Old Age, Invalidity and Family Benefits*. 1996.
Panoutsopoulou Kass. *Social Welfare*. 1980.
Papaflessa, Th. *Basic Programmes of Social Protection*. 1984.
Perrakis St. & Lixouriotis, J. *European Social Space and Communal Social Charter*. 1990.
Raphael Mar. *Sociology and Social Administration*. 1978.
Stathopoulos Petr. *Communal Work. Theory and Practice*. 1990.
Thomaidis Xen. *Research of the Social Protection Institutions from the Ancient Days Till the Revolution of 1821 in Greece*. 1973.
Zarras, J. *The Problem of Being Old in Greece*. 1974.

Selected Bibliography

Bibliography in English

Amitsis, G. 'Greece', in: Pieters, D. (ed.) Social Security Law in the Fifteen Member States of the European Union, Antwerp: Maklu, 1997, pp. 147–170.

Amitsis, G. 'Current Policies and Reform Plans for the Greek Benefits Framework', in: Benefits & Compensation International, 31 (7) 2002, pp. 12–19.

Katrougalos, G. 'The South European Welfare Model: The Greek Welfare State, in Search of an Identity', in: Journal of European Social Policy, 6 (1) 1996, pp. 39–60.

Papadopoulos, T. 'Social Insurance and the Crisis of Statism in Greece', in: Clasen, J. (ed.), Social Insurance in Europe, Bristol: The Policy Press, 1997, pp. 177–204.

Paparrigopoulou P. 'The Distinction Between Basic Pension and Contributory Pension: The Paradoxes of the Recent Reform to the Greek Pension Scheme (Laws 3863 and 3865/2010)', in: Pensions, 2011, 16, pp. 51–62.

Paparrigopoulou P. 'Report for Greece', in 'The Political Economy of Pension Reforms in Times of Global Crisis. State Unilateralism or Social Dialogue?', International Labor Office Working Paper No. 37/2012, edited by H. Serfati, Y. Ghellab, pp. 68–71.

Paparrigopoulou P. 'Constitution, Social Rights and Economic Crisis. The Case of Greece', in jønstad, 'Velferd of rettferd, Festskrift til Asbjørn Kjønstad', 70ar, (edited by) K. Ketscher, K. Lilleholt, E. Smith, A. Syse, ed. Gyldendal, Oslo, 2012, σ. 449–461.

Sissouras, A. & G. Amitsis. 'Social Security Policy', in: Kazakos, P./Ioakimidis, P. (eds), Greece and EC Membership Evaluated, London: Pinter, 1994, pp. 248–259.

Index

The numbers here refer to paragraph numbers.

Index

Index

Index